Sour Milk and Stolen Honey

Marianne Azizi

Published as an e-book by Marianne Azizi

Sour Milk and Stolen Honey

Copyright: Marianne Azizi

Published: 22 March 2014

Publisher: Marianne Azizi

The right of Marianne Azizi to be identified as author of this Work has been asserted by her in accordance with sections 77 and 78 of the Copyright, Designs and Patents Act 1988.

All rights reserved. No part of this publication may be reproduced, stored in retrieval system, copied in any form or by any means, electronic, mechanical, photocopying, recording or otherwise transmitted without written permission from the publisher. You must not circulate this book in any format.

In the case of brief quotations embodied in critical reviews and certain other noncommercial uses, these are permitted by copyright law.

For permission requests, please send an email entitles, "Permissions" to the following email address –info@chocolatecakeandwords.com

A note from the Author

This is a work of non-fiction, and is factual in its entirety. All the facts can be supported by documents, witnesses, and evidence. Ilan Azizi bravely gave his full permission to be named in this book, and all those associated with him who contributed to this entire experience.

Some names have been changed, but only a few.

Copyright © 2014 Marianne Azizi

About the Author

Marianne is a writer of real-life experiences. She has fulfilled her ambition to write, and this is her non-fiction debut which has been written using her own life experiences. She lives in England and enjoys a happy and varied life with family and friends. Away from the keyboard, her passions are football and living life to the full, in every way she can. Marianne has combined her career in behavioural work with decades of understanding the fascinating aspects of humanity, and the beauty of life. She draws upon her strength and compassion to tell wonderful, true, and enriching stories.

Acknowledgements

To my wonderful editor, Tabi, at Chocolate Cake & Words who has been my teacher, mentor, and friend, bringing this story into the world.

For my mum who was the fountain of unconditional love and faith, and looking down on me always.

For my family who supported me emotionally, financially and practically.

For my dear friends who supported and encouraged me - Marie, Manny, Carol, Graham, Sue, and Elaine - and many more friends, too numerous to mention.

Thank you all for your love and patience.

For the people who shared their stories with me, and even for my faithful cat, who purred on my shoulder, keeping me company as I wrote, night and day.

Marianne

For Jan,

For never doubting me, and walking in my shoes every step of the way with me.

The Israeli civil court has ruled that *"unlawful infringement of personal feelings as a result of not honoring a person's basic right to shape his life as he wishes constitutes an infringement of the welfare of that person, and it is encompassed by the definition of injury."*

I kept my promise, not just the marriage vow. It's the promise I made when my husband begged me never to give up on him. Just at the point he was losing his identity. That's what happens to hostages eventually.

Would any new wife say no to such a request? Almost seven years later the cost of this promise has been a personal tsunami. Would I still have made the promise to stand by those words if I'd known what it would do to me? Now he is barely known to me. Not only are his human rights in tatters, but so is his ability to reason with anything but fear or hopelessness.

It is my free right to fight for my liberty and the freedom of someone who has forgotten what it looks and feels like. It is just a whisper in the air, or a lingering memory of a life not lived, of two personalities in one body, recalling the sounds of laughter, and the simple things. A yearning for the mundane most people take for granted and then the frustrating inability to get it back.

Being free is the absolute right of a human being in a democratic world, to live a life and not merely an existence.

I am going to be liberated after nearly a decade in chains. And with my freedom I will shine a light on those who would keep me imprisoned in this situation.

The battle itself is proof of *my* freedom to fight. Imagine a world in which decisions are impossible. The facts are there but action is impossible. Imagine a world where entrapment and loss of freedom is normal behavior, and shouting for help to the world can bring no justice. I am fighting against an entire culture and their system, a country. And the very person I want to free, I'm fighting him too. I have asked myself a thousand times why I'm doing this but when something is so clearly unjust, a stand needs to be taken. It's difficult to understand how it is acceptable for a society to stand back and watch the murder of my husband's spirit. I stand for truth with friends and family who have stood by me, whilst his friends and family have created the injustice. The Israeli system has colluded with these personal agendas rather than for freedom and human rights.

They picked the wrong woman. Despite everything and his almost inaudible cries for help, I cannot and will not give up until freedom is achieved.

Chapter 1

Naked, my body young, lithe and supple, immersed in the water again. Shame and humiliation were coursing through my veins.

"You hate all things Christian. You reject your family and friends, and turn your back on all your past."

The words reverberated and echoed in my head. At least three men were watching me. I felt like a hypocrite. Who would be able to believe in a religion which bred such hatred and fundamentalist instructions from the outset?

I was standing in the Mikvah, a bath used for ritual immersion in Judaism. My studies said it was for purity after menstruation or childbirth, and of course for the final procedure in the ritual steps I had to take to become a Jew.

Down into the water I went, praying to some God somewhere for this to be the first and last time I would ever do this. Down a few steps into the small pool of water, fully submerging, and then instructed to go back up the steps. Disconnected and retreating into a personal space, waiting for it to end.

Finally, after seven plunges, I stood, wiping my eyes, stinging with tears and water, and they said, "Now, you are Jewish. Mazaltov."

They turned and walked away, leaving me with an attendant to wrap me in a bathrobe, cleansed from my past life, approved and legal to embrace a new life as a Jew. It was 1988. I had no idea that the pool was prohibited to men, and the ritual usually entailed three submersions with women only, usually by appointment to protect dignity. How could I know? I was just doing as I was told.

It had seemed so easy to agree to this conversion. Being spiritual and not religious, it was a simple accession. It was a fast track project, just business to them. Learning everything was compulsory, yet assimilating anything, or believing it in a heartfelt way was impossible in the short time it took to complete the enforced education. Even though there could be no failure, as the money was our assurance.

I'd agreed to this for my fiancé, who wanted any children of our impending marriage to be automatically Jewish. Always through the mother, a non-Jewish man can still make Jewish babies through a Jewish woman. I had become Jewish for this reason alone, to acquiesce and commit.

The final day was a blessing, months of studying and tests ensured I passed with flying colours. I was not only Jewish, I was an Orthodox Jew.

Champagne glasses clinked as my future family advised me to forget everything I'd learnt. The purpose of the exercise was purely Zionist, keep the Jewish line going, but not to worry about observances. The hypocrisy was there to see, but I had no time to absorb just what I had done.

I slipped blissfully into bed, although the worst part was over, the nagging fear reared up within me. I had no idea how I could spend the rest of my life being

Jewish, trying not to be Jewish. Never wanting anyone to think I was born this way, or even chosen to be in a race of people who spend their time either denying their heritage or being aggressive and arrogant about it. The Jewish nation regards itself as the chosen people who would have all the rights and entitlements. The truth of this, as I came to experience it, was beyond anything I could imagine.

In the quarter century I've been involved with Israel, the attitudes have become even worse. The name of their game is, use short-cuts, always make money, and deny everything. I didn't want to own this conversion or its consequences, and at the time I was more than content to have done something else to please people I loved. It wasn't right. I hoped this bending of the rules was for a good cause, and done with the best of intentions, but the lies and corruption of the authorities couldn't be the best start for my connection to Israel. It could not be undone, so I had to live with it. I tried my best to see things in a more positive light.

The hours preceding the humiliation of my baptism had involved testing my ability to display my religious knowledge, particularly the thirty nine rules of Shabbat, the things you cannot do on the Sabbath. Learning them both in Hebrew and English, I faced a group of rabbis seated at a table bursting with an array of food, fruits, biscuits, and a wide selection of beverages. They expected me to know the specific blessing for each type of food, and say the appropriate prayer before eating or drinking.

If the Head Rabbi had covered the table's contents with one all-encompassing prayer, there would have been no requirement for me to pray. With no idea if the overall blessing had been done before my arrival, my mind was a blank. I refused all offers of food and drink, terrified to make a mistake. A bilingual lawyer was with me to urge me on and explain the process. (There is always a lawyer in Israel where there is money to be made. Israel has the highest number of lawyers per head of population in the world. In 2010 it had one lawyer for 170 people, compared to one lawyer for 295 people in the USA, and the population in Israel is 50 times smaller!)

Haltingly, I began to recite the thirty nine rules. I was speaking words I barely related to in my own language; winnowing, sifting, tearing, and sewing for example. There was no mention of everyday life, like driving, or switching lights on and off. Just a regurgitation of ancient work practices, all prohibited from dusk on Friday, until dusk on Saturday. Some of the ancient prohibitions have been translated into modern work practices now, and anything high tech is forbidden during the weekend.

I had to write the letter confirming my hatred of all Christians, and rejecting my family. It was to be read aloud at this gathering. I hated every second of it.

The irony of it all is, I paid money for this fast track conversion despite learning all they required. In today's currency exchange, it would be nearly £7000. They said it was to encourage gentiles to become part of the Jews without the hardship. Converting usually took years, and they didn't want people to be deterred, especially when it involved marriage, because children would be automatically Jewish. Doing it quickly was a Zionist principle. The task was complete, and the change to my life was irrevocable.

My life had altered so quickly, and driving back to a celebration for my ordeal, I could hardly believe only a short year ago I knew nothing about the people or the land of Israel.

My first visit to Israel was just after the Intifada began, in 1987. The word Intifada, translates from Arabic as uprising. The Palestinians started a campaign against their oppression. As tourists on holiday, my friend and I only realised the seriousness of the situation upon our return to England.

My friend Sharon and I had decided on a trip to Eilat with an impromptu need for a break, and after being told not to worry about any troubles there although the town was bordered by Egypt and Jordan. We had never even heard of the place until we visited the holiday store, and were sold on the idea of something exotic. I'd been working so hard to build a new business, and wanted to treat Sharon. Whenever I had some money I usually spent it on others, giving treats or creating memories. I'd promised her if she came I wouldn't spend constantly. She agreed, both flattered but as with most people, a bit uncomfortable with generosity. It is harder to receive than give, and I was becoming an expert at giving. Why not? I'd earned my money, and wanted to share it. With barely any knowledge of the country or its politics, we went with high hopes of sun and a good rest.

Chapter 2

Arriving during Passover, a major Jewish holiday, our hotel had no bread. We didn't know about this special holiday so just thought it was poor accommodation. My pal smuggled eggs, cheese and crackers every day from the breakfast table to see us through the day. On various trips, the Israeli guides did all they could to cover up the unrest. At one point, we'd been asked to sit on the floor of our coach as a 'safety training exercise'!

During this holiday I met my first husband, a young 22 year old, who was visiting Eilat for the weekend. He was so different from people at home in England, a dark eyed handsome man. His background was Moroccan and he had the look of a Spaniard. So full of energy and confidence, it drew me to him. He told me later he'd known in the first instant that he wanted to marry me. As far as he was concerned it was love at first sight.

He was different from the men back home and I fell in love with him very quickly. I could never grasp how he could be so smitten with me. The Israeli women at the time were all so beautiful. Dark eyes and luxurious dark hair, to me they were the epitome of sophistication. They were always so beautifully made up even on the beach. Not at all like me. I would come out of the water looking like a drowned rat, nothing like a glamorous Bond girl. My attention to my appearance was sparse. A quick check of myself to make sure everything was tidy, a bit of make up for a night out, and always a sigh as I wished I was just a little bit thinner.

At 5'6" and a size twelve, my friends couldn't understand my occasional moans about my figure. I suppose I never saw myself through the eyes of observers and never really accepted compliments fully.

Sharon and I enjoyed a trip to Jerusalem. Leaving the hotel to aimlessly wander the busy streets during the evening and 'get lost' in the city, we experienced a bustling neighbourhood, ancient and modern, cobbled streets so narrow, full of orthodox Jews and Arabs rushing around noisily talking and getting on with their business. The beauty was intoxicating. It was another world. We didn't pay attention to the landmarks as we wandered through the city. We just soaked it all up.

The alphabet was different too so we couldn't read any signs to help us get back to the hotel. On our eventual return we were severely ticked off by our tour guide as he learned we'd been in East Jerusalem – the West Bank. Perhaps if we'd been informed of the risks we would have chosen differently but innocence is a great protection for a tourist. It was a cauldron of cultures which had cast a spell on me. I wanted to stay forever. I wasn't settled in England. It was cold and rainy and so dour in my view. I was too young to understand the benefits of our democracy and freedom at the time and Israel felt so fresh and free spirited.

A bad bout of dysentery from the tap water in Eilat curtailed many further excursions into the country leaving us confined to the hotel pool for almost half of our holiday. It was desperately hot, sweaty, loud, and exciting. And meeting my husband to be was the icing on the cake. Our sickness was so bad. We had to sit just outside our room to have constant access to the toilet. We couldn't even manage to get to the hotel pool. After a few days, we'd decided if we could get half way to the nearest pub we'd make the effort to have a night out. After all half way meant there would be no going back! It was that night in the local English styled bar that I met my new man. I had dressed to kill, in a deep blue shirt which enhanced the colour of my eyes and dark hair. We had a wonderful evening, talking until dawn. Sharing an early breakfast we enjoyed a fabulous day in Taba, a resort which has since been returned to Egypt. It was occupied territory in 1987.

I was on a new course in life, and I didn't even know it. The country was full of foreign tourists in 1987, especially in Eilat which had drawn many young men seeking a holiday romance during their holidays. I was fortunate to be involved with a good man, but even then I didn't notice how the country sucked up rational thinking and lured me into such spontaneous behaviour. A year later I was preparing for my wedding in Israel.

Chapter 3

I was brought up strictly in the Catholic faith. My father was extreme in his views. There was no leeway in his beliefs and I rebelled against the rules from an early age. Questioning everything, I soon came to view God as a figure head of many religions and it made no sense to me as I observed people kill and die for the same deity. Despite my uncertainty I was an obedient child and developed a sense of obligation and duty, with or without God's finger pointing down and accusing me of terrible sins.

Discovering the world of business and selling, I found an escape route for being dominated by my personal weaknesses in relationships, and worked my way to the top of the tree in almost every field I was in.

Fiercely loyal and protective, the role of a boss was a pleasure, my main requirement of others was honesty, to tell the truth in all things, and to stand up for what is right. My father had the same principles, which to this day I have honoured, and I still feel blessed to have the same characteristics. To have no fear of the truth, which he told me would be a lonely road in life, most people didn't want to hear it, read it, or act upon it. I had grown up with an irrational fear of rejection and this flaw propelled me into the world of sales. Professionally I mastered the art of minimising rejection and not taking everything so personally. Yet still, at home I was compliant and willing to please.

I felt ashamed of my conversion in part, as I had been true to my heart but not to my deepest instincts. The fear of rejection and putting myself to the test of being loveable as I was, meant taking a risk I wasn't prepared to take at the time. But if I'd thought it challenging to grow up as a Catholic, it paled in comparison belonging to one of the most misunderstood religious groups in the world. I was jumping from one extreme to another. Both religions were fundamental and in Israel religion was not just a way of life, the laws were dominated by it too.

I put the memories in a mental box because thinking too much about my catholic upbringing wasn't going to change anything, except my mood. I concentrated on eagerly preparing my nuptials, with the aim of putting some of my own European flavour to it. I wanted to put my own mark on my wedding, especially once I'd learned I couldn't even speak at the ceremony. I waited for my friends to arrive in order to make plans. The rebel inside me awoke, and I needed my own personal stamp on the day.

My first wedding was held in Israel with hundreds of guests. They bring money so it is easy to have a lavish celebration because the wedding almost pays for itself. It was my first experience of either a Jewish, or an Israeli wedding. With my Christian background I knew that brides enjoy the planning as much as the day. They choose bridesmaids and plan the reception. I was bitterly disappointed that there were no vows for me to say.

It was inconceivable to me that I would have to make a commitment in silence at my own wedding. Only the groom is permitted to speak. Whilst very excited to be getting married, my heart was saddened for my family who were not able to attend. My father refused to come, and the others had small children, so the expense of travelling meant it was impossible for them. I had just a few close friends coming which lifted my spirits.

There was no Hen night. It was a Hina, meaning Henna in Hebrew. My new family were of Moroccan descent bringing many of their customs and superstitions with them. I had less than a dozen hardy British friends who travelled to see my exotic foreign wedding, and explore the Holy Land.

One of my friends was bitterly disappointed with Israel. She was a devout Christian who wondered when we would visit the genuinely Holy peaceful sites, of which there were none in the town of Nahariyya. Her biblical knowledge only stretched as far as the famous sites. Her perception was the Holy Land was full of sacred places and the rest of Israel was just a place. Two separate places, she wasn't too far off the mark.

Nevertheless they enjoyed the Henna Party but I drew the line at being painted on my hands and feet with the dye. Also I didn't really fancy having an egg tied to my head. I didn't understand any of their customs at all, and I felt very self-conscious. I'm one of those people who will start searching for things in my handbag rather than be called up as a volunteer in front of an audience. Being the centre of attention was wonderful but being painted was horrifying.

I was full of relief being with English people and speaking my own language again. It was the most comforting feeling in the world to speak naturally and use my humour. A second language with humour is the most difficult thing to master. After the distress of my conversion I decided to enjoy myself. It was so much fun to chat and feel my brain beginning to work again. Usually full of conversation, I had been so quiet in Israel for the past weeks, and stringing a few Hebrew words together gave me no satisfaction. Breaking with their tradition, I asked Sharon to be my Maid of Honour and put some tweaks into the preparations at the venue. Two days before the ceremony I was required to go back to the Mikvah to be spiritually cleansed for my groom. Full of reluctance, the memories of a few weeks before surged into me, I was still raw and full of trepidation about being naked in front of those men again.

"No, no, don't worry." my future mother in law assured. "You'll be robed, we will all be throwing sweets at you, and it will be fabulous. No men are permitted to go into the Mikvah." The people who had assisted me had clearly got a nice perk from the bathing.

I reeled at her words. It was my first taste of the absence of empathy and detachment of these people. They could be so kind and accommodating but it was all for their own agenda. Not only had I endured the secret scandal of a quick conversion, but to learn of a complete break disregard for their own rules was a shock and now I was being urged to bury it. Strange people, I thought. Taboos were broken for expedience so I broke one too. I hired an Arabic wedding photographer. It caused ripples, but he was talented and good fun.

The photographer spent the whole day with a couple before their ceremony which took place after sundown. I wanted someone I was comfortable with, and perhaps subconsciously we were both underdogs. Attitudes at the time meant Arabs and Jews didn't always mix in business. For the photographer this was a major breakthrough. For me he was the best man for the job.

There is no Best Man in an Israeli wedding. The major honour was to be asked to be the driver for the couple during their special day. There was only one person in the frame for this job, our dear friend Ilan. One of the worst things, was when I could manage a few Hebrew words, they would be met with cheers or a pat on the back. It was as if I'd been a baby taking their first steps. I felt exactly like a small child, stumbling around and learning to communicate all over again. I was still a foreigner and this period of my life has developed in me an empathy and kindness for all non-English speakers ever since. I reflected on the cruelty of people and it was the inevitable teasing which brought Ilan into my life, as a very dear and honest friend. There could be no other person more suited to driving us that day than someone I could trust.

It was not until almost seventeen years later that the knowledge and comprehension of my early connection with Ilan dawned on me.

So, Ilan was to be our driver for the wedding day. Custom dictates the ceremony must take place after sundown, so the daytime is spent in preparation. After a few hours of pampering, I emerged from the hairdressing salon in my off the shoulder wedding dress, the train as long as I was tall, to be whisked away to various scenic spots for photographs. I'd never experienced an Israeli wedding, and was in the flow, with no idea of what would be happening next.

Sharon was also in the car for the whole afternoon, looking resplendent in her royal blue silk gown which had been made especially for the occasion. Looking out from a boat hired for a short trip, I saw the coastline of Acco and was filled with happiness. Ilan was an excellent choice of driver and took good care of us. Finally we arrived at the hotel for the ceremony.

It is customary for the bride, groom, and parents to greet guests as they enter, so we were lined up ready to meet and greet. Music was playing and a table was heaving with delicacies. The food was actually sculptured and presented a feast for the eyes. Once all the guests were in, I was placed on a throne like seat to greet all the guests again, whilst the groom went and settled the legal requirements, the main one being the 'ketuba'. This is a Jewish marriage contract, written in Aramaic, with all sorts of promises between man and wife, but the main part being a nominated sum by the groom which represents his bride's worth. Hearing a few gasps, I learned I had been worthy of a million shekel ketuba. I think my fiancé was totally in love, and perhaps a little naïve, as this sum had to be paid if we divorced. He must have been very sure at the time.

Staying in the moment, I shook hands with hundreds of people, unable to speak Hebrew to respond to their comments. I was a little afraid of being left alone, but my new family did their best to make me comfortable.

It was all noise, chattering, music, food, and for me and my friends, very exotic. I was caught in the flow of the day, not knowing from one minute to the next what was going to happen. Letting go as much as I could, I truly felt part of Israel and one of its people.

Our English guests were at a complete loss with the etiquette at the wedding, and unable to understand Hebrew I kept toasting and eating at all the wrong times. It was hilarious to watch the video later, my guests and I were out of sync with everyone else, but in true English spirit they drank and danced, living up to the image of the English abroad! There were hundreds of guests, and I found it daunting as well as exhilarating to be the centre of such a huge occasion.

The best part of my marriage was having two wonderful children. I worked harder than ever, trying to build a good home and a bright future.

Unfortunately, the relationship broke down only a year after my second child's birth, and I had little choice but to press on as a single mother.

The spectre of the religious conversion had never left us. I tried endlessly to do the right things, observing the special days which my husband picked and chose to do. He wasn't particularly observant as I had been taught, so the inconsistency was difficult to manage. He never worked throughout our marriage, so I was the breadwinner and a mother. Every year, like clockwork, the tensions would mount from around September until Christmas. I wanted our children to enjoy the festivities, not with any religious involvement, but Santa and a Christmas tree wasn't harmful in my eyes. My husband had even celebrated

Christmas before the children were born, but for a third of every year of our marriage, the desire I had to make the season full of excitement was quashed. I got my own way each time, but it eroded the marriage year on year. I kept the Jewish observances as expected, and realised very quickly if it wasn't truly in my heart, or had come from birth, it would be impossible.

Even worse, coming from a Catholic background, obviously half of the children's family were in a different camp to the Jewish side. At least there was never an argument about who to have round for Christmas.

The fissure grew and my unhappiness with it. Working all the hours available, with two young children and no support was too much for me. I saw a future in my mind's eye which was intolerable, and with all the courage I could muster, I filed for divorce.

My husband was a young man, married at only 23, naïve in life experience and he had a fear of Christians. It was no surprise given the indoctrination I received in the conversion. To be born and nurtured with this attitude achieved such an ingrained view of the world, nothing could change it.

It was the most absurd event which sealed my fate. Our last Christmas was the final straw. Yet again the 'discussions' had begun, and I wasn't allowed a tree. With a good friend in tow, and despite all my protestations and reasoning of trees not being based in Christianity, I had an alternative.

Returning from a garden centre, I proudly dragged in a display Reindeer! It was bright green and about a foot high and two feet wide. We could put the presents under his legs I joked, and lights all over his body. He was furious, and before storming out of the house demanded I returned it and get a tree. I didn't need telling twice. It was a tragedy in my eyes that the religion and anti-Christian conditioning could bring our marriage down. Obviously having a partner who doesn't provide isn't helpful in a marriage. Not all Israelis have this viewpoint or intolerance to the customs of others, but I should have guessed at the beginning when asked to convert. How I felt wasn't really in the equation, and the consequences of his request brought in a new generation who couldn't embrace the Jewish faith either. As their mother, despite all efforts, I couldn't feel it or believe in it enough. I believed my trips to Israel were all but over and steadily built a new life for myself and my children.

Chapter 4

Ilan had hypnotic brown eyes, with a penetrating gaze holding both innocence and hidden depths. His serious face was transformed with his warm smile, and I could sense his whole being was engaged in real joy. His grin was one of a young man, a man with all to live for, who could melt every corner of one's heart. He was an industrious man, very proud of his work, always giving one hundred per cent. He had a presence and charisma which I was drawn to from the outset.

One time, he'd pulled me away from a crowd and said "You must learn Hebrew. People are teasing and playing games with you, and you don't even know it." I was grateful and never forgot that kindness.

He never flapped or panicked in those days. He was a man who could be abandoned in the middle of the countryside on a survival course, and yet still eat like a king and sleep like a prince. His extensive army training both in conscription and later as a volunteer every year had rounded him into a very competent man.

Getting to know him took years but at the time he was an ally and a friend on each visit, showing consideration and hospitality with a gentle nature, which was an oasis of calm for me in an otherwise unfamiliar, aggressive environment. No wonder he felt like he didn't belong as I never saw him raise his voice or lose his temper. He didn't fit the mould of the typical Israelis I had come to know.

2004

I didn't want to go back to Israel again. My marriage had lasted almost ten years, and had eventually ended amicably enough, but after my divorce I'd had enough of going back and forth to Israel. It had been four years since my last visit which was for a family wedding. I'd now been single for almost six years and the last thing on my mind was romance. However duty called, there was another family celebration on the horizon and I had no option but to attend. My brother joked with me a few days before my trip, "Maybe you'll meet someone!"

"In Israel?" I'd snorted, "I'm done with that country and the men in it. I've had one Israeli husband already. This is just a duty call."

I should have listened to my own words. If I'd stuck to them I'd be living a completely different life right now. I had never been prone to casual relationships, and I was definitely closed to anything serious. I was a busy working woman and had buried the fact that I was also a single female. There would be no complications entering my life, I was determined.

It had been a few years since I'd last seen Ilan, but there he was the night I arrived, just as he always had been, asking to see me. He looked great. His hair had receded and gone grey but his eyes still shone with friendship. He was holding a little girl, his daughter. I hadn't known and was surprised, as it was a seven year gap from his second son.

The visit was akin to stepping into a war zone. To stay with my ex in-laws wasn't the brightest idea, but it had been the only option. My ex-husband and I were at a very low point, my in-laws were incredibly hostile to me. They had a completely different view of our breakup. Half-truths and keeping a good image made sure that after years of avoiding them there was little chance for me to set the record straight. The tension was getting to me and I needed an escape. My ex suggested to Ilan that he take me out for an hour or two. Ilan duly arranged an evening of diversion. He was thrilled I was a single woman, though surprised as he had only just learned I'd been divorced for six years.

We sat and chatted like old friends and I realised it was the first time we'd been alone. He wasn't happy in himself, very restless and finding it hard to open up fully. Looking into his eyes, it felt like I knew him, really understood him, and I told him so. We found that we had a mutual, irresistible connection. I can't describe it as they do in romance novels but I came back to my room late at night a different woman, knowing the depth of our connection was beyond the expectations of my rational mind.

No touch, no kiss, and yet that evening had opened something very deep inside me. I write all this because to understand how I could endure the life I had to come, it's important for me to recall the first special night. It was exactly the same for Ilan. We both knew our lives were going to be changed. There are not enough words to come close to how it felt other than, I felt alive for the first time in years with no doubts of our destiny to be together.

At the end of the visit I had no intention of returning to Israel ever again, and on my last night Ilan and I went out again to play pool, a nice safe environment for us to be in. There was a disconcerting chemistry but not a single touch was shared between us. We didn't even share a peck on the cheek in greeting. There was a shared knowledge of something so deep and there would be plenty of time for physical connection.

The second evening with Ilan, he told me all about his own marriage. They were together in name only and he was desperate to get out of the marital home and start afresh. It clearly made sense given my own divorce had been a secret for so long. In fact I think it was only Ilan who had learned of it. Image was important to them so a considered failure wasn't exactly advertised or openly discussed. It confirmed to me again that Ilan didn't have an open relationship with his own family, as he admitted he had not discussed his situation with them. Matty rarely visited his parents' home just as I hadn't gone back to Israel since my divorce.

Ilan was separated from his wife Matty. They lived in the same house, and she was later to testify in court their marriage ended in 2003, a year before I met Ilan again. So I knew the marriage was indeed just a front for image over many years. Ilan told me as much.

Since he didn't know I was divorced for so long it was no surprise for me to learn image and reputation meant people could be sparse with the truth.

I'd met her a few times, Ilan's wife. She was well known in our circle of friends for being a volatile woman. She had a short fuse and a very short, quick temper. She was not particularly pretty, of average height and build. Her eyes were the darkest brown, almost black, and she had a shock of hair which Ilan told me was the bane of her life and she spent hours trying to straighten it and control it.

He described her compulsive tidying and cleaning, which he said was to the point of OCD. He felt her brashness covered her low self-esteem, but events might turn out to prove him wrong. Her family origin was Tunisian. Ilan told me he'd begged her over the years to see someone about anger management and her severe PMT. He'd confided many times to her mother to try and influence her to get some help. She was a very intense woman and I had always got the feeling she could erupt at any time. My ex and I saw them each time we visited. I sensed a volcanic personality and I knew from Ilan they'd had countless arguments particularly about his parents. She despised them and it would be the one thing I would have empathy for.

So Ilan spilled his pain and dreams and we became kindred spirits. Being a particularly private man, it took many months for him to tell his parents about us. It was in England one evening after we got together. He called them to break the news. At a much later time, my ex told me being with a friend's ex was taboo, particularly in that neighbourhood, and perhaps he was right.

But it would be Matty who would shape our future. Her actions and the knock on effect, combined with a cultural lack of empathy, and a court system which colluded with her was to change many lives irrevocably. It was to change Ilan from this gentle vital man, into a cold hearted shell of a human being.

The morning of my departure from a very unenjoyable visit, Ilan came to say goodbye and pulling me to one side, whispered that he would call me at the airport before I departed. Then he said he would talk to me every day for the rest of my life.

This is not a romantic novel, but I need to convey what an instant and deep commitment we had, and to all those who saw this as a lustful midlife crisis, I must make it clear; they were so far off the mark. I trusted him with my life almost immediately.

We made our commitment to each other through long distance phone calls and we knew we wanted to marry before he arrived, even before any kiss. Not a 21st Century relationship at all! It was so special and it was mutual. Ilan knew exactly what he wanted before he flew from Israel and I waited in the UK for his arrival with the same goal. It rarely happens this way, if ever, so of course the bond was a deep one. Our first week together lived up to expectations, and his departure was incredibly difficult for us both. He had to return to make plans to tidy up his life in Israel, and move to England.

He informed Matty of his intentions to move to England. He told me her only comment was she would decide how and when their divorce would be done. At the time, it seemed almost too easy, but veiled threats were there.

Ilan and I were settling down in the UK. But it seemed Matty had decided Ilan's life would not be his own and we were not going to get any peace. I never really knew how she could take the actions she did, and for so long, but her agenda was as clear as day. Ilan would have to fight for his freedom to be with me in the UK or pay exorbitant amounts of money to the system.

Not a man to be idle, we had to find a way to get Ilan work. By sheer coincidence, someone in a shop recommended a steel fabrication company for us to approach. I visited the factory to be met by Manny, the owner. In my early days in sales I'd done a lot of cold calling and was accustomed to talking to strangers so I breezed in confidently.

"Do I owe you any money?" he asked me brusquely.

Tall and sturdy, Manny had black hair and piercing eyes. I was initially intimidated but displayed confidence, falling back on my selling skills.

"I would like to hire a bench from you for my fiancé." I said. "He's moving here from Israel, and would like to start his own business in stainless steel."

"First time anyone has come in with that line before. Ok why not, pay by the hour and we'll see how it goes."

It had been simple. Ilan and I started in earnest. Manny and Ilan were to become the closest of friends and formed a deep brotherly bond. They were similar in some characteristics. They were both hard working and honest, with a good work ethic. Manny's parentage was Spanish which blessed him with Mediterranean looks which was incongruent with his cockney accent. Ilan was of a slimmer build, receding hair and a ready smile, compared to Manny who was quieter and more moody, whereas my fiancé would chat to anyone.

Both had intensity when working but they shared common interests and enjoyed each other's company. They helped each other in their respective skills. I used to laugh at times watching them sitting in our kitchen, doodling and enjoying their companionable silence intermittently broken by several cups of tea. Quite a different picture from two women chatting together!

At the time I still felt a little awkward with Manny's strong gruff character but we would eventually form a strong friendship to this day. He was the link to Ilan's work and future and had the kindest and most generous heart under the surface. Working together Ilan and I were building a foundation we hoped would last a lifetime. We spent most of this year going back and forth to Israel to try to tie up loose ends there and also link Ilan's existing business to the UK to give the enterprise an international flavour. He was sure in the long term it would be good for Abe, his partner, who was worrying about being left alone to run the business there.

Matty called frequently and when I answered the phone she would tell me all was ok. It seemed so civilized, which at the time made sense as the marriage was in name only. But despite her outward calm manner by the end of 2004, she'd prepared an enormous file for the civil court, preparing a No Exit Order on Ilan, with expressions of fear that he would steal the house, amongst other things!

The document floored him. "Full of lies." He said. He didn't know how to respond, just reading and rereading the file in disbelief. But he had to return to Israel to fulfil a work contract. His business partner was desperate and though it was too great a risk to do alone and Ilan felt a strong sense of responsibility and promised me he would be away for only a few weeks.

This was my initiation into Israeli law. No expertise or reasoning would be able to break through the twisted system. I just didn't know it then. A No Exit Order is a paper which prevents a person from leaving Israel. It is often used in divorce, to allay fears that one of the spouses could abduct children or not pay child support. Also it is applied on debtors, so they cannot flee the country owing money. The idea that Ilan would steal his property was ludicrous. I imagined it being smuggled out brick by brick and couldn't stop laughing at the scene. It was deadly serious though. No matter what spurious charges had been written regarding Ilan and his intentions to provide or not, the intention of this document was to impinge upon his freedom and I also felt sure it was designed to separate us, giving us little chance of building a new relationship.

I'd been in Israel for almost three months that summer, and on my return had fallen seriously ill from a mosquito bite. I was suffering from high fevers and had an emergency 999 callout once already. That was enough for Ilan, and he flew back to England. I remember him telling me later Matty had been furious he'd gone to save 'his princess' as she called me. But his actions here genuinely saved my life. Still, when he knew I was on the road to recovery, he reluctantly had to return to fulfil his major work contract.

Whilst Ilan was away, I was extremely nervous about the file Matty had put in the court. I had started to read up about No Exit Orders. There wasn't much information and I was very naïve. All I knew is he needed to get back home to me, despite his professional responsibilities.

He also had a medical problem, tendonitis. It had been affecting his hand for some months but he refused to go to the doctor. Ilan wasn't fond of doctors. He had a real fear of them and still went to a paediatrician instead of a GP.

Whilst we'd been together in Israel during that summer, I'd managed to get him to visit a physiotherapist who diagnosed surgery was required. He could hardly lift a glass, his wrist hurt so much. So during the visit he'd decided he'd have the procedure. For all his bravery in life he really was a baby when it came to medical matters. I've always been instinctive, and I'd woken up one morning with the strongest premonition of him needing to leave urgently, it was so strong I called to tell him I had booked him an indirect flight back to the UK, first stop Vienna.

He trusted my instincts. His faith in me was total. He had a sense of dread himself, and knew his time to leave was imminent. The No Exit Order becoming effective was only a matter of days away. So just a few hours after his small operation, with his hand bandaged up, he grabbed his things and departed for the airport, telling no one of his plans until he was through the passport control. For Ilan, it was like The Great Escape, he was convinced he would be stopped at the airport.

He was on his way home and I'd been right. Matty called me, screaming and shouting. She wanted to know where he was so I replied honestly that I didn't know.

He was airborne so I couldn't pinpoint his location and hadn't lied but she was raging. She must have called dozens of times during his journey claiming she had a special relationship with her 'husband', and this was just the beginning of our troubles. Feeling very nervous, unused to such confrontation I waited for Ilan to call in Vienna to confirm he was connecting to London. I didn't hear so I just waited at the airport hoping he had made it safely.

He was the last one coming into arrivals and our relief was palpable. To see him safely back in England and away from her drama filled me with calm after the anxious night of waiting at the airport. Though we'd been together for such a short time, we welcomed each other as if the separation had been years. Matty called all night, over and over again, we couldn't really make much sense of it. It was a couple of weeks later when the No Exit Order on Ilan was ratified but he was safe in England and there was nothing she could do about it.

She and a member of her family were coordinating a plan which would entangle me in a battle to this day. At the present moment she still has the ultimate power to lift Ilan's No Exit Order without any discussion or judge. The key to his normal life was and still is in her hands.

Our bond deepened as we shared the same values, goals and dreams and the only stress in our life was that Ilan could not return safely to Israel, fearful he might not be able to leave again. My family and friends were delighted with our union, it seemed only people in Israel disputed Ilan's right to choose.

Chapter 5

2005

We hired a lawyer in January, after the Christmas break and although very happy in our new relationship the shadow of Matty hung over us. The bigger problem was the No Exit Order. What added to the stress was Ilan being prevented from speaking to his children and she'd also prohibited them from visiting his parents. She had told him his whole family was not fit to see the children. We didn't know how to defuse the situation and against Ilan's beliefs of her being reasonable we had to find a lawyer and be prepared. She wouldn't calm down and they had some terrible telephone conversations. We had to record them for potential evidence and placed the transcripts with our lawyer. This ensured she couldn't deny her own words at any time in the future. She declared his family unfit to be with the children, and her fury was unceasing. Nothing Ilan said, or anything he offered in terms of money or security would assuage her temper.

So much for the initial courtesy she had shown. She seemed to be on a wild rampage and swore revenge on Ilan and his family, particularly his father. I had never heard anything like it in my life. I'd heard the saying 'hell hath no fury like a woman scorned'. What didn't make sense was the fact they had not been together a year before Ilan and I had met again and she also had a boyfriend. At risk of another cliché, this really was a 'dog in a manger' scenario. She couldn't bear the fact of Ilan and I being so much in love. I'm sure this was all about pride and her image.

When I describe image as being all important to Israelis, it cannot be underestimated. The truth and the stories told bear no resemblance to each other. It was such a waste of energy, and even more it was outrageous behaviour given the fact Ilan was paying every month almost £1000 for her needs.

Despite the tensions, we had to build our own lives. Ilan made a tremendous impact on my life. Our new business was full of potential and Manny and Ilan had become firm friends and colleagues. It was as if we had two lives. One in England full of joy and the other with a spectre of Ilan's freedom of movement being restricted, something which was his Achilles Heel, and one being used to a destructive effect already. We tried not to make it the central focus of our lives but it was impossible to relax fully with the knowledge that someone else had control of our future. We were inseparable. All the months of conversations on the phone every day meant we knew each other pretty well before we were together. There was mutual respect and genuine love. We were two halves of a whole, the sum being much greater than the parts. Friendship was paramount and the foundation of our relationship. It was great being together. Romance and laughter filled our house to the rafters. I couldn't imagine life without him and he couldn't imagine it either. But our fear of Matty and her actions were always present.

We were building good contacts for the new business and working so well together. At home Ilan loved the garden, and grew a herb patch just outside the kitchen window. He loved cooking, and having his own fresh produce was no small pleasure. He'd told me the story of how his father had got rid of his dog when he joined the army, something which had broken his heart, so I bought him a beautiful Border Collie puppy, which we named Jack. Ilan spent hours training him. I learned much later walking him didn't make him tired at all. It exhausted me to build up to almost ten miles a day with him. The dog needed mental stimulation. But it did make me fitter than I'd been for years. Ilan integrated almost immediately into the English lifestyle, and won the hearts of my family and friends. It was idyllic and I had to keep reminding myself, this was all real! We shared our happiness, but the strain of things not settled in Israel kept a blight on it.

Ilan offered everything he had in agreements but never to her satisfaction. Six months had passed. We'd written countless times to finish 'the story' as they say in Hebrew. In Hebrew the term is 'ligmor et ha-sippur'. They tended to talk of divorce as a story or a movie in their language. No drama there then! Everything was so full of hysteria and I began to feel like a Buddha comparatively. I could see why Israelis told me England was so quiet, even boring. Appreciating my country as never before, I was the only calm person and my mistake was to assume that rational thinking would prevail.

As a divorcee myself I knew things might be heated in the early days of separation but Ilan was desperate to see his children, or at the very least talk to them and was still prevented. He'd told me from the beginning he believed Matty to be an intelligent and reasonable woman, despite her anger issues, and still believed after half a year eventually she would calm down, and also the court would see how unreasonable she was being. He wanted to stay in England, and marry me but her actions were stopping all our dreams. Of course, divorce was hard, yet they'd hardly lived as man and wife before I arrived in Israel. She'd written in her testimony this very fact, so her cries and indignation seemed disproportionate to reality. I understood people and their behaviour through my work as a consultant, and thought it was accurate worldwide. I wasn't so confident in comprehending the Israeli culture, but I felt it would be obvious to the courts with evidence that she was behaving in an extreme manner. Israel is like no other country on earth, I would learn just how stubborn and arrogant it was. This woman had barely begun her campaign, and our naivety was to come at a big price.

We hired a lawyer in Israel, warning him of Matty's inability or stubbornness to listen to any reasonable offers. This would become a repetitive mantra, with each lawyer having to learn the hard way, and our suffering increasing because of their refusal to listen. Letters went back and forth from her lawyer to ours. It was clear to see she wanted a lifetime guarantor, and the content of the letters seemed to indicate she was desperate for the Get – a Jewish divorce. This is a critical document in Israel. There is no civil marriage there, only a religious marriage. In Jewish Law marriage is viewed as sacred, and a divorce involves agreement of three parties, the two married people and the religious court. This is the key to everything. Keeping people together is ancient Jewish Law, and should be applied.

If one partner does not want to divorce, then usually the court will try and involve mediation or extra time for a couple to settle issues between them. Also a Get cannot be given if there is no agreement. This is usually done through the civil court, known as the family court. A file opened in one court cannot be defended in another and in Israel to be a defendant can be costly and inconclusive. Matty had already opened every issue she could think of inside the family court, and then refused any agreements. She wanted everything, the house as a gift, a lifetime's child support PLUS a lifetime guarantor. It was ridiculous. All we wanted was to live in peace, pay our way and plan a future.

Chapter 6

The legal system in Israel is like a bowl of spaghetti. The courts are not connected to each other, so it can be simple to play one off against the other. Civil, Religious, and the third player in this quagmire is the Bailiff. They tend to issue No Exit Orders easily, which could be unlimited. The civil court issued them for a set period of time such as 6 months or a year. Matty had placed one in the civil court and one in the Bailiff. It felt like shooting a dead man after stabbing him, a pointless exercise.

During this time, we were advised to give her everything and not get involved in court battles. Women could say anything and the defendant's word of honour meant nothing. The sticking point during this year was the house. Ilan was insistent he wouldn't just hand it over as a gift. Usually the law decrees a splitting of assets, or the property could be used as the Guarantor. We had read up on it but couldn't seem to get this point agreed on with our own lawyer, never mind her. As I said in the beginning, where there is money to be made, there is always a lawyer to be found.

The most irritating part is of Israeli lawyers charging a fee up front, with promises of all being settled quickly. Imagine in England paying any business the whole amount ahead, and then hoping they will still keep an interest. It's not human nature. If things got difficult lawyers always lost interest and the representation became sporadic. Then it became a blame game.

Files passed like a relay race from one lawyer to the next, who claimed the previous one had made mistakes. What a business.

I don't believe any of them sustained passion and commitment with the exception of one. To file a defense or a counter claim also cost thousands. The race was on in a divorce. There is a rush to either the civil or religious court, or who can get the file in first in the place most advantageous to them. Matty had filed everything she could think of, but hadn't actually opened a file for the Get in the religious court. Her weapon was to withhold this until she had a financial agreement, and I sensed she would use Ilan's desperation for freedom of movement as a method of emotional blackmail.

Despite all this new education for both of us we were strong as a unit and I never considered the possibility of an unreasonable outcome. I had put my mindset into work mode, a place I rarely failed in, and was able to separate my emotions to concentrate on negotiating. To me it was business, the business of just how much money it would take to get the courts to agree or to force her to agree to our offers. The trouble was there were no precedents in Israeli law to work on. Different judges and courts made independent decisions which could vary. We didn't know what to do. We'd never been to court in either country, having lived honest and decent lives.

Eventually, the only recourse was to go back to Israel. Ilan had received a letter and in discussions with our lawyer was persuaded Matty would lift the NO Exit Order if he just went back and signed an agreement. I would have given her everything just to get this nonsense finished and worry about things later, but the issue was one of a guarantor.

Coupled with the No Exit Order, the assumption was automatic. Ilan would be an absent father, and never pay child support. It's the way of things in the system. This meant he would have to supply a Guarantor who lived in Israel to compensate for anything he might not pay. The criteria for this person were set very high. They had to be of a certain age, income and well-travelled themselves. No one was generally prepared to risk their own lifestyle for another, even a close family member. Trust disappeared, and the cultural fear predominated. It actually made me sick, when I remembered how much my family had helped me over the years and how much I had given to people myself.

She was getting financial support every month, and a good amount. The concept of Ilan outside Israel created some paranoia and fear he might stop paying one day, and there would be no recourse. Of course it wasn't going to happen. Ilan was paying even without contact with his children and we were committed to supporting them. It was a common value between us. So a guarantor in Israel is a rarity. Even his own family members were reluctant to sign their name securing his future payments and be liable for any missed ones. My own family was prepared to but Israel doesn't accept foreigners for reassurance. All it told me was how stubborn Israel was. Zionism was rife, and losing one citizen was an anathema to them. The problem was Matty only wanted his father as his guarantor. He was a pensioner, but she believed he should still do it. The point of it wasn't for security, it was to pressure his father, we both knew from the conversations which had taken place she wanted to hurt his family. To this day, I am relieved we recorded some of them. I can remember sitting on the sofa one morning listening to them talking.

"Your father talks about me." she shouted. "If I catch him on the street, I will spit on him and take ten years from his life, like he did mine. I won't sit quietly with this, I have nothing to lose and you know that."

"Don't go near my father." Ilan warned.

"Don't mess with me. If I see him I will humiliate him until he wouldn't be able to walk. He better not mess with me." she ranted. "I will do exactly what I want, I don't give a fuck… If this is my destiny in life, if God chooses it, then it will be that way… I don't want your father's money. I don't want money from her. She is a germ and after two years she could sue me that she gave money and wants it back. My lawyer told me. Find another way to give me money." she screamed.

We were recording the call, listening in amazement and horror. I knew people could be heated during stress, but she was furious and determined in her words. Her screaming and shouting was permeating into the peace of our home stealing our harmonious atmosphere. She continued.

"That's it, this is my condition, and two months before the year is finished, you need to give me a guarantee that you are coming back to Israel, and you will give me security that you will keep paying my maintenance. Ok. That's what I and my lawyer have decided. From her, I don't want to take money. He told me not to take the money from her whatsoever. Do whatever you want now. Open a savings account open a bank account, *your* money only. That's it did you hear what I said? This is my solution."

Uncomfortable with her demands and attitude, I watched for Ilan's reaction. He responded calmly throughout, but looked at me in dismay.

"If you want cash, no problem, I can give you cash." Ilan prompted, as she'd insisted upon no cheques.

"Ok, if you don't know how to behave like a human being... you force me... you force me... from now on... I don't accept your behaviour now, for sure, and your father is in the equation... believe me that I won't rest until I have paid him back. I will sort it out, so that he will be dumb all his life... I promise you that his evil and his behaviour, that I wish him the worst cancer in the world. Ah... ah... I pray that he will get it...I will celebrate it all over town. He is a piece of shit, that's why. You have his genes." She continued with barely a pause for breath.

The conversation continued in the same vein until Ilan said,

"Have you finished speaking?"

She blew up. "I didn't finish yet, I told you what I want, I am not going to accept her money. I don't care what you will do. I need to get money from YOU. I don't know how you are going to sort it, after a year, after 10 months, think about an answer, you have a lawyer, let him work and break his head for a solution. How can I get security that you will keep paying me? That's what I need, that's it. Think about it, this is an instruction from my lawyer not to take money from her. No way, never will I accept money from her. She will give you... I don't know how... I am not going to take the money from her."

Where the money came from was clearly a concern for her. Perhaps it was her pride but money is money when it comes to children, and our money was being paid into just one account, so there was no difference to me. We held hands as we listened to regular tirades pulling us back to a part of our lives which wouldn't go away, despite our desire.

We endured many more phone conversations like this, and one of them was a prediction of things which actually came to pass.

Ilan called her to try and arrange to see his children on his return to Israel. "You understand when I want to come and see the kids. I can come?"

She retorted. "No, only if you will go to court."

"There is nothing in court." he insisted.

She threatened him. 'If you will come, I will bring the police here."

"You can bring 10 policemen!" Ilan retorted.

She repeated. "I will bring the police, and then we will see if I have court case or not. You don't understand. You try and come to the house, and you will see where you will be spending the weekend."

He persisted with his desires. "You don't understand that I can come to the house when I want?"

It sounded like goading from her. "Come, come to the house, and I will call the police and you will see what a court order is!"

"Let us check it, and I will see what you can do." he responded angrily.

We knew there were no court orders preventing him from seeing the children. She had made the decision herself, hence no contact.

"Ok, just come and we will see what a court order looks like Ilan. Not like you think, and your father thinks, we are not playing games. We are straight people, we are smart people, we don't give people bribes under the table, do you understand me?" she shouted. It was her usual decibel range, I couldn't remember a time when she didn't shout.

"Who is giving bribes to whom?" Ilan asked, intrigued by her comment.

"It's not important, leave it, just leave it. You are so stupid and you are garbage... I didn't decide it, the judge decided, and the social services. The social services decided that you can't see the children. I didn't decide it, the opposite. No way are you allowed to see them. It went to court, and I have a court order that you can't see your daughter."

She was lying, there were no orders existing then, and wouldn't be any. It seemed she was living in a different reality.

Ilan tried over and over to explain he'd offered everything required and more.

"Yes, very funny. I am glad of the day you left my house, as I had quiet in my mind. You don't know how peaceful I am." she bellowed.

"I don't hear that, I can hear you are still angry. I thought you would calm down, and it doesn't look that way." sighed Ilan.

"No! With you I can't relax. You are the only person I can't relax with. To hear your nonsense, just to think about it I... I am losing my temper. I reach to the conclusion that you are the only person that drives me mental." She was shrieking now.

He tried to reason with her. "No one died, people just changed"

"Good! You are talking stupid. You are fucked, you are autistic." She started yelling again.

"I am autistic. I am whatever you say I am." He looked across at me and rolled his eyes, she wasn't listening to anything.

"Yes, yes, right, with your ugly behaviour. I just don't know." She continued with barely a pause.

"If I am so bad then let me go." Crossing his fingers, he mouthed his hope to me.

"Give me my money. Give me money in time, and leave, I don't hold you." she railed.

"I offered you money for 1 year, and you didn't want it!" he was getting frustrated.

Matty lost her temper. "You didn't give me money for a year, 5500 shekel, it isn't enough, and I have told you on advice from my lawyer that I am not allowed to take money from *her*."

I wondered why she was so obsessed with the idea that any of the money would come directly from me. I reasoned it was just pride and ego, which was far more crucial to her than the welfare of her children.

"You will get the money from me, it doesn't matter the source." he reassured her.

"From her, I am not allowed, it is forbidden for me to take money from her. She could get crazy after a year and come and sue me." She continued relentlessly.

"You will get the money from me." He repeated.

"You better understand. I don't deal with her, if you want to you deal with her. With people like her, I don't deal. You have the responsibility for me, it's enough for me to have one crazy person on my head, and I don't need another one. You understand me!? This is the advice from my lawyer – he saw exactly who he is dealing with." She was at screaming pitch.

We didn't understand a word of this, or what her intentions were. Then, Ilan froze as she continued.

"Never mind, you want me to go to court and cancel the stop order for the border, you think you can solve the problem like this, you are stupid if you think you are going to do it."

"Ah, now I understand, I really understand." He replied angrily. It was all about controlling his freedom. She'd finally declared her true intention.

"You start to behave like a human being. Like other people and you pay me and I will go to court and say that this man is OK now. If it takes 5 years so be it. You don't keep the agreement. We can't go with this agreement to the court." Mally threatened.

There was so much vitriol and bitterness from her. We had no idea of what would settle her down, for money, property and the business wasn't sufficient, we knew we had a battle on our hands when we returned to Israel. *Who was this woman?* I pondered the question. She seemed to have a feud with Ilan's family but more ominous were her promises to control

Ilan's freedom with no fair exchange. She was woman who would see her threats through to the bitter end.

In June 2005, Ilan returned to Israel. I stayed in England. It couldn't take more than a few days I thought. For a week we spoke on Skype and Ilan was incredibly stressed. He told me the moment of landing in Israel was a nightmare as his freedom to come home didn't lie in his hands at all and it was terrifying, but he assured me an impending case would conclude matters. He wasn't a resident of Israel anymore, his base being in England, and believed one of the countless agreements offered should stick or they could be cobbled together. I told him to give her anything she wanted, just to do it. Their conversations had unsettled me and this wasn't a game – it was real life.

The night before his case he and I talked all night on Skype, sharing a virtual bottle of wine, one in each country. The separation caused a physical pain in my chest. We all want the love we see in the movies and I had it. But I missed him so much and the real threat of him not coming home and our fate being in the hands of someone adversarial really frightened me.

Seeing him via computer was barely enough. My predominant thought was I should have been there with him. The next day I waited anxiously for news and by the time it was 4pm Israel time I knew matters had to have been decided either way. Something was wrong or Ilan would have called me.

I contacted our lawyer Sam, who told me Ilan hadn't been in touch with him that week, and if there was any case he was certainly unaware of it. Standing in the garden, with the aroma of the herbs and newly planted rosebushes, I sank down, my legs just buckled under me. My world changed in an instant, and nothing felt right. We'd talked all night, Ilan had sounded confident of success. Nothing was making any sense at all. There had to be an explanation, and above all I wanted to know where he was.

In a rage, I located him through Abe. We talked and he told me things weren't going well but he had not wanted to worry me thinking he could sort things out within the week, though in truth he wasn't coping. There had been no court case. Ilan had tried to buy himself some time, hoping he could reason with Matty and come home. His reasoning had left him. To have no freedom of one's own and the feeling of being trapped cannot be underestimated. But for the right of freedom being in the hands of an enemy using it as a weapon is terrifying. Imagine being ordered for surgery, knowing your worst enemy had the scalpel in their hands.

It is incomprehensible to most people to have an idea of how crippling it is to experience. Ilan's desire for freedom was imperative to his character and well-being - intrinsic to his healthy functioning but the paralysis had brought out what I called a lie, and what he called self-preservation. He was ashamed of himself, he couldn't manage the situation. So he'd hidden the truth from me and being such a proud man hadn't reached out to his own family either.

This was no surprise to me. They had no comprehension of the struggle of freedom, and as typical Israelis I would learn unless it was a personal experience even blood relations were not helpful. I recalled then someone giving me a throwaway line about Israelis saying I'm here 24 hours a day if you need me, until you ask, and then I am suddenly very busy! Ilan knew this better than I. His freedom was not an issue to anyone but himself, and of course to me. Despite all of this he had lied to me at a critical juncture.

I had to fly to Israel. I was angry and disappointed with him. I wasn't sure if I could trust him again.

Preparing myself to give him a piece of my mind face to face we met at the airport. After one look at him I knew beyond doubt Ilan couldn't flourish in Israel especially if captive behind the borders without free will. He ran from the waiting crowd as I came through arrivals, and swept me off my feet, hugging and kissing me. Just for a few moments we were the only two people in the world. As we held hands and walked, it was only then I felt the tension. It was palpable. We were not in a normal situation. All around us were ordinary people meeting and greeting each other. It was like watching a movie, when you know the central characters are in a conspiracy, but this time it was me who was in the film. Only when inside the situation, can it be appreciated how helpless we were.

We were in a bubble, the thin layer separating us from reality. Sounds of laughter and conversations were muted, my senses heightened from the drama which was unfolding. He was the father of her children and she was cutting the roots of her own tree of life. His eyes smiled, and the worry couldn't be erased from his face. All thoughts of admonishment faded away and I knew I'd done the right thing by flying to be beside him. The idea of constant separations interrupting the flow of life was unbearable.

Matty had enlisted her brother in law into the situation. He'd been calling and getting involved from the outset, 'mediating a solution' as he called it. More likely it appeared he had been getting Ilan to talk and give away his weakness and vulnerability. I was to get proof of this agenda during my visit. I persuaded Ilan to pretend he'd managed to lift his No Exit Order. Matty's brother in law was taken aback, and using carefully rehearsed words Ilan chatted casually.

The reaction was not the one Ilan wanted, but it seemed very clear the agenda was to keep Ilan trapped. He'd taken a lawyer for Matty very cheaply, who had drawn up an agreement. Ilan just wanted to leave so he'd signed it without scrutiny. We took it to the office. On the same morning Ilan had arranged an appointment with the Religious Court (Rabbinate) to complete the Get. We genuinely believed on this day all would be concluded and he'd be on a plane home.

Not a chance. Suddenly her brother in law wouldn't take phone calls, promising all would be well in the morning and the agreement would be ratified in the family court but never doing it. Finally Ilan visited her lawyer who did accept the signed agreement and asked Ilan to stand outside. Within a few minutes, he was called back in and the picture had changed completely as the demands began again. 'Feed your children, get more money, and don't be unreasonable'. Her lawyer ordered. Time passed and after 4 hours of waiting, Ilan's other meeting time had passed and we had nothing. If only Matty had understood at that time Ilan would have given her everything, and she could have lived a lavish lifestyle in Israel.

Our own lawyer Sam was out of his depth, thinking us overly suspicious and had pulled away. What is it about this country, I asked myself. Just when people are needed the most, they go silent or disappear.

We sat in a café in Haifa, crying into each other's arms in despair. There seemed to be no answers. Matty wouldn't accept anything. After half an hour of self-pity, I decided we needed a second opinion. It was impossible to believe Ilan couldn't leave Israel; it was just not in my psyche. We went home. I scoured the internet, and found an English lawyer whose husband was Israeli. We were so fortunate to learn they were available the same afternoon in Tel Aviv. We took the unratified agreement and drove to meet them.

Chapter 7

Withheld for legal reasons, I have to change the lawyer's name, so I'll call him Alan.

Alan was not only a giant of a man but a giant character. He was thorough, efficient, and could see at once Ilan was in a state of shock. He had little English and I matched it with my limited Hebrew. I had no choice but to handle the discussion, as Ilan was sitting in a stupor. I recalled the day he'd told Matty

"Whatever you want to do to me, don't mess with my freedom."

She'd done exactly the action he most feared and he was cursing himself for handing his weakness over on a plate. Alan agreed to take the case and then began to read the agreement. He was horrified. It was a license to print money and keep Ilan trapped forever. It had been Ilan's lucky day things had not gone to plan, he told us. He dropped the bombshell by informing Ilan he had not needed to come back to Israel and all matters could have been resolved whilst he was outside the country. The fact he was now back meant it would take more effort and more offers to be able to leave. But he was sure he could manage this. What a relief. Ilan felt so safe with him but what a blow to learn this was all unnecessary. The power was back in Matty's hands as he was trapped inside Israel's borders.

We had been so naïve.

Up to this point my Hebrew was limited, confined to a few conversations. I'd picked up some useful business words when staying in Israel and working with Ilan in his company. Not that stainless steel and building terms would be useful in this scenario.

Blessed with a photographic memory and the ability to learn rapidly, this was a crisis and all my skills would be needed. Not just the mental skills but also the qualities of patience and unconditional support. I was frustrated, as in English I knew I had the vocabulary to turn the whole thing around and bring about a win-win result. My business skills were working overtime.

His first action was to travel to meet with Matty's lawyer, who was most disconcerted, and uncomfortable. He repeatedly asked where our original lawyer had gone. I began to suspect they thought he was easy and they could thrash through a killer agreement, but not anymore. Alan was formidable and concluded we would meet in court. I was waiting in the car outside, a déjà vu from the previous day, but this time I felt in safe hands for the first time since I'd arrived.

The dynamic changed so fast. I'd hired one of the best barristers in Israel and their local lawyer was an amateur by comparison. The empowerment we felt was intoxicating. I had no doubt our man would win the day. What a day it would be.

We arrived at the family court and knew the moment she entered the building as we heard the shouting and noise she brought with her. I was intimidated and afraid of her. Ilan's freedom was on the line and I couldn't sense one opportunity for negotiation. I was told to wait outside so seated myself in the court café at 8.30 in the morning and settled down with a book I had brought. I never got past the first page, the words of the first line repeating in my brain leaving me unable to concentrate at all.

There was a couple working in the café who were so kind. They gave me some homemade grappa, a type of alcohol, which was gratefully received and under normal circumstances might have made me giddy. Despite being unable to eat a thing the alcohol didn't affect me. My nerves were frayed yet I somehow had to find the patience to sit for almost four hours. I knew there was a recess as I could hear her voice raised and sounding angry. She entered the café. It took all I had to sit calmly, pretending to read and keeping my eyes well away from any contact. Trembling inside, I prayed for Ilan and Alan to arrive. She sat in a position where she had her back to me, her own lawyer able to see me. Angry just wasn't the word I could use to describe it.

The atmosphere in the café had changed. She was eventually asked to leave, as her loudness was disruptive. It was akin to a tornado crashing through the building. I'd never seen such an out of control and angry woman like this before.

Alan sat down next to me, instructing me to smile and laugh as if I'd just heard great news. It was all for her lawyer's benefit opposite me across the room. Then he told me things were not going so well, the judge was a Zionist, and we'd need to work hard to overcome his stance. There it was, Zionist. The difference between being Jewish and Zionist is the latter has a compulsion to keep all Jews inside Israel. This was deadly serious; our future lay both in her hands and a Judge who didn't know us.

Alan said we'd need to be prepared to offer a reasonable amount of money, six months hopefully, but possibly 12 months. Was I prepared to go so far, and was Ilan? He instructed Ilan to make some phone calls and act happy and confident and then smiled, telling me perhaps I was the secret weapon after all. As soon as Matty had seen me, she'd gone into a rage, and Alan hoped it would result in her not thinking clearly. Patting my hand and reassuring me, he told me to try and breathe deeply to get the colour back into my drained face. People had been looking at the uproar and thankfully as she'd gone I was able to gather myself together again. Ilan and I hugged as they returned to the courtroom and I was there alone to wait for what was to be another four hours.

Waiting is an art form. It is a skill which requires practice. I wouldn't want to recommend acquiring this to people in life, but this kind of waiting - in an empty room - fills your head with wild thoughts and fears flood in. It takes a determined effort to throw the useless thoughts away and concentrate on the hope. I think it is one of the most difficult activities I had to learn and this was a baptism of fire. The café closed and I had to leave the building, not knowing if normal life would be resumed or if Ilan could come home. I was frantic on the inside. Could it be she would have the right to determine our lives? Would the court see reason? Divorce is not a crime, and the punishment should not be captivity. The conflict of trying not to think or letting thoughts control me was rife.

The heat was like an oven outside as I exited the court, so I quickly crossed over to the nearby shopping centre and found a quiet corner in a bustling restaurant, this time deciding a glass of wine would calm my nerves. Ilan called me.

"Where are you?" He asked.

Quickly giving him my location, my next words were "Did you win Ilan?"

"I don't know. We are on our way to you now".

I could have spilled the contents of my stomach right there and then, had I had any.

Although the café was only five minutes' walk I watched every stranger passing and after what seemed like an age there they were. Ilan looked shell-shocked. I was bursting for news. If it had been me I would have given the news immediately but of course this wasn't my culture.

"Take your husband home!" Alan said. "You need to deposit 70,000 shekels within a maximum of seven days and that's it." As he said it, Ilan listened too as if for the first time himself. I wanted to know everything, all the details.

"I was right Marianne. You did disturb her. She was out of control when we returned. She was using her mobile phone repeatedly and the Judge got more impatient as time went on. She had demanded money and security for all her life. The judge had become very impatient with her, telling her nothing in life could be guaranteed."

Finally relaxing I could begin to enjoy the story, at last we had some sanity returning to our lives.

"I was worried about the Judge." Alan continued, "He was a hardliner as I told you during lunch but Matty's lawyer couldn't control her. She was interrupting all the time, and someone even popped their head through the door to say she was so loud it was disturbing other rooms! There was a turning point when the judge exploded and told her to be quiet. He'd finally told her there was an offer of a year's child support on the table. She'd refused, demanding more, until the judge had said, it's one year or 6 months, take it or leave it, and if you can't answer, then I will decide it to be six months!"

I didn't need much imagination to picture the scene. The only times I had experienced her as being calm and quiet was when she had been planning something, and despite my joy I felt a pang of sympathy and pity for her. Ilan was sitting at the table, and listened as if he hadn't been there inside the courtroom.

"She had realised then she had to accept one year, as nothing else would be forthcoming, and with great reluctance she'd agreed. The judge had told Ilan she was a very difficult woman, and he should leave the country as soon as possible, and stay in open places until his departure."

So the judge had seen too. She was so intimidating and both Ilan and I were slightly afraid of her.

Alan added, "The things which had been said of her intransigence had not been exaggerated. Ilan needs to stay well away from her and Israel too."

I clasped Alan's hands with deep gratitude. Ilan went to the restroom and on his return Alan asked, "So Ilan, tell me about the work you have in England? What plans do you have? I want to know all about it."

As Ilan started to talk, Alan winked at me and then whispered to me, "I did this case for you because his soul was in peril. Not just his freedom. She is one of the most extreme characters I've encountered and I warn you now to get out of Israel and don't ever come back. Now go and get the money, it's almost £10,000 and you only have seven days to deposit the money. I have a feeling she won't readily accept this and might makes things difficult, but call me if you need me."

He gathered his papers and gave me a big hug and left us.

We'd actually won! Ilan just hadn't absorbed it as the eight hour case had exhausted him. We'd won! Oh My God! What a day.

We travelled back to his parents sharing this private moment, Ilan's phone ringing incessantly, but we didn't answer any calls. It was our victory and an imminent return to reality with England just around the corner. What joy we had, the judge had ordered them to find some kind of peace during the next year and Matty was ordered not to put any No Exit Orders on him for the upcoming twelve months. Free at last. An expensive freedom, it was almost £10,000 to give to her, and nearly half the amount again for the barrister. Ilan was elated as he also had a cheque for 50,000 shekels at home from his partner, relieved this wouldn't be a major burden for us to find the whole sum.

Our joy was to be very short lived. His parents were waiting for our return. They were sitting outside in the porch, their faces unfathomable. Ilan jumped out of the car.

"We won." He called as we entered the gate.

"No you didn't." replied his father, "You lost."

Ilan was surprised and aghast. "No, not this time Dad, we were there, we won. Trust me on this."

I knew immediately what had occurred, as we had told no one and I was determined we were not going to be brainwashed against actual events.

"No Dad, you are wrong, we won." Ilan repeated.

"So where are your papers to prove it?" his dad demanded.

Both parents looked thunderously at us.

"Don't worry, we won, and I can go home." Ilan persisted.

Something was wrong. I watched in horror. His own parents didn't believe him. They didn't want to believe him more to the point. There was no joy, no enquiry, nothing. It was just accusations and a cold dark mood. Ilan's mother looked uncomfortable and tried to defuse the situation by offering us food.

"Well Ilan, you won't be going home as you put it, and also know this, the cheque is not good." His father stormed away with those words and so did Ilan, down to the basement room we were staying in.

"What was all that about?" he raged. He was so hurt and angry with his father yet again.

"Don't worry," I said, trying to calm him down, "Let's call Matty and get her bank details then go and cash the cheque. My credit card will cover the rest." I assured him.

But Matty was having none of it. She refused to give her bank details and refused to even talk about the judgment. We called Alan.

"I suspected this would happen Ilan, don't worry. Get the money and I will have to come back up and hand in the cash to the court. Seven days remember. This could be a delaying tactic." Alan informed us.

Our happiness was dented, but not defeated. We left the house and went up to the small village of Maalot to the bank to cash Ilan's cheque. Yet another shock awaited us there. The cheque bounced. There were no funds in the bank to cover it. Ilan's joint account in the company had been taken over by Abe and there wasn't enough money to pay.

Ilan had no idea his name had been removed from the account and I don't think I'll ever forget the murderous look in his eyes. The realization dawned on him. Gossip must have travelled like lightening after our case, and somehow Ilan's father had known the cheque was a dud. This meant only one thing. In the event we would win the case, a contingency had been arranged. The cheque Ilan had received for his share of the business was never going to be cashed. Ilan's parents knew this and it could only have been through conversations between them and Abe.

We were putting two and two together. Perhaps Matty knew the cheque was a dud too. If she was refusing to take the money she must have known and the only source of finance would be our account in the UK. She'd said she wouldn't take anything connected to me. How many people were involved we wondered?

The relationship between Ilan and Abe was broken in that moment. Ilan drove to his factory, his anger cold as the stainless steel inside. Abe saw him and knew instantly Ilan had discovered the truth. He looked genuinely afraid. I would have been too if I'd been him. I held Ilan back as much as I could. The treachery was apparent to us both. Parts of Matty's file could only have been written with Abe's input and there was clearly a plan to prevent Ilan living the life of his choice. This was a sinister situation and I wanted us out of this primitive land.

But I had to transfer cash and my credit cards wouldn't allow me to do this from Israel. I had to return home to make a bank transfer and we only had seven days to achieve it. With our weekends and Israeli weekends we would only have four of seven days to deposit the money into the court.

I said my farewells to Ilan at the airport, promising him I would arrange it and he'd be home within a week.

This time, although we hated these goodbyes and separations we knew it would only be a few days.

Getting money transferred to Israel is a feat in itself. First I needed to find an organization to do this quickly and directly. My bank was not able to do this within the time frame. It was stressful, difficult and a full time project. So much paperwork was involved. I needed to have the money in an Israeli bank, cleared, removed and deposited in the court. Seven days, or the judgment would be void. It wasn't just my imagination. Matty was making things more difficult. She'd got the judgment for money but wouldn't accept it directly as the court had ordered. It was ridiculous. But I was now fully aware money was never the root of this. It was a weapon, and becoming all too apparent she just wanted to make things impossible for us. Some of her promises on the phone were coming true.

Not to be defeated, the money was transferred and then we learned because it was Israel it would take a number of days to clear, unlike any other country in Europe. It was there but inaccessible and the time to get it would mean the order nullified. I made so many calls to banks here and there and eventually the money was released. It was filed in the court, and a glorious piece of paper issued to Ilan releasing him from the No Exit Order.

Ilan was on a flight home the same day. Won or lost? Who knows? I thought reason had prevailed and we would have a year to get calm. Surely she would have calmed down by then; she had a boyfriend so nothing made sense. But she was still his legal wife and held all the rights and this was the problem. It prevented him from getting papers in England for residency. A nagging doubt pricked my mind as my account details were in the transfer and she'd made threats of holding him to ransom. A year seems a long time but it worked both ways. A year to build bridges and make an agreement, or the time spent to plan more court cases.

But my partner was home and we'd had a lucky escape. I have to include the letter below which Ilan wrote to the lawyer Sam. Because this legal practice was not unique, the letter evoked no response and I was disgusted with the legal representation and also the fight for Zionism. I did believe the sum of money for one year was a normal judgment and would base many of my future actions on the innocent belief that the judicial system in Israel had some regulations. It was almost two years since their separation and still Matty was erupting like Vesuvius. He had a narrow escape and the fear permeated his letter. Israel has no mercy for its citizens, none at all. Everything comes with a price tag. What right does it have to charge so much for legal help, especially with the number of lawyers that earned their living from so much misery?

Chapter 8

Dear Sam,

I want to confirm in writing that I no longer require your services on my behalf. I think you need to be clear about my reasons why. I have copies of all my correspondence to you, from 22nd January, when I first contacted you. I gave you explicit instructions on 3 occasions to go to the court and prepare a defence for me regarding the border. I wrote to you explaining that the border was not to be a bargaining tool for the agreement I was trying to make with Matty.

I also instructed you in Israel on my return when I visited with Marianne to go to court and prepare me a case to defend on the border. You on NO OCCASION, carried out those instructions for me.

You indicated to me in your office that you could get me released in a matter of hours, and then told me that it would probably take a week, knowing that I was trying to arrange a flight back to England within a couple of days of that conversation. This took place in your office on Sunday 3rd July. You couldn't even tell me on that day what had or hadn't been placed in the court regarding the agreement. We suspected the signed agreement hadn't been lodged by xxx, and you were sceptical about our mistrust, yet didn't chase it for me.

On 4th July, when we learned that the agreement hadn't been lodged, you advised us to meet with xxx as soon as possible regarding the guarantee situation with my father. Though you yourself couldn't come *and attend the meeting. You said on the phone that the border could be sorted out as late as Thursday 7th July, before my intended flight on 8th July.*

I never heard from you again, even though I again instructed you to get on with the border issue as a separate agreement.

I subsequently took the advice of another lawyer on 7th July. On 13th July a defence was submitted to the court, and a case was given for the 20th July. After 8 hours in court on 20th July, I was granted a release from the stop order, and also the maintenance order of 10,000 shekels a month, which was a second stop order weapon.

I have now arrived back in England. The whole process took 3 weeks.

The advice I have now received from my lawyer has horrified me. Firstly the agreement you recommended I sign was not going to release me from the border, it was a suicide note.

The agreement I signed offered the following to Matty, just as a few examples.

There was no child support agreed. The extras I had promised would have more than doubled the 6,000 shekel per month payments, plus the children had the right to sue me for the child support.

Matty had the right to claim a MINIMUM of 16,000 shekels a month maintenance from me for the rest of her life.

I signed away my rights to ever renegotiate or dispute the agreement.

I agreed that she could close me here for the rest of my life.

There is NO SUCH THING as a guarantor on maintenance in the way you were leading me.

The house should have been the guarantee from the beginning. Not my father. As I had tried to tell you from the beginning.

To think that my lawyer advised me of this is just too much. I have been the subject of emotional and financial blackmail, and signed under extreme duress. How is it that you never read the nuances of that agreement and advised me against this? Also, the advice I have been given is that I NEVER, UNDER ANY CIRCUMSTANCES, needed to return to Israel.

As a result of my return, I spent two months in Israel, causing untold damage to my work here, losing clients and money. I was not aware until July, that there was a maintenance order for 10,000 shekels per month. It had been granted in February, and you didn't inform me. As my proxy, I believe from your correspondence with me that you had no knowledge of the cases against me, nor the exact reason why I had a stop order. I am now aware that several laws were breached for the stop order to be given, and would have expected that you would have made me aware of this. According to my lawyer, the fact that the agreement was never lodged in court saved my life. I have been physically ill and suicidal through this. How could you have recommended such a destructive course of action for me?

On a personal note, I have endured 7 months extreme stress, and you are the main contributor to the situation. I have no intention of paying you any money, and in fact will be looking at what action I can take against you for the totally misleading and bad advice which you gave me. Your representation almost destroyed my life, and I cannot tell you too strongly that you will be hearing from me in due course.

Yours sincerely, ILAN AZIZI

Despite our victory, and Ilan's freedom secured for a year the divorce issue was paramount. Ilan was still unable to speak with his children. Matty was still stubbornly refusing to divorce. Simultaneously, we were building a beautiful life. The garden was blooming, our dog a pleasure. Work contracts were in the offing and we were more in love than ever, our friendship and mutual respect deepening daily.

We enjoyed things normal people did; going on days out; concerts, west end shows; our mutual passion for football; seeing family and friends; long walks; movies; playing cards and games, and living our life in peace and quiet. We had something worth fighting for but time was passing with no agreement between Ilan and Matty. He was afraid. What would happen next year if things were not concluded? How could he get a work permit if he was not divorced? So of course, we spent a lot of time trying to resolve this too.

Letter writing became more than a hobby. We tried everywhere to get help. We contacted the Beth Din (religious court) in London, tried the Reform Synagogues, and wrote to people as far and wide as the USA and Australia. Our local MP couldn't see a problem either. I knew this problem was bubbling away, ready for another eruption, but trying to convince a stranger was proving to be impossible. I had never been as contented as I was in my relationship and would take on Matty myself if that is what it would require.

Since his return Ilan repeatedly begged Matty to release him, she continually refused, and even worse she blocked all contact between him and his daughter. I was powerless to console him. My emotions ranged from feeling pity for her and being incensed at the long term damage she was doing. She was a mother after all and this was unhealthy behaviour. He wanted his oldest son to visit us which was another nonstarter.

I called Matty one afternoon and asked her how much money it would take for her to release Ilan from the marriage. I will never forget the conversation. She told me she wanted to destroy Ilan, either by hospitalization or death or madness, it didn't matter which, and money was not the issue. She sounded like madness personified. She had already told Ilan if it took five years to break him, then so be it. She meant it. I know they were not empty words, because if they were empty, then I wouldn't be writing this story.

I hadn't been a soldier in a war as Ilan had but I'd fought my own battles over the years and it takes a few near death experiences for one's antenna to spot impending danger. I might have been all kindness and openhearted to those who knew me but underneath I am not a woman to be messed with.

I received news that my father was seriously ill and it was a probability that he would die. I loved my dad despite his extreme methods of bringing us up. I took after him more than I liked to admit especially in terms of persistence and honesty. I never quit anything I started even if it took an age to actually get started. He was never a man who would call for a chat, his calls usually a summons to come home and face the lectures of how I should improve; stop letting people walk over me and deal with financial problems as my generosity got me into so much debt.

I know he loved me because everyone told me so, except him. He couldn't actually say those words to me but I know he was proud of me. Because I was born with a survival instinct and a strong sense of empathy I could sense moods just walking into a room, right from childhood.

It is one thing to be a soldier, conscripted and obeying the rules of command, but it is quite another to be nearly murdered in your home and find a way to escape a madman. Just after my 21st birthday I'd had the misfortune to date a man who was seriously emotionally disturbed from his own army experience in Northern Ireland. It was a short relationship, only a month or two and I ended it. Something about him just didn't feel right. He had other ideas about this closure of mine and on Christmas Eve I returned home to find him sitting in my living room, which had been trashed. I saw that he was drunk, several cartons of wine splayed across the floor, and red wine splattered on my walls. I tried to leave but he locked the door and yanked the phone wire, leaving me trapped.

Initially indignant, I was soon to learn of the real peril I was in. He beat me black and blue, over and over.

Sitting on me and punching me to semi consciousness. I saw the headlines in my mind of 'girl found murdered' and no, your life doesn't flash before your eyes as they say. It was just sheer terror. I had to find a way out of this. At some point he was exhausted and had slumped in an armchair breathing heavily, at which point I dragged myself up to him and told him how amazing he was, how much I loved him. It was purely instinctual.

He responded by looking up and touching my bleeding face. My ribs were cracked, and the excruciating pain almost took me back to oblivion. But I wanted to live and the only way was to get out of the house. The funny part of this is I had purchased a car some months before very cheaply, because it had no reverse gear! All I could think was hopefully if I could get out there would be no cars parked in front of me. With cajoling and sweet words, I managed to persuade him to let me go to the shop and buy more wine, a few cigarettes and we'd sit and talk. I took my car keys and stumbled to the front door, the only thing spurring me on was to get into the car. My hands really did shake as I tried to get the key into the ignition and the knowledge that I would have to hit a car close by to escape.

This crazy guy suddenly saw through my trick and had emerged from the house with a giant kitchen knife, trying to get into the car or smash the windows. I had no time to be terrified, so concentrated was I on the task of driving away and I succeeded. Arriving at a family member's home, I collapsed at their door covered in blood. Yet I was reluctant to call the police! They did and I was told it was one of the worst cases of Actual Bodily Harm (ABH) they had seen. On Christmas morning, when my mum arrived to find out why I hadn't gone to church, she was greeted with a daughter she didn't recognise. I was taken to hospital and had all my wisdom teeth removed, with a broken jaw. Stitched up and with a face swollen like a hamster my mum and dad took me to their home.

A week later, having been watched by hawk like eyes by the family, on New Year's Eve I sneaked out and went to this man's home where he lived with his mother. When she opened the door all her protestations died in her mouth as she saw the state of me. All she said was he'd not eaten or slept for a week since the incident. Her eyes showed me all the shame I needed to see.

On that night, I forgave him for what he had done as I knew without the forgiveness there was no moving on for me. It took months to recover and the company I worked for, an advertising agency, didn't want me to prosecute because of image. Yes, there it is, the word image again, all about others saving face when I hardly had a face of my own left. My dad was wonderful, strict and Victorian, but wonderful. So I disappointed him and tested his faith when the traumas of that event lead me to try and take my own life. There was no counselling in those days and I couldn't handle it in the end. The lessons I learned during this time were that I gained a super sensitivity for spotting hidden agendas, lies, and self-preservation for life.

Dad was dying and as complicated as our relationship had been, I'd never given up on him. If Matty thought she would take my soul mate to hell, then she didn't know who she was dealing with. He was inexperienced in real life, as are many Israelis who have never lived outside the country, and my dad's imminent demise had brought all the memories and also all the strength back flowing through my veins.

I think Ilan sealed the love and commitment from my family in December of this year. My father was dying. He'd had a few close calls, but this was really it. I drove like the wind on the news of his imminent death with Ilan by my side. The time had come. Ilan never said a word about my driving speed, though told me later it was well over 100 miles an hour.

At the hospital were my mum, sister and one of my brothers. It must have been so hard for Ilan to be in that situation. But he was so supportive, getting coffees and providing unobtrusive strength. He'd lost his grandmother, her dying in hospital, waiting for her final son to arrive so she could let go. It had sounded like an episode from The Waltons; how she had waited fully compos mentis for her final son to arrive to say her goodbye.

She'd been Ilan's inspiration, the true love in his life and a woman who had shaped his life so much. He'd told me all about her unable to continue so often through his tears. So I was aware the memories would be flooding back to him of that. He'd never seen any other deathbed event. Since my dad had been 65, he'd given me presents from the home at each visit saying this might be his last day. He was convinced he was going to die. Twenty years later, he was going to be right. This man, who had shaped my character and my enduring years of therapy to deal with who I was because of him, was now struggling for every breath. There are moments I celebrate my old faith and as Irish Catholics we stayed for hours, singing, telling stories, with our eyes constantly on him wondering if this breath was the last one.

My father passed away in the early hours of the morning and my mum hugged Ilan asking him to take care of me. He did indeed, holding me all night as I sobbed and cried. He was with me the next day to collect the death certificate and register it. I'd thought it would be easy but it was far from it. The most influential man in my life had departed. He had loved me, I knew it, and he was so proud of me, wanting more for me always. Thank you Dad, despite all our difficulties, I still turn to you in my heart for advice. Then there was my dear Ilan, such a rock, always there and fully aware he didn't require or need any attention from me.

He was solid and just present to the situation. He was the best of my father, my mum told me so. I am eternally grateful to him for how he supported me. He continued by his tender care for my mother; taking her out and doing odd jobs for her. They also had an incredible bond of real love and my mum felt she had adopted another son. She took to him instantly as he did her and he often told me she was the best mother figure he could have had. He saw the unconditional and un-possessive love she had and admired her greatly. She would go to the ends of the earth for him, she said, and would keep her word as events would show.

Chapter 9

2006

What a wonderful year it started out to be. Our relationship went from strength to strength. We had some wonderful trips, to Hungary, France and a fabulous holiday in Portugal to meet with my close friend Jan. She and I had met on 9/11 on a plane. We were passengers coming from Aberdeen to London. The flight was taking ages to land and as we circled round Heathrow we'd struck up a conversation. We became firm friends from that day, a fateful day for so many.

We went as a family unit and had so much fun. Jan and her family took to Ilan immediately, and she was delighted I'd finally found happiness. We laughed together from the beginning to the end of our trip. It was the perfect place to forget our worries and live just like normal people. The trouble was, the year of peace was almost up and we needed to finally resolve what felt unresolvable.

It was almost a full year since Ilan had been home and every night I was relieved to fall asleep in his arms, knowing we'd wake up together but that peace of mind was disintegrating by the day. I had practically forced Ilan to sit down with the outstanding files Matty had, and he wrote in Hebrew as I dictated in English. He hated concentrating on it but Matty was still simmering and coming to the boil on occasions with no agreement or divorce in sight.

Each time we'd got one step forward, events out of our control conspired to block our way. One was a strike of stenographers in Israel of all things. Another was the US Presidential visit, which put a hold on court proceedings. Then we achieved a major breakthrough.

It appeared that Matty was using a lot of internet dating sites and by sheer coincidence she'd been chatting to someone we knew. He had contacted us to say he was sure it was Matty, using a nickname Metushka. The background all added up and unless there were more women in Nahariyya her age with three children the same age and an estranged husband living in England then we had hit the jackpot. There was no doubt it was her. One of the most disturbing notes in her profile was a sentence she'd written regarding destroying her cheating husband, and finishing his life. We kept a copy of the page. She'd written *it was against her nature but she couldn't stop it*. So not only was she dating, she was still looking around. She had variations on several sites of divorced or separated people. We told the Rabbinate to request again that they forced her to divorce, but it was extraordinary. They claimed the evidence wasn't enough.

"Do we need photos of her in bed?"

"Not particularly in bed. That would be an invasion of privacy." was the response.

This was all nonsense I thought angrily. How hard should it be for a divorce, when both parties were with new partners? I had no idea what it would take for the court to set Ilan free from the unholy alliance. It was time for a plan. We decided to hire a private investigator to follow her. Bearing in mind that we were in England, it wasn't easy to guess her movements. Ilan had been receiving secret calls from his son on certain days during the week when Matty was out.

It is very expensive to hire someone to sit outside a house to watch and wait for movements, and we were warned it could take weeks of surveillance and would cost a fortune. We had to pick the right moment. We told the investigator to go that very evening when we believed she might go out.

We struck lucky. She had gone out with her boyfriend, which the experienced investigator testified was a long term intimate relationship by the nature of their body language. She'd also gone out to his flat until the early hours of the morning, leaving her small children alone. It was just what we needed. Nothing in the bedroom as the rules stated and we'd got the information we needed.

We had acted on the advice which they had given, which was drip fed. They would tell us what we needed; we would do it and then they'd feed us a bit more. There was nowhere to get full advice from the outset. My love affair with Israel was well and truly over. I couldn't understand the reticence of the court.

Meanwhile Matty had appealed for a delay through the religious High Court. Her behaviour seemed insane to me and to Ilan it was a vendetta he could see no way to end. We saw videos and photos of her. Ilan could barely look at her without a shudder and I was overjoyed with our concrete evidence. She must really have believed she was untouchable.

It wasn't enough. Despite Ilan and I being together and Matty ensconced in a long term relationship, there were still not enough grounds for divorce. Was marriage itself so sacred that people who hated each other had to stay spliced?

This was not the agenda. I was to discover it was pure Zionism. A design to keep Israeli Jews together come what may. We were knocking on the doors of every court and none of them were interested. Maybe she was untouchable. The only thing I held on to was she had to sign a declaration in her lawsuits agreeing if anything she had written was damaging to Ilan's life or income potential, she would be liable and could be sued. What a pipedream I had. No one is liable in Israel for damage. It didn't work this way in real life.

We prepared ourselves, knowing the year was almost up and we pushed hard for answers. Ilan offered everything. There was no reply from anyone.

Then we had a momentous interruption to our lives, as the war between Israel and Lebanon began.

Nahariyya was in the direct firing line of hundreds of scud missiles. We couldn't go back now. Ilan was beside himself with worry for the children. One night,

Jan and I were talking on Skype when Ilan received a call from his son. He was inside the building at home and was terrified. We could hear the sound of rockets. Jan heard everything. The terror and helplessness was almost too much to handle. Ilan was begging his son to go to the shelter but his son was screaming and crying. As a parent it is an unimaginable pain to be on the other side of the world and not be able to help your own flesh and blood.

Jan was frozen in horror listening to the conversation. Ilan was shaking and trying to calm his son to move downstairs to the shelter. Those of us who heard the call will never forget it. We wanted to bring Matty and the children to England no expense spared to ensure their safety. Matty moved away from Nahariyya over the next few days, calling for money but refusing to give any account details for us to transfer something for assistance. She claimed we could steal her money if we knew her bank account number! What ridiculous paranoia. Ilan begged her to come to England but she refused and wouldn't tell him where they had gone. It was an agonising time for us; watching every news channel to get information. Ilan's parents moved to Tel Aviv, my ex's family stayed put. We had friends and family in danger and we learned a scud had hit a neighbouring building to Ilan's home there.

There was no point in flying to Israel if we didn't know where anyone was. We just had to watch and wait. It was one of the most stressful times of our life. One million people from the north of Israel were displaced during the war and 42 were killed. Anyone who has loved ones in a conflict zone will understand how the powerlessness and lack of knowledge can engulf your whole existence to just one focal point.

Mercifully the war ended in September after only two short months which felt like two long years, and as quickly as it had arrived it had ended and normal life was resumed in Israel. We worried endlessly during that time, watching from a neutral country which also showed the brutality of the war and the deaths of over 1000 Lebanese people from massive airstrikes.

The world made Israel stop before a ground war started. I wondered how the Israelis could live and endure such trauma so regularly. Of course I feel for them and always admired their tenacity and ability to survive, yet they were so heavy handed in their military responses and the war was a draw, a ceasefire, but the PR war was won by Lebanon. The issue in Israel is they just don't care what the world thinks because they don't live in the world, they live in 'The Land' – Ha Aretz in Hebrew. It's described in a way that anything outside is either a threat or inconsequential. Their cultural paranoia brings them their own disasters.

We had to concentrate again. Ilan had a pending case against him for alimony for Matty of a minimum of 10,000 Shekels per month and she wanted it backdated. They were still not yet divorced so she felt she had a claim for wife maintenance too. Ilan sent a letter to the court, offering his business and everything he owned. Unsurprisingly she refused.

I was certain she wanted revenge; though I couldn't really understand the depths she was going to. But I was worried. We visited our MP and expressed Ilan's fear of returning to Israel but it was not regarded as a country which actually abuses human rights. Israel was an ally of the UK so our fears were dismissed out of hand. We contacted lawyers in the UK to enable him to have 'leave to remain' which is a visa allowing him to stay without citizenship. He hadn't been in the UK for long enough and no one believed his freedom was at risk. In fact he was only a few weeks short of the requirements. We were brushed off by everyone we approached for help. The continuing *legal* marriage was the problem.

"Tell her the truth, try and appeal to her sense of fairness. She must have some humanity inside her." I whispered one night as we cuddled up on the sofa.

"No way! She won't listen. She's trying to destroy me. You and I both know that. You heard the things she said. She's not going to stop now, and I'm not going to tell her how desperate I am. She'll use it to her advantage." He said.

In the end I persuaded him which was one of my biggest mistakes. I had an innate belief in the goodness of people and innocently thought Matty had some kindness and compassion somewhere in her being. I believed if she could manage her anger and have some self-control we could all live a better life. Ilan was the father of her children and her financial security. In my mind the war should have been the sort of event to bring people back to their senses and grasp what was more important in life. No matter what her issues were, I had to believe she was a mother who would see it was damaging to fight constantly with their father.

Reluctantly, Ilan made the call.

"In the long term I will be able to pay you double what you are asking for. I will always take care of the children's needs. I will help you as much as I can. You can have a better lifestyle than you ever had before."

We waited and listened, praying for her to understand the bigger picture. Her response was the opposite of what we wanted.

"In your dreams Ilan, I haven't even begun yet. I don't care about the money."

There had been a ceasefire in Israel but not in Matty. She hadn't even started with her own personal war.

Financial security was bottom of her list, it was clear to see. It was due to that call that I lost all my empathy.

I called Jan to ask her advice a month later.

She reminded me, "Don't forget the call we heard. It still haunts me. She left her children inside when the bombs were going off. I think she is capable of anything. I don't have a good feeling about this."

"I know Jan but surely the war would have changed her priorities. So many people were hurt in Nahariyya. It must have been terrifying. Even she must have learned something from this and I thought she would have seen sense." I urged.

My hopes were dashed. No matter how hard Ilan tried, or how many offers he made, Matty was intransigent. He'd had calls from his son crying all the time about his mother's aggression and the children were afraid of her. We'd been horrified to see their change in behaviour just approaching their own home, becoming tense and shut down emotionally when minutes before they'd been full of life and laughter.

The stress was overwhelming Ilan and I wanted him to relax so he could be better prepared when we needed to return to Israel. All he could think of was the close call we'd had the year before, how much money it would take to sort things out and a real fear of the courts not giving him a chance. I surprised him with to a day trip to Venice to take our minds off everything. The vision of Venice on approach from the boat is something I hope everyone could have etched in their memories. Better than any TV documentaries, it took our breath away. Stiflingly hot, but a place of beauty, we plodded around all day taking in the smells, sights and sounds of this epic city. Ilan was mesmerised and we put it down on our list of possible venues for our wedding which we desperately wanted. It was never in doubt we would marry, just the doubt of when we would be free to. The day out did its job and we returned later the same day relaxed and happy.

We'd gone just for a few hours so had no luggage to carry. But on return to Stansted Ilan was refused entry. We were told to sit and wait to be interviewed. Ilan didn't have his Israeli ID with him, and was terrified. I noticed about him, the more afraid or anxious he was the quieter and more still he would become. I told him we must tell them the truth of our situation but he was more concerned that he could be deported to Israel without his ID which would land him in prison. He had a flashback to the case over a year ago, waiting for someone else to decide his fate and just couldn't handle sitting and waiting yet again.

Although Matty couldn't hurt Ilan for a year, he felt fear of all authorities, and for the first time in England he was afraid. So was I. All these geographical borders were between us, and our peace and happiness. Getting out of Israel, getting into the UK with lines on the maps of the world deciding who was acceptable and who wasn't. I was angry and scared myself and all I wanted was to issue a tirade about injustice.

It took over three hours, sitting and waiting, well past midnight, until there were barely any passengers left. Then we were interviewed, separately and together.

We had nothing to hide, no stories but they said Ilan had overstayed in England over a 12 month period and must leave. I asked which 12 month period, from when? They didn't explain, just repeatedly said he couldn't stay in England anymore. He begged them for mercy and we explained our situation and how we'd been trying to get help. They were kind and urged him to sort out his personal problems and as he had no ID for Israel he could have only three more weeks in the UK, and then must leave by 8th December.

It was a devastating blow. I regretted my impulse to go out of England that day as our security and peace had been shattered. We had no option but to focus ourselves on Israel and it took a supreme effort to pull our attention away from our life. It was that very life we wanted to preserve so we had no choice. I resented Matty with all my being as she wouldn't leave us in peace. She knew how to play with the system in Israel and we had no idea of how much collusion the state had in condoning vendettas. Perhaps Ilan could stay here illegally, as many do, but our integrity wouldn't even consider it. If only I'd known there were potentially other options but I didn't.

So the date was set for 8th December and eking as many final allowed hours as we could we flew at 10.30pm with an hour and a half to spare. We landed at 3am on 9th, which is a very important date and time to remember.

Ilan had a case arranged in the family court and also one for the Rabbinate. When we landed, the familiar oppressive feelings washed over us and we prayed it would only take a week. We had plans for the Christmas break and had also found a place to marry in England and our guest list was written.

It just couldn't be allowed to take too much time. Ilan was so well prepared in defending his alimony case and it was struck out immediately. It was our first success and without a lawyer this time. Ilan handled it so well in the court, bursting with papers and references. In Israel, if not represented, then a case can be heard relatively quickly as the view is a layman will not be competent enough. But Ilan defied the odds and we were faced with yet another scene with Matty. She didn't like losing and this was two in a row.

I had to return to England as there were so many family commitments there and left Ilan to it. I was confident that his next case would be fine, that he could force an agreement, get the divorce and be home before Christmas. The Rabbinate was expecting them on 24th December. I prayed to the Universe the courts would see sense. Ilan had the evidence from the private investigator of her relationship and believed they wouldn't be allowed to stay married; it was against all Jewish Law.

But it was not to be, the case was a fiasco. One rabbi didn't turn up, so the full requirement of judges was missing for a judgment and even then she still refused. It was a crushing blow. That Christmas was miserable for me and sitting in the bedroom with all Ilan's things around me I was desperate, angry and scared. Who did she think she was? What kind of court system would allow this extremely bad behaviour? He'd barely landed and then he was trapped again. Expletives across the page, she'd done it again.

An immediate case was arranged for 31st December and Ilan explained how we'd been unable to pay during the war, and for 3 months couldn't support the children so he offered his pension to cover it plus any future money for another 6-12 months. He had been able to come home the previous year with a year's money ahead, so we expected the same outcome again from the same court. Not an unreasonable expectation, despite the games which were being played. The judgment, by Judge Bergman, was that he wasn't resident anymore, and should not be expected to remain in Israel, she wanted them to settle things amicably and gave them a week to do it, failing that to return and she would order an agreement by the court. It was clearly written with details of Ilan not being a resident of Israel and meant that he shouldn't have barriers of exit.

This was great news, I was missing him so much after two weeks and we celebrated this on Skype looking forward to his return and our impending nuptials. The Universe didn't like us. It couldn't do, because the next day that Judge left the position leaving a vacancy which was not to be filled for a year and no other judges would be allowed to take the case! What a disaster.

Chapter 10

2007

Ilan took another lawyer. Matty placed a request in the Bailiff for another No Exit Order which was refused due to anomalies in her request. It didn't take her more than a couple of days to resubmit and get it ratified. So we were back in the same nightmare from 2005.

There was no money owing, everything had been agreed but there he was, still in Israel. The court had ordered her to receive his pension to cover the arrears during the war. She had demanded half of the pension for herself. They had rejected her plea and she was delaying the receipt of the money, trying to imply he was not paying. More games and the court did nothing. He offered her the house again; a year's money and everything but the clothes he stood in. He was uprooted, away from home with work waiting; a month's wage could pay for everything.

This was a massive problem not only for us but for Manny too. He'd promised Ilan he'd take care of me and our customers until Ilan returned. We'd hoped for a week, and it was past that already.

True to his word, Manny was a regular visitor to the house and spoke to Ilan regularly on Skype. He prepared letters for Ilan to take to the court showing how much work was waiting for him and all the new customers we had pending. Our customers were sympathetic and very loyal. Ilan's work was of the highest quality and they were prepared to wait. Manny expressed the urgency of Ilan's return as he was the one with the stainless steel expertise.

I tried again on the advice of a new young lawyer Ilan had taken. We were told if we deposited one year's child support into the bailiff, Ilan should be able to leave, just as before.

He promised to be there to meet us, so I booked a flight to Israel that evening. Arriving at 3am, we drove from Tel Aviv to Haifa to put in the request. The lawyer didn't even show up. I was disgusted, yet reminded Ilan that when we put our heads together we were better than any of these lousy lawyers. We wrote the request, offering the same period of time as had been previously accepted. If it had been ok once we still couldn't see how it couldn't be a second time. I was obsessed that day to get results and fly home with him. This was to be a whole day of waiting. We chatted to staff in the bailiff. They had got to know us well, joking it was our second home.

There were others waiting for decisions, similar to ours, to be able to leave Israel. One or two of them asked us how long our 'story' had been going on. On the discovery of our time, we were horrified to learn that some people had been trapped for almost 10 years, and we were novices in the court system. I refused to believe them; perhaps they just were not smart enough or had done terrible things. I denied to myself that these sad tales could be norm and not the exception. I was wrong. This was second nature in Israeli courts, and affected women and children too.

I ran back and forth to various banks to extract enough money for a year. All before the decision had arrived. By early afternoon this forlorn group looked hopefully at the lift doors each time they opened to see if the court secretary would be the one exiting full of good decisions for everyone. I never felt so far away from civilization as I did during this time.

Ilan was pacing, sitting and going through a multitude of emotions. It was down to me to be the calm and reassuring one, emotions which were nonexistent in me. We reasoned it out together. They must agree. We'd written about all Ilan's work contracts, our assets, ability to pay even more and even wildly offered to pay another year's support within 6 months. Begging for freedom like animals we were. I felt humiliated and ashamed and desperately angry. The decision arrived. Ilan punched his fist in the air and shouted "Yes!"

The first line of the decision agreed with us. Ilan was not a resident, and could be free to travel. Our offer was acceptable. I hugged him and started to run to the lift to get the money exchanged for his freedom.

"Wait Mar, wait." Ilan was sobbing. "Look at the back page."

I couldn't read Hebrew, and Ilan was too shocked to translate fully. Haltingly he told me the decision. *You can leave the country with a deposit of 600,000 SHEKELS - £100,000. Also 3 guarantors must be provided, each between a certain age and income bracket. You have a number of hours to achieve it, and submit all information to us for approval.*

It wasn't a yes and it wasn't an outright no. I didn't get it. Twice he'd been told he wasn't a resident, so I couldn't grasp why a non-resident would need to provide an Israeli guarantor. At this point, Ilan had the same rights as a foreigner.

We were told it was a typical judgment, one that no ordinary person could fulfill. Anyone with this kind of money wouldn't be in the bailiff in the first place. Israel doesn't make life so straightforward. It uses words to defend itself later to lie, to pretend that of course people are free. But the sum demanded would take Ilan's youngest to the age of 44. What madness to ask any human being to find this kind of money and to an age greater than Ilan was now. Ilan learned the first lesson in a system designed to break human spirit.

I was inconsolable. There was nothing to be done. We would never use guarantors and put someone else in Ilan's hell and we certainly didn't have £100,000. It was more like a ransom note than a court judgment. We had a few hours left before my flight back. I had only gone for the day. We held each other so tightly I wanted to be inside his skin and not my own. At the airport I was in such distress I wanted to leave my body and the airline had to move me up to first class, wrap me in a blanket and treat me for shock. I didn't stop crying for two days. The cruelty and inhumane way we'd been treated was beyond compare, and my anger raged because Israel claims to be democratic. That's the biggest lie of all to the world. It is an outright lie to extort money and breach all international human rights laws. I hated Israel, and had every right to.

Weeks had turned into months, six of them already. Another ally of Abe, a Bedouin emerged into the story, the new Messiah in Ilan's search, the new miracle worker. He would need a sum of money, around £8000 to 'arrange' to lift Ilan's stop order. And surprise surprise, the money was needed immediately. I didn't particularly like Ilan when he was desperate; he was so abrupt and demanding. He talked like they did.

"Get me what they demand, be there when I call you." His manners had left him, and it was all due to the stress.

I did as he asked; dredging compassion from deep within and agreed we would find the money. I went on a mission asking all those close to me to trust me and lend me the money. I collected the full amount within two days, people making very large personal sacrifices; my mother's life savings, brother's tax bill, my close friends' mortgage deposit for her new house and my child support.

"Hurry up Mar, get it sent." Ilan kept urging.

I had driven all over the country the day before to collect the money and I rushed to the Post Office to transfer it, texting the reference number to him.

He called me. "Which bank? Where? Which branch? Work it out Mar, hurry."

It was so unlike him to talk to me this way.

I wasn't at home when he was making these calls. I thanked my mum silently for the loan of her Fiat Panda. My car had been repossessed due to not paying any attention to my own affairs, something which could have been avoided. But in her little car, given with a big heart, I managed to run around to achieve the Bedouin's demands.

"Go home, find the branch, hurry." He urged impatiently.

I felt resentful and taken for granted but obedient to the end result, I did it texting him to let me know when he'd got it. Hours passed; I heard nothing and received no news. I was burning calories just with tension. Would this be enough to bring him home? Finally, I learned that The Bedouin had received the money and they'd been having lunch to decide strategy.

The Bedouin spoke with me on the phone. "It's great, well done, the money is here, but the question is, do you want your fiancé on a plane tomorrow? Just how much do you want him? I'll need another £1000."

I told him, pleaded with him that we'd sent all we could.

"So sell your computer, sell whatever it takes, we just need a little bit more and I guarantee you'll have your fiancé in your arms by tomorrow night." He said. I was being manipulated and I knew it.

What else was I supposed to do? It was so close; I removed the rest of my savings and sent it. My stomach was knotted; my heart throbbed so much. I could feel it in my fingers and hear it in my ears. Just how much money and how much trust in these strangers could I endure? Days passed, still no news. Ilan seemed almost comatose with distraction. I couldn't reach into him as we faced yet another potential disappointment. I wasn't sure if he could withstand any more in the environment he was in with no people really supporting his desire to come home.

Matty was indifferent and cold. She couldn't see the damage she was doing. If she could, then it can only have been deliberate to hurt so many people. She was far too intelligent to be ignorant of the consequences, Ilan was falling apart. My family were on a knife edge, having trusted Ilan through my words and were hoping to see him within days. My anguish was spreading like a virus. All this wasted energy, which could have been used for really positive things.

There was no flight, no news, nothing. So yet again I flew to Israel wanting to meet the almighty Bedouin. Ilan told me to keep my eyes down and show respect for the culture. I was having none of it. Confronting him I saw the look in his eyes and he knew I knew. But Ilan was demur and deferential. I, on the other hand, was a raging beauty! Any traditions I was expected to respect were off the table. I was an

English woman, from a sensible culture. Instead of looking down I looked him right in the eyes. I remembered I was a Western woman, full of energy and passion at this point. I demanded the money back, or my fiancé home.

The Bedouin made excuses saying these were legal fees. I was on fire with a determination I can't describe. Above all, this was my mum's money. Yorkshire had been in the midst of their worst flooding in history and it had taken her hours to drive the one mile to the bank to get a special cheque for Ilan. She had NO doubt about this, because she had no doubts in me.

The Bedouin was a superstitious man, and I decided to play on this, so I took flowers and leaves from a basket, added salt, pepper, ketchup and made an abstract drawing. Abe knew I had spent some time in Trinidad. I'd been there for a few weeks on a consultancy contract to investigate the potential use of Obeah and its destruction in a workforce there. Obeah is the Trinidadian form of Voodoo. I had loved this work.

Trinidad has a caste system, differing levels in society and had a reputation for being a violent country. I always take people as I find them and those suffering the most had the most generosity. I had no fear as even in this remote island I saw the good in people. Sadly those in power don't always remember their own goodness as power is certain to corrupt. In the course of my work I had protective gifts of flowers and fruits outside my front door. With a healthy respect for any belief system, I admired the poorest and most superstitious people there. So many of them were living in cardboard houses, needing a rebuild each time it rained. I enjoyed drinks in the local pub, which was the size of a small kitchen in the UK. I treated them with respect and they protected me.

I was privileged enough to enable them to have some of the basics; fresh water to drink, a bed to lie in during rest breaks and to see their dignity returned to them. I was warned off many times by ex-pats telling me not to get involved. It was better to leave people to sort out their own problems.

I was stubborn in my aims and the trip reaffirmed my deep belief if people are given respect and dignity they will respond in kind. It was difficult to assimilate myself back into life in the UK. People complained about things which were insignificant in my view. I felt that everyone should have the experience of living in poverty once in their life to understand what it really meant, rather than the complaints of sky TV having useless channels or uncomfortable chairs in the office. It was one of the most rewarding times of my life.

Events in Israel were in stark contrast as greed was the predominant motivation. I had an urge to airlift every one of them to somewhere outside Israel and teach them a lesson in humanity and humility. One of the most valuable lessons I had learned in Trinidad was the belief in superstition being strong enough to change behaviour. I had no real idea of how to perform Obeah, but the Bedouin didn't know.

Returning to the restaurant, I instinctively knew the Bedouin was hiding upstairs. *Not such a bigman after all*, I thought. Standing the menus up on the table I finished my artwork with a few more condiments.

In practiced Hebrew I said to the waiter: "May the smell of failure reek into this business and all who do damage will lose everything."

It is true that blood can indeed drain from a face. The swarthy waiter paled instantly. His body was imbued with fear, his feet rooted to the spot. With my heart beating wildly, I left. Within minutes the threatening calls started.

"Ilan, look after your girlfriend, for now it's serious. We can kill her you know. Who does she think she is?" The Bedouin raged.

I'd got to him, I knew it. Respect him? Not when he'd stolen the money my family had given in goodness. I would have committed a crime to retrieve the funds. To be so blind with anger is a sick empowerment and shows the veil between those who do the wrong or right thing to be fragile and easily torn. Perhaps it's the surrender into evil and wrongdoing which gives these greedy people their energy I thought. We decided to take these superstitions to the limit, in the hope the money would be returned, but sadly before my flight home it wasn't to be. I wish I could say more about this episode but I need to protect myself.

People have very long memories in Israel, with little chance of reconciliation or understanding.

In November, I visited again and it seemed Matty's games would reach a crescendo. She tried to get a one sided court order to prevent Ilan accessing the house, claiming he was violent. Yet again my instincts were on fire and a premonition of this enabled us to prepare a defense. We were informed she'd gone to the court and we arrived just in time for Ilan to see the judge with her. The judge decreed Ilan to be harmless and that he could have access to the house and Matty lost her case.

She was incensed with rage, asking *me* if I was getting some pleasure from these games! Outside the courtroom she started to scream abuse.

"Come on Ilan, come home and fuck me. I'm your wife, it's your job. What do you want for dinner tonight? *She* can't come and watch. She's not welcome! Well?"

It was so awful, we both hated confrontation and this was beyond anything she'd screamed before.

Continuing to shout obscenities she then looked at Ilan and waved a hand in dismissal of him, saying to me,

"Him? He's nothing, nothing, he's no one. It's *you*. I need to break you and I will – through him."

She walked away still screaming in Hebrew but my mind had ceased to be able to translate. In that particular outburst her words stayed with me. They were to haunt me. She never said anything she didn't mean to carry out. We were learning this all too quickly.

"Ilan, what are we going to do? She knows you have a right to enter the house, and was ordered to give you a new key." I asked him.

Still burning with the humiliation of this public outcry, Ilan replied.

"We'll collect the key later. She's out of her mind. But the judge saw through her. That's why she is so angry. I don't know what she will come up with next. Try not to worry."

But I knew she meant every word she was saying and would do everything to achieve it. Despite all our protestations of her behaviour, the authorities shrugged them off. I wondered if this battle was normal to them because for me it was nowhere near reality.

As we left the courthouse I speculated how far she was prepared to go. Ilan wasn't coping well, despite his calm attitude. His doctor had even written on his medical record he could be a suicide risk.

Matty didn't give Ilan the key that night. She spent most of the evening with her lawyer trying to find a way to appeal against the decision. Court judgments meant nothing to her.

Just before I needed to return to England, on the last evening Ilan and I went to the house to see his kids. I waited downstairs, seated on a wall outside the building. The next thing I knew the police had been called as I'd been considered a threat. She was just warming up. She was clearly outraged with the decision of his accessibility to their home.

I returned home to England, and it wasn't long before we discovered just how far she was going to take things. Ilan now had access to his house, so he could go *inside* and visit his children, a very unwise move, as police had advised many times that all she had to do was cry rape and he'd be arrested.

I reminded him of the phone call she'd made almost two years before when she'd threatened him if he tried to come to the house. If it was common knowledge to the police that women could play tricks to have a man arrested, then I was certain she knew it too. I didn't want him to go in without a witness. Naïve as he was I thought he would heed this. But the next thing I learned was that Ilan had been arrested. She'd done just what she'd said; her son had called the police to say his dad was raping his mother. Of course, Ilan was arrested and taken straight to the police station! This movie was in full flow. A bad 'B' rated movie. Ilan was ordered to stay away from not only the home, but the whole city for 28 days and both of them were ordered to have no contact with each other. But it didn't end there.

The next act was to name Ilan's parents' house as his, claiming to the Bailiff she was owed money. They received a knock at the door with demands for goods, which terrified them; they were easily led into hysteria anyway. Poor Ilan, he had to go with his father to the bailiff to state obviously it was not his house and an order was issued stating she couldn't do it again to them. In my view the seeds had been sown. There was no way they would want to help Ilan leave Israel as she'd prevented the children from seeing them and was on a rampage. Consequently Ilan was proven not to have done anything except to fix the bathroom that night. How she had coerced her son into such a betrayal was unthinkable.

His parents were protected so who was left? It had to be me for there was no one else left to target.

During the same month Ilan called to say the police wanted to talk to me. I was back in England at home working on my computer and she'd cooked up another farcical tale. A complaint had been filed accusing me of trying to murder her! She gave the date and claimed witnesses saw me trying to put my hands around her neck. It was so funny I laughed at the absurdity. I had called her a couple of days before suggesting we talk and try and relax. I'd only been back in England for a week but perhaps she had assumed I was still in Israel. It wasn't really so funny as on 1st January 2008 I travelled again, to prove I'd been in UK on the 'said date' and the case was dismissed.

But of course the damage was being done repeatedly with no thought for the consequences and still she would not go through with the divorce. Holding him chained (in Hebrew – Agun). It is not allowed in Israel, and she was sanctioned which meant her driving license was taken, wages frozen and it still it did not deter her. She was forced to deposit money as an assurance of showing up to the Rabbinate (religious court) and each time she claimed to be sick, refused, or appealed. It was out of control. She had a boyfriend. We had the photographic and video evidence of this and still she wouldn't let Ilan go.

I was later to ask the question as to whether it was *her* tactic, or just a general cultural tactic to get money or avoid paying money. Either way, I couldn't understand how a court system could accept and endorse such adolescent behaviour in their community. It's so obvious to me now. The people who work in authority were citizens of Israel and had no ability to separate their own thinking from the people. I can't count the times Ilan told me the country was primitive and animalistic and the only way to survive was to become the same. He was losing his humanity before my eyes.

One year had passed and still Ilan languished in Israel needing to work, back in the company he had owned, but not a part of it, not wanting to commit but running out of inner resources. We ended the year recapping on events. We were parted by borders with no help there due to what looked like a terror campaign. The lawyers we hired could not believe what we were dealing with, until they faced her and she refused all reasonable agreements and offers, just demanding the house in full, which was totally unreasonable. It was unbelievable given Ilan had offered it to her several times and she'd refused it or ignored his agreements. We were living in an emotional war zone and could see his children were taking the brunt of it too. God knows if they were going to be emotionally damaged by this 'War of the Roses'.

Chapter 11

2008

We promised ourselves, one more push. In Ilan's mind the calendar year was his time in captivity. So he felt he'd been there for two years though I knew it was only 13 months. He was desperate. His problems paled in comparison to the mess I was in at home, trying to handle the financial losses, keep the business afloat and stay strong.

At last the religious court had run out of reasons to delay. Matty was forced to sign the divorce or face prison. She cried; she was angry and extremely bitter. Ilan was present and ecstatic. It was such a contrast in a divorcing couple. The bitterness between them had reached epic proportions. The Rabbis had watched the videos from the private investigation and questioned her coldly. For once she was on the receiving end and apparently cried with humiliation and displayed her usual resident anger. Yet again I felt a pang of sympathy for her as I know divorce isn't easy but she had been doing everything she could to keep us apart. After 4 years of it I was glad this part was over.

Over the time I had regularly urged him to give her the house for it really wasn't as valuable as his income potential at home but he had been so stubborn, at one point promising it to her then withdrawing at the last minute in anger. It was another of his big mistakes. I often wondered if things would have been settled that day. I had no idea that Ilan had removed his offer of the house, and I'd seen her scouring the pages, searching for it. She'd believed him, and so had I. Ilan had second thoughts, feeling robbed of his life's work and couldn't do it.

But despite her anger, she wasn't legally entitled to have the house AND keep Ilan trapped. I say legally entitled, but the law never came into it. I felt she had lost all reason as I could have bought the house twice over myself or given her money to last a lifetime. Our problem was the mesh of lies tied up in various courts and our inability to cut through the beaurocracy.

Although the divorce was done, the matter of the house and equity still lay in the civil courts. What was firing me up the most was no one wanted to listen. He wasn't a resident of Israel when he'd arrived, yet after a year trapped against his will he was subject to the laws again like any other citizen. The decision from Judge Bergman had been pushed under the carpet. I felt like a high voltage battery about to explode whilst simultaneously trying to be normal.

It was very rare for a divorce to be granted without an agreement of splitting assets, but this had been exceptional. It wasn't going to go away in a hurry, far from it. No offers were going to suffice and I tried myself a few times by calling and asking her.

"What do you want Matty, what do you need?"

"I'm not interested in money." She snarled. "I don't want your money. I don't need any money from anyone. Until he is crazy, takes his life or dies, I'm not done yet." Ilan wasn't surprised at all when he heard the conversation; events were proving to him that his life was worthless from her viewpoint.

She wasn't going to agree to anything but money was all she demanded over and over when talking to the courts. We knew she wasn't motivated by money. Telling a court it was revenge was ignored despite all our evidence. It was all out of control. She'd even squandered most of the deposit given in 2005 because it was from me!

But on the day of the divorce he'd whooped and hollered, and called me on Skype to celebrate his freedom from her. I've never seen a man so happy and my old friend Lizzie came on Skype to share our joy. He wanted to marry me instantly and started making plans for our wedding, to bring me to Israel and make me his wife. He was desperate for this wedding but at this point I was becoming aware of his instability. He was so desperate to come home and believed our marriage paper would increase his rights. It wasn't the marriage I had planned.

I also felt some reservations, not about him, for my love for him was never in doubt. It was the nagging feeling which came from his lawyer's assurances the wedding would be his 'Human Rights Ticket'. I didn't want that desire playing a role in our marriage.

Ilan wanted to marry me the next day but it was forbidden because of a special Jewish holiday of counting days 'Lag B'omer. He tried though. My friend Lizzie and I flew over in the April, shortly after his divorce. Ilan was manically happy to see us and showered us with amazing hospitality. He had missed her so much.

We went together to get his ID changed to divorced as required by law and Ilan rang many rabbis to find a quick wedding even for that week. Lizzie was horrified about the energy in Israel. She didn't like it at all.

Unfortunately for her she had fallen for Ilan's brother Eitan and they had initially met outside in a neutral country, now here she was in his. They spent some time together and I could see how happy she was but had serious doubts as I knew Eitan had a lover and had recently been separated from his wife. He was an interesting character. Not wanting to do business with his surname, which is Arabic for precious, he'd changed his to the Hebrew word instead which was *yakir.* He'd been very shy when I'd met him in the '80s and when I'd met him again he and I had become good friends. He confided in me regularly, telling me of his relationships and affairs.

Ilan used to be surprised at how much he told me. His own marriage had recently failed and Matty and his estranged wife were friends. He believed in lying low until a woman became reasonable and was terrified of having a similar divorce to Ilan. He was a man good at keeping secrets. He had a certain obsession with Lizzie but I didn't think he was good enough for her. It was during our trip Lizzie told him she'd given £3000 to help Ilan to leave through The Bedouin. Money we still hadn't recovered. Eitan didn't look comfortable with her independence, or perhaps it was that he wasn't happy at the idea of Ilan leaving Israel.

They looked a fine couple. Lizzie, tall and very slender with long blond wavy hair which she despised and I envied, Eitan, a chunky overweight man who knew what to say to a woman to get his way. I didn't think the relationship had a future. I knew he was playing the field, more often than not with Russians. He wanted someone like me. He wanted what Ilan and I had.

Leaving Israel isn't just difficult for its own citizens; it is a challenge for anyone. To enter is simple as no visa is required and very few questions asked. But leaving is a different story. When Lizzie and I arrived at Ben Gurion Airport I warned her.

"They will ask a lot of questions, Lizzie." I explained. "I know people who have been internally examined; had all their belongings searched over repeatedly and one of my old friends was held for so long when I first married here they almost missed the plane!"

"It can't be that bad!" She replied with some concern.

"Don't say I didn't prepare you." I warned, smiling.

I hadn't prepared her at all with those words. Entering the airport Lizzie was taken to one side and grilled. They wanted to know her movements, and when she told them she'd come to see Ilan to plan a wedding, they asked if she also wanted to marry an Israeli! They took her bag and put it through the X ray machine at least 3 times, and then took her away.

I had no idea what was happening and no one would tell me. The plane was boarding and she was nowhere to be seen. I didn't know what to do and asked over and over about her welfare. I was assured not to worry and she was in safe hands.

I boarded the plane with great anxiety to see Lizzie already seated, alone! They had questioned her to the point of exhaustion, taken her to a room and showed her a video about Israel and escorted her to the plane before boarding.

"Thanks Marianne!" She said. "You didn't prepare me to expect such an interrogation. It's crazy. I can't believe they can put a person through all this just to leave the country. Entering maybe, but leaving?"

"Oh Lizzie, I'm so sorry. I forget that you are not used to this place."

"I think they suspected me of being a drug runner or something worse." She said. "If it's like this for me, no wonder Ilan is having so much trouble. They have an attitude that it's a betrayal for anyone to leave here, can't say I'm looking forward to doing this again."

In the coming three weeks before my return to Israel, it was time to prepare for another wedding. It was going to be a completely different occasion to my first Israeli wedding. Ilan wanted only to make me his wife. I wanted to marry him more than anything too, but our plans to marry in England had been abandoned. I resigned myself to the knowledge I'd never have my family witness any marriage I entered into. Still hoping we'd be able to have our commitment in England one day, I went in search of a wedding dress. I found the perfect one, not an official wedding dress, but a soft, cotton long summer one.

For the third time in my life, I had to go to the Mikvah. I needed a certificate to prove to the Rabbinate in Israel that I had been religiously purified. I found one local to me, which was a small place, and the bathing this time was dignified and private. It was another job done and paperwork ready to show my cleansed and spiritually prepared body. I wished fervently it wasn't in Israel, but I'd also bought into the belief of our marriage giving Ilan more rights to leave. It was even written in law, when a man remarries, his income must include his new wife's welfare too, so it seemed realistic to suppose they wouldn't hold him away from both his wife and his income in England. That's how my naivety was still working. Despite not being Ilan's wife anymore, Matty still held the cards.

Lizzie and I flew back to Israel again for my wedding on 28th May. There were no hairdressers or beauticians this time, so Lizzie helped me to do my hair and make-up. We prepared at Ilan's parents, who were on holiday. Despite the small scale, or miniscule scale, I was still excited, with this time only one friend with me.

Ilan and I were married with only one of his family members present - Eitan -who was disgusted with the marriage and face to face rejected me from the family, storming away. Ilan was oblivious to it all, so euphoric was he to have finally got his dream wife. Eitan had made sure both Lizzie and Ilan didn't see his anger. It was nothing like my first wedding in Israel. There were no fanfares, no guests and no reception. The rabbi who performed the ceremony took us to his synagogue, so we'd have a few people there.

Lizzie took a few photographs, as we didn't have all the trappings of professionals to record the event. Ilan wanted us to be man and wife. It was what we both wanted, but our England wedding had been cancelled with all our friends, and yet again I was married in Israel without my family.

He and I went alone for a meal in a beautiful open air restaurant.

He was attentive, romantic and overjoyed. At last we were man and wife and I felt it didn't matter where it had been done, or who was there, it was right and proper. I was more familiar with Israel now, the light and the dark side, and twenty years later sitting in beautiful surroundings; with no wild party, I was joined to my soul mate at last. Nothing could have been more perfect than that moment.

It wasn't quite so perfect for Ilan.

"Abe says he can find me someone to get me out of the country." He said optimistically.

"How can you even begin to trust Abe? Why would he suddenly want to help you now? It's a trick Ilan. Don't fall for it, we'll find a way, a better way." I said.

After the debacle with the Bedouin, any ideas or help Abe offered was untrustworthy.

But Ilan was emotionally high, a desperateness in him as he said,

"It doesn't matter. I know he's not to be trusted. He's told me it's for free, the man in question apparently owes Abe money so he said if he took me out the debt was cancelled. I can't stay here. You are my wife now and I can't let you go. It will be alright."

I didn't realise how desperate Ilan's feelings were. He wanted to come home, more than any other point in his captivity.

We had a marvelous few days taking Lizzie to the tourist hotspots. Eitan came occasionally, calm and cool, behaving as if his outburst on our wedding day hadn't occurred. Ilan finally saw how much I was struggling. I couldn't sleep without pills, and had tried to hide them from him. He was more determined than ever the plan would work.

After a few days I had to return to UK. Ilan didn't want to drive us to the airport. Neither did I want it. We decided to say our goodbye at the local train station. It was much quicker and would spare us the memories of parting in airport terminals again.

On our return flight, Lizzie and I talked at length.

"Mar, I remember Ilan so well from our first meeting. I know how much in love you are with each other." Lizzie began.

"I know you do Lizzie. But you definitely have something on your mind. Aren't you happy for us?" I enquired.

"Of course I am. I love Ilan as one of my closest friends. Look how he is with my children. When you are busy working, he always has time to chat to me. We're like two old women over a garden fence sometimes." She laughed. "But the marriage hasn't changed anything. Matty isn't going to just let him go now; in fact I think it is less likely. She can hurt him more by keeping him from you, now you are legally married. I've seen enough over the past four years, and listened to you endlessly. I have a really bad feeling about the whole thing. These past two visits to Israel have been an eye opener for me. It is a really stressful place and I don't think Ilan is well. I don't believe he's handling things well at all."

"Lizzie! He was ecstatic to marry me. I know the family wasn't there, and I think he engineered it that way, apart from Eitan." I answered, knowing deep down that there was some truth in what she said.

"Mar, you were too busy to notice but since we left Ilan, I have been too upset to talk about it. Did you see the look on his face at the railway station?" Lizzie asked.

"What look?"

"I cannot describe the devastation. The look on his face was as if he'd just seen someone die. Mar, trust me on this one. If Ilan doesn't get out with the crazy plan of his partner who I don't trust either just by looking at him, then I think this will be a pivotal moment for you both. I'm warning you that's all. Tread carefully. I think Ilan is heading for a massive fall and I'm scared for both of you." Lizzie poured the words out so quickly.

I sat back in my chair, taking all her words in. I've known Lizzie for almost 30 years, and had depended upon her through this crisis. She was fond of us both, in love with Eitan, yet able to spot things as an observer, especially as she wasn't caught up in the romance of emotion of our farewell to Ilan. I hadn't seen anything like she described realizing I'd just wanted the parting to be quick, positive and easy for me. I had a strong sense that she could be right.

I had no experience of how to deal with him. The trauma was rubbing off on me. Like a virus I was infected with misery and despair then highs and lows. Everything he said and did, I was taking personally. I felt terrible for him, as just a few days after our marriage, Matty went abroad with one of her children without asking Ilan's permission, something normally prohibited. It looked like a slap across the face, as if to say 'you may have a new wife, but you can't travel'. He was devastated.

I could see that Ilan's desperation would make him believe anything and listen to anyone who promised him liberty. People looked down on him, became indifferent, even uncomfortable with his blatant need. They could see he was trapped, and were thankful it wasn't them, but no one wanted to reach out and help, and the help was so small really; to put pen to paper and trust this man they'd known all their lives. A belief in his integrity to work hard and pay his child support every single month rather than assuming that overnight he would be an irresponsible lazy person because he did not choose to live in Israel. So he was going full steam ahead trusting in the black market route he'd mentioned on our wedding night. More worrying, he confirmed again it was all for free. There were no altruists coming forward, not when there was an opportunity for making money. I didn't believe a word of it but he was blinded. I had little faith for his return either by the black market or the justice system. Desperation was becoming a disease and I was relieved to be in a more civilized environment to find the cure, and bereft without him again.

Once home, I searched for a Plan B. My hands ached from all the typing, eyes strained from internet searching. Googling to find human rights groups – somebody out there who would be my champion. Trusting the universe, and by God, the universe had really looked after me.

I was increasingly worried about Ilan's desperation and full dependence on this one 'escape' route especially as I didn't trust the source. He couldn't bear the idea of sending his new wife from Israel and not being able to come with me. Lizzie had been right. My house was under a repossession order and his calls became wild with desperation, but not for my plight, for his own. After my return he called me nearly 50 times a day as he waited for 'the' call – the one that would tell him where to be and when.

I wanted the Plan B, a contingency plan. No matter what I suggested he was hell bent on Plan A. But I was beginning to understand that he never really knew how to think things through under pressure for that was my job, my gift. I decided to wait, be patient and see how things went. My heart was aching again after our week together especially now I was his actual wife. He had arranged it so quickly knowing his parents would not be there for the ceremony. I could still see Eitan's look of derision, clearly not happy that Ilan had married me. I should have seen the signs, they were there. But all we wanted was to be together and we didn't care for the opinions of anyone in Israel. One last push, one more effort was all we could concentrate on.

The courts were painfully slow and we saw this as our golden opportunity. Maybe once Ilan was out of Israel other people would concentrate on some healthier activities than this obsession to keep us apart. I couldn't really understand the motivation at the time.

I acted alone. I contacted a newspaper, tried to grab attention with a headline – I'm going to tie myself to the railings of the Supreme Court in Jerusalem unless you free my husband! I got their attention. I had no idea of the consequences to my credibility and career, so obsessed was I. Returning to Israel just a few weeks after our wedding, I met with the facilitator of

Ilan's impending freedom. He seemed ok and genuine enough but I feared that he was not the decision maker. One evening when sitting together, Ilan's tears fell unreservedly. It was a moment which was to change my life. My husband, my soul mate was falling apart. There was only one choice I could make.

"Mar, promise me, promise me, because right now I'm scared for myself. I feel like reality is slipping away. I am starting to forget what real life is like, I am losing myself. I can smell England on you, taste the freedom but I'm losing it. Promise me that no matter what happens, who I might become, if I lose it all that YOU, you will never give up on me because I am really afraid"

I held him in my arms as he cried and I made the promise, the promise. He knew I always kept my word.

"Yes Ilan, I promise, no matter what happens I won't give up fighting for your freedom."

There it was; the promise. My character would be put to ultimate tests and keeping or trying to keep my word was going to cost me everything. If I'd only known then what I know now I would have done things differently, but the universe has a plan, and the lessons were not just mine, Ilan had some lessons to learn too and wasn't about to learn them any time soon.

A few days later I saw my article, just as I had asked for. *'I'll tie myself to the railings of the supreme court in Jerusalem.'* The headline blared from the Jewish Chronicle.

Ilan was still obsessed with his boat to Cyprus solution and all my instincts were screaming that something was going to prevent it. After all, the helper in question was Abe's colleague, and whilst we both knew Abe had a hand in Ilan's affairs, Ilan was forgetting the level of treachery, but I hadn't. We were married of course, but this event was a major turning point, or an even better description, a plummet for our love and future. Ilan had only one focus which was to get out of his hell. He reasoned that he could restore the balance between us after he returned. We had already started to act independently. Newlyweds already ripped apart.

Ilan called, the date was set.

"Book me a flight from Cyprus. I don't know exactly what time but sort it out, it's going to be tomorrow." He said.

I searched endlessly for flights, trying to decide if I should travel and get him.

"The boat will drop me somewhere in Cyprus." He was so stressed he could barely speak.

I was knotted up with anxiety, excitement, fear, the whole thing. So was he, he was taut as a violin string. This was just too dramatic and too much. I couldn't work and I had delayed a start in my new contract of work as I was unable to concentrate .This was it. The nightmare would be over just short of two years in

Israel and soon he'd be back here in my arms. Phone calls pinged back and forth and then the moment was upon us. Nothing existed in my life other than waiting for his call. I still didn't expect his words despite my reservations.

"He lied Mar. It was a joke, I'm standing here with my bag, and he's not here, he sent a text to say it wasn't the right time, maybe another week. It was a game." Ilan said desolately.

As the shock rippled through me we started to argue, both vying for the most pain. This became my very first real lesson in trauma and how someone reacts to it. I was defiant, indignant and wanted action. Ilan was stupefied, not comprehending the news and not able to see the bigger picture of Abe's betrayal. We didn't know at the time just how deep it went. The contrast of our ways of dealing with it and the distance geographically was a turning point.

I still remember the date, around 18th September 2008, less than four months after we'd married. I'm certain he had an emotional breakdown. Maybe I did too. The stress was unimaginable. I was out of my body with rage and disappointment. I couldn't believe it. He decided he wanted a break from the effort and for the first time in our relationship, he didn't Skype, didn't text and didn't call for almost 3 days.

The court battles were still raging but Ilan's psychology was changing and this was the pivotal moment because he never received treatment for this trauma, though he would beg and ask for help several times in the future. Lizzie had been right. From love to nothing in one moment, it doesn't bear thinking about.

He finally called after three days indifferent, cold and uncaring.

"So I didn't call, what's your problem!" He said aggressively.

Who was this person talking to me? I didn't recognise him. I marked the date as his first 'breakdown' date. He was indifferent, had probably been drinking and had a real fuck you attitude. Why I didn't actually act on those signs I'll never know. I wanted to trust his manhood, his ability to calm down and rethink. Like me, like I would have done.

When he'd been here in England he was always in control and able to recover from disappointments. I wish I'd known how wrong I was at the time. The lines in the sand were about to become muddied and I was the one who was going to keep moving them. I could almost kill myself looking back, why didn't I act, go out there and sort him out there and then? But I didn't.

He was becoming a bit calmer but the damage was already done. I just didn't see it fully with all my consciousness at the time. I took matters into my own hands but all our subsequent conversations became about freedom, finishing the problem and giving what money or ransom had to be given. Do what had to be done and we'll worry about it later. It was not the way to have any healthy relationship but we were not in a real and healthy situation anymore. We were part of a game, a game I would learn all too soon. One in which power, jealousy and control would play a major part, and my dear Ilan, he just wouldn't have the strength to endure it, not in the end.

He had finally calmed down but was not the same man.

I found a lump. Oh my God, a lump. I was stupefied. I told him but his own trauma and being emotionally shut down meant he refused to acknowledge it fully. He just wasn't interested. This was a man who'd flown to save my life once and now this news was as important as the weather forecast. Where was he? Who was he? But he was still mostly 'there', coming and going in his conversations and I was so desperate. All these years and our daily calls were dwindling. I was losing him, as he was losing himself. The fear in me gripped my stomach, I could actually lose him. We hadn't even started married life yet. But despite the torment I was still going to have to deal with things myself. A lump and the house being ordered for repossession! I could barely take in how things were disintegrating. I was becoming blind to everything, the only thing filling my mind and my life was how to get him home. Surely then he would be the person he always was.

I waited at the hospital alone as I didn't want to tell anyone. All the thoughts of being ugly and maimed were running through my head. Would this be the deal breaker? Maybe I could lose my breast. I can't say too much about this event as it was secondary to losing my home and Ilan being so closed down. It should have been a major event but my soul was already suffering enough, it didn't really touch the sides of my pain. How demeaning is that to people who've gone through the same fears. In no way can I say this wasn't important but I was so out of my own body it just seemed like something else to deal with.

The lump was large, but removed. They said it could have been from stress. How could I not even feel things? Friends have been traumatised when it had happened to them. It is a major life event and family and friends pull together. I'd been and returned as if I was at a dental appointment. There was a job to be done which was much more important, which was to restore my family. But it was all beginning to fall apart as my credit cards maxed out and the repossession was looming. I couldn't answer the phone anymore, I couldn't face the debt. I started to avoid calls, trying to put things off. I knew it was wrong and they'd catch up with me. Suddenly after years of success and wealth, I never realised how well off I'd been, I was facing ruin.

But it would all get better as soon as Ilan came home. I was sure, so certain of this. I was convinced that if Ilan could just taste one day of my life, he'd wake up and see how much we were both suffering for it was not just his story.

For Ilan it was the period when it was only about him. He had no ability to connect his behaviour to the effects it had on me. He came on Skype one day and left it open, whilst I rang the mortgage company and begged for release so I could sell my home at a massive reduction to stave off bankruptcy. He ate a couple of meals, watched a movie during the entire day I was on the telephone checking regularly on me and at last he seemed to really understand the enormous stress I was facing. He was very distressed, but it didn't last.

His mantra was always,' if I can't be a man for you there, I don't want to hear anything'.

It looked so cut and dried for him, powerless to help; he would shut my problems off in his mind. I was losing him and I knew it on some level but the obsession was taking over. I wasn't prepared to lose my marriage to circumstances and neither to his emotional trauma. Nothing else mattered. It was a matter of principle. How could this woman using such destructive actions decide not only his life but mine too? It just wasn't going to happen. I couldn't know that the treachery and deceit would be passed like a baton in a relay and finally end up in his hands to do his worst.

My house was sold in the nick of time, a new credit card had arrived in the post and I maxxed it out to pay for the deposit on a new rental property. Moving was awful. I was no longer a homeowner after decades of hard work. I downsized to a small terraced house.

Don't get me wrong, I'm not a snob or anything but I'd worked diligently to get where I was and it really hurt. I'd had my share of ups and downs financially but this felt like it was in a good cause. Ilan's earning potential was great here, we had promises of contracts and I had my own career in consulting, it was just a blip. An 18 months blip I was certain couldn't be sustained. But my head was all over the place, I was totally engrossed and obsessed with this ground hog day problem. I think both of us were losing sight of the reason for this endurance test which was to win the day, ensure that love conquered all and we would prevail. I couldn't handle the pain. The wedding had fulfilled our dreams of love but had been performed in the wrong country whilst he was a hostage. How could we survive?

I liked my new home. It was small, with a beautiful large lawn surrounded by trees and open fields behind the wall of Leilandi plus the added benefit of an enquiring squirrel who crept up every morning to my conservatory. I had placed my office there, a very narrow space spanning the back of the whole property. I boiled in summertime for at times it reached 40 degrees and froze in winter, shivering in the minus temperatures. I was to be in this house for four years, the first four years of my marriage, lost in anything but this nightmare. A pattern was starting to emerge. After the move I was determined to galvanise myself for a concerted effort.

Christmas number three. I marked the calendar on anniversaries, birthdays, special moments, counting them, special days and memories and now the third Christmas. We had no money and could barely pay the bills. Things were getting desperate, and the more desperate I became the further Ilan was pulling back. He seemed totally disinterested in my problems. In fact I found myself having to chase him constantly to get answers on the phone. On Christmas Day he wouldn't answer. I needed those moments to be reassured he still wanted to come home. But he was ebbing away. The one topic conversations just were not sustaining our love. He became secretive, refusing to talk about everyday things there as he said this meant he was giving in and he veered between extreme interest in events at home and total disinterest and apathy.

He also veered between resentment and jealousy of my life to wanting to keep a toe in the water of the life he was missing. I was heading from one disaster to another and oblivious at the time to the damage I was doing to my family and friends.

He might have had a stop order but the real prison was the stop on my heart and my normal life. I could see no way out of this. But giving up wasn't an option at all.

I didn't know how to be 'normal' anymore. To get on with life even with friends and family there is only so much people can listen to. I should have been in the honeymoon period of life and instead everything was falling to pieces. I was so connected to Ilan, his trauma was rubbing off on me and finding its way into my life too. I called an old friend of mine in the USA. The sort of friend it was easy to speak to, and get straight into how things really were.

"Hi Sue." I greeted her.

"Oh Marianne, it's so great to hear from you!" Sue replied.

We chatted for a while about the election, Obama had just become the first black President and Sue loved to talk about politics and human rights.

"Talking of a good cause, when are you going to break your silence on Israel?" Sue asked.

"I don't know." I sighed. "I've almost given up the ghost. But you are the third person in as many weeks to ask me, and I don't believe in coincidence as you know.So, I sat on it for a bit, and thought, hey the universe must want something. I am no hero, and not looking for glory, my pride had been totally squashed, having lived on charity and help for the past year and having learned to not only graciously receive but to even ask at times. Just because Ilan is losing his mind I shouldn't give up Sue. It's such a scandal and so many people there are invisible hostages."

"I thought you would have been settled into married life by now." Sue was furious. "Why doesn't the world know about this blatant abuse of human rights?"

"I tried, I really did. But I've been torn with different advice. My instincts have died, I have no feelings apart from lots of rage, feelings of betrayal and anger at Ilan, Israel, anything, the system, the bloody economy, you name it, I have been relatively paralysed." I wanted to cry as Sue held the space for me to rant.

"Come on girl, what are you going to do?" Sue asked. "You can't give up now."

"Well, I took up my meditation in earnest again and cleared myself and then I've begun my major campaign to get more information. I have scoured the internet, writing to anyone who has had a bad experience in Israel. Lawyers, individuals, you name it. I have gone on forums, and really found some terrible information. Foreign nationals trapped there, unable to leave, their freedom taken, I can see the connection – if they can hold their own people, and they don't say anything, then of course how could that actually be abusive to do it to the Palestinians? It is so clear. Obvious I know. Meantime, you would curl up at the stories I have."

It was so good to pour out my frustration, and in doing so I could feel the energy and determination rising up in me once more.

"Any Americans affected?" She asked.

"Oh yes, a lovely American guy I found. He goes on holiday with his Muslim Israeli wife and kids. She files for divorce unbeknown to him, and wham. A prevention of exit order on him, can you believe it. Then he received a request to pay over $5000 child support, and all sorts of other claims. He was a lost soul in Israel, no language, nowhere to turn – so went to the US embassy. They send a couple of officials to check things out for him, and they 'disappear' into prison. After a week, they are released and tell him he's on his own, no help forthcoming now. He has overstayed, his visa was only for 3 months. They tell him pay 100k, and guarantees etc. and he can go. His salary is nothing like that income, they won't give him a work permit for Israel. Hey, he's in the shit. But luckily, he escaped with an old US passport, and two years later can get no recourse to justice. No one in the States is interested. No-one!"

Sue was shocked and angry. My friend is like an Amazonian, getting up and fighting for causes. She always felt like someone who could have challenged things immediately and I would be happy to stand behind her. This was no lady to confront and her vitality was filling me up. I'd been running on empty for some time and a new voice was doing me the power of good.

"He's a mild example." I continued. "So I trawl, write, nag, nudge and insist. I ring and network and finally got a couple of journalists of national newspapers, not tabloids, who are looking into it. We'll see. I have had lots of emails and some potential solutions to Ilan's personal situation.

But it is so much bigger for me now. I just got an email from a chap who went to his son's bar mitzvah 10 years ago and is making a statement in the Knesset in December hopefully with some media coverage. Wants to join forces he says but afraid to contact me. He says people are watching."

"Yeah right." Sue blustered. "I'm certain people are watching. Don't think for a minute that Israel doesn't know what's happening. You need to be careful."

"Am I bothered?" I laughed. "Not really. It can't get any worse."

Ending our long distance call, I felt refreshed and empowered. Sue and I had met on some deep personal development workshops in America and had got to know each other on a level many people never reached. If she believed in me, then I had to get up and keep believing in myself. My love and determination just had to keep me going. The compulsion imbued every part of my being. It was back. With the knowledge that maybe 30,000 people were trapped in Israel, I couldn't stop now.

I received a call from a lawyer, an American who had started practising law from Yale in 1965 and had gone to *change the world* in Israel. After a few years she became a vet, that's how much she couldn't handle things. But she had got drawn back in and occasionally worked for free telling me she would take over from Ilan's useless egotistical young brat of a lawyer. Good stuff. She would also give me all the information on everything she knew for the newspapers, and begged me to keep at it, saying that only breaking this open by a lay person would change things. I received similar comments from another

American lawyer, fighting this primitive abuse for 25 years, who told me when I saw him in August with Ilan.

"I can see your husband is broken, I can see flaws in your representation, but I also know it's more than that. I keep trying to draw you back to just discuss Ilan but you are compelled to discuss the bigger picture. This is rare. You are eloquent, forceful, believable and full of integrity. I have a strange feeling you could change this. It will take someone from the outside. Most get out and keep quiet, or move on. But I feel you might just be someone who could do this. I am trying, we are all trying, but the wheels move too slowly and it is known but not universally. This is a third world legal system. Please go and do it, for all of us."

Phew! I took the words on board but I couldn't pursue my aim to chain myself to the railings of their supreme court. I was so close, had TV and newsgroups interested, but Ilan's own lawyer thwarted it on grounds of fear of how he would look! There it was - image again. It was only ever about image. If lies had to be told, it was part of the act. The lawyer's ultimatum put so much fear in Ilan, I couldn't act. Ilan was afraid of being abandoned, and without me by his side he wouldn't manage. It was inhumane, and a clear avoidance of doing the right thing. I'd never been so near to a culture which operated on image and lies, and this drive was the perpetrator of all the smoke and mirrors I now see so clearly.

Despite my failure I had to just get up and try again. I could feel my senses waking up with renewed purpose. I wasn't sure if I was the person to expose the internal issues but I did have more energy and focus, so I can only assume that as my lovely mum said.

"You were put here to use all your skills, you must do this, it is your destiny. I'm sure one day it will help at least one person."

I hoped she was right. I had no idea of how we would eat at Christmas. We were desperately short of money. I didn't know where this would lead me, if anywhere, or what would happen, if anything. But I felt in my bones that this activity was not just for cathartic or therapeutic purposes. Beyond that, I didn't know.

I just could not bear to read and hear of people who couldn't imagine walking down a street of their own choice, seeing a beautiful building somewhere outside of that wretched hellhole and having a freedom of mind, body and spirit. It just forced me on. I couldn't let this go unheard anymore. I just couldn't. It was not a cause, it was a necessity, that's the only way I can say it. I trusted each day I was in, and looked no further. I was in a place that was totally new to me, unknown territory, with none of any old associated feelings of helping or saving. Truly, it was just a job that had to get done, paid or not and that's all there was to it. Somehow I had to get the information into the public domain. Ilan's breakdown had changed me fundamentally as a person. I loved him and would do whatever it took, but something else was bubbling away which was the need to hear of all the others trapped too.

It was scary if I thought too much about my own survival, gas bills, electric and other financial commitments. We were totally broke. I'd never been there before. I couldn't even think too much about it, or it would take me down again. Even writing about it would bring the memories surging back.

Chapter 12

I knew it wasn't just Ilan suffering at the hands of the system. I had searched the internet, Googling with the words 'No Exit Orders'. Unsurprisingly very little came up in English, yet I was convinced there were more people out there. I just had to find them and persuade them to talk. I want to expand more on my friend Rick, who I'd mentioned to Sue.

I'd come across Rick Myers, an American, who had been fighting to get justice. His story was one which touched my heart, and changed my picture from concentrating just on Ilan to a bigger one. The Israeli system seemed to have little focus on children, and more attention and desire on making money.

Rick had escaped from Israel after being held by a No Exit Order, an illegal judgment, but since then had been fighting for his right to be with his children from his base back in the USA.

His story opened my eyes. He'd met and married Ranya – an Israeli Arab woman – in 1998 whilst he was working as an ex pat in Israel. After their first son was two years old they were living in the USA. When she became pregnant again, Rayna wanted to be near to her family for the birth of their second child. Sadly for Rick, the marriage didn't work out, but worse than that, he became a victim of huge abuse from the Israeli Justice System.

When I read the latest email Rick sent me, its tone struck such a chord. I recognised my own feelings in his words and saw his depression was similar to Ilan's. Just between Rick and myself I can count dozens of lives disrupted and destroyed by financial demands of the system. Lawyers have got rich and enjoyed their own freedom, family holidays and peace of mind making their living on our desperation. We have struggled to finance our need for justice and have our families restored. Rick is now a criminal in the eyes of the Israeli authorities, prevented for almost 7 years from the joy of being a father participating in the lives of his children. He had a No Exit Order imposed upon him as an American Citizen, with an arbitrary demand of $300,000 deposit, $12,000 per month child support and no freedom to achieve it. It was done with no compunction, denying him all his human rights. His life as he knew it was obliterated in an instant and his values of truth being his salvation were decimated.

As he struggled to find a way out of Israel, caught in a catch 22 situation, it was his expired US passport which saved him. He had spent almost 6 weeks languishing in Israel, and like me had resorted to searching on the black market for people who may be able to smuggle him out of the country. Rumours persisted of people such as this, and of course many people played the role of saviour with empty promises and equally high demands for money up front.

Using both current and old passports, Rick weaved his way through Ben Gurion Airport, bluffing his way on to the plane. But as he flew to freedom, he had to leave behind his two young sons, the very essence of him. Damned if he left, damned if he stayed, he felt, like many more before him and probably many more to come, that fighting outside Israel was the better option. The trap is those left behind don't have the mental freedom to co-operate with rational thinking.

Rick wants to be a proper father. It's not such a tall order. But not all fathers are allowed this right if connected to Israelis. First the money, lots and lots of it, then the possibility of very limited access. Rick won a case in Israel for joint custody. But when he tried to have his children, he was treated like a downbeat useless man by the courts. He found himself at the mercy of disinterested judges and game playing lawyers. He was advised to give up the ideal of truth, and get down and dirty like everyone else. The same advice Ilan was given. Ilan was advised to lie, cheat and do anything to destroy 'the other side'. But he couldn't. So I received the brunt of his frustrations as his personality split into two.

Ricks foreign status reduced him to an unworthy person, unable to have a voice and unable to get help from his embassy. I identified with his grief. He was naïve and ignorant of the Israeli judicial system. There is no one who can or is willing to give the full picture. Where's the sense in that?

In his email I could see he now knows the money spent to fight all the nonsense lawsuits was a waste. No politician in the USA is interested in helping him or his American children; their vested interest in Israel is far greater than the acknowledgment of human suffering which their budgets are funding. Four television appearances haven't helped him either. Human Rights Organisations have ignored Rick's requests. Their response is, 'Israel does not abuse human rights after all they have a realm to defend.' Just as my newspaper article didn't help me.

People tell Rick to 'move on, his kids might look for him one day, and he needs to get a life'. He's stopped talking about it to new people, and has put his broken record monologues down and locked his pain inside of him. All his court victories are worthless and unenforceable. Just like mine. Israel keeps its people and charges a fortune in the process.

Rick can't beg for his rights nor demand them for him and his children. His ex is the law, as the courts nearly always ask an ex to endorse a judgment. The plaintiff in the family court is a winner from the outset, male or female. No truth is able to overturn a story and first impression.

Rick and I inhabit the same desolate world in which the sense of loss becomes a part of the psyche. Time cannot be regained and the future is filled with a mere wisp of hope of one day, maybe one day, our worlds will be righted as those we love and miss are restored to us. But the time passing, coupled with the brainwashing, means it will probably never happen. I don't want to think negatively, I must keep fighting.

He is tenacious, believing love and determination will conquer and right must be might. But every day a part of him dies as he struggles on. He is just one of many individuals whose life was broken by the cruel system which treated him like an animal and all the more difficult as a foreign citizen. Ilan is an Israeli citizen but wasn't a resident and Rick was treated the same way, and as an English woman I received the same treatment. Ilan was alone, with no family support, their Zionist principles overriding his heartfelt desires, and trampling over his dreams and his hopes and finally his ability to feel at all.

I knew Rick and I are not alone. We had both heard so many stories. I had been shocked at the amount of people in this situation. The silenced victims, people who had the misfortune of loving an Israeli, or an Israeli loving a foreigner and actually believing they can live outside Israel. Of course Israeli people travel and see the world, but the spectre of No Exit Orders is there in the shadows, easily attained by someone who they may upset and can exert the ultimate power. It's not just divorce; it can be an alleged debt. It's a very easy document to obtain, despite what the publicity says.

Rick languishes in the USA, as I was in the UK, and many more I've learned of, knowing Israel has no care for family unity or children with both parents in their lives.

The trickle of stories and testimonies coming to me didn't help Ilan at all. There was no solace in numbers, rather the realisation it was a huge issue. Those free to travel don't understand, until it happens to them. I was told the number of people with these restrictions was well over 30,000 per year. I didn't know if the numbers compounded every year, but some of these orders had lasted a lifetime.

The connection between the suicide rate, no exit orders, and being alienated from their children was apparent. When a man is reduced to nothing, and needs a dozen jobs for stupid demands, it is understandable that suicide becomes the only option. I'd been urged by lawyers and many Israelis to keep on trying. They told me to get the story out and make people understand the horror of being trapped with no crime. The murders of estranged partners made sense. If a person couldn't be free, then better to serve time in a prison without the financial pressures.

I had no choice but to press on. If only Matty could let him go.

Chapter 13

2009

In the beginning there was light, love, and hope, so much hope!

On our first anniversary Ilan was so down he told me he couldn't go on. We were getting nowhere. Over 18 months had been spent in such a waste of energy when we could have just been living like normal people. We were too far in to turn back but I couldn't see any way forward. Ilan was tied in knots in the court and since the boat disaster he'd been trying as hard as possible to get Matty to agree to let him come home. I felt it would never happen. I couldn't imagine what pleasure she could be getting in the 5th year of this vendetta. I had never experienced anyone who could keep the pressure on for so long to prevent someone from actually living a normal life.

Freedom was essential to Ilan for it was his identity and time was killing him. Despite all efforts there was no interest from the courts either. She had everything her own way, and we knew there were discrepancies and lies in much of her paperwork, especially in the claim for child support from the beginning of 2003, and her claim that I'd tried to cause her physical harm when I wasn't even in the country.

I needed a call on this special anniversary but despite all promises to talk Ilan had disappeared. I called his family home, but they said they had no idea where he was. (Something I would learn was their mantra). I was desperately worried for Ilan who had told me he was going downhill fast and had started smoking cannabis to deal with his depression. It was a lethal combination. So I called the police and reported him missing. Wouldn't anyone have done the same? Not only worried, the neglect was hurting me. I felt abandoned myself. Having a passport was not a document for freedom. I was just as trapped as he was. I couldn't enjoy anything in the world whilst he was stuck. But I needed emotional support from him, to keep the flames burning. The police went to his parents, and eventually I was able to speak to Naomi.

"'Ilan is in a terrible state. He's not coping well at all." I told her.

"'I don't believe you. He looks fine to us." His mother replied.

"No, he's starting to take stuff to numb his feelings. I'm worried sick about him. Please help me. I love him. I want to be with my husband. He needs to come home." I pleaded.

"You are not the right woman for him." She said. "He is my son. You stole him; you stole our wedding day by doing it in secret. I will do anything to make sure you are not together, as long as I'm alive. Also, there is a watch missing in our home, does your friend Lizzie know anything about it?"

I was distraught. She was flipping from one topic to another but her message was clear.

"Enjoy him while it lasts." I said. "You can't hold him forever. He needs his life and I will find a way to bring him home."

The gloves were off. The cards were on the table. Any manners I had were gone. This woman, his own mother, was going to let her son die inside. She was oblivious to his feelings, full of her own selfish needs. I was filled with determination and indignation. Who were these people? If Ilan hadn't the strength then I'd have to get him out another way. I'd heard plenty of stories about people escaping on boats, we'd travelled the length and breadth of Israel in the past searching for someone, so I decided I would go in from abroad and get him that way. Despite Ilan's failure through his no good partner, and though I had no idea of how or who, I knew it was worth a try. There had to be a way. After informing Lizzie about the call she was equally determined being so worried sick about the state I was in.

Despite many emails to Eitan she'd heard nothing regarding Ilan. We decided we had to take matters into our own hands. I was boiling inside at other people deciding for me at my age whether I could live with my own husband. It was way out of control. I didn't really pay attention to the fact that it was taking my own life way out of control too. It was more than love, it was the principle. To have a strong principle is a very expensive and compelling path in life and I was more than willing to take it. The principle took me on a mystery tour.

I checked out ex pats in Cyprus, Lizzie and I both asked around, searching for anyone who was prepared to make a trip to collect Ilan and bring him back. We waited and waited and then decided to go there and look for ourselves. Can you imagine, two middle aged women flying out with no idea of what we were going to do! We landed at the end of July in searing heat and got a hotel for the night. Then armed with a litre each of water, we walked and walked, hardly noticing it was over 40 degrees, not eating, just walking from boatyard to boatyard. Eventually we ambled up to a spot, and were assailed immediately by an English speaking tour guide.

"Ladies, a boat trip?"

Well, how can you casually say you want a private hire to Israel, just like that? But I did. We were introduced to someone who said he'd take us and a deposit of £2000 sealed the deal. I'd borrowed money just days before from a credit union, explaining exactly what I needed to do, and they were incredible. Yet again borrowing but blind to the consequences or thought of failure. So half the money was already gone but the yacht we had chartered was a beauty, named Escape. We couldn't believe it; perhaps fate was leading us to the solution at last. Lizzie, my magnificent friend, took the role of the *project leader* and we talked to Ilan on the phone. He could barely register that we were so close and I ached with the proximity.

"Hi Ilan, it's Lizzie, how are you?" she asked.

"Hi, I'm boiling. It's so hot, you cannot imagine."

"I think I can. I'm in Cyprus with Marianne. We are only 150 miles away from you and it's bloody boiling here too." She giggled. "We are going to get you home Ilan. You need to be at a certain place at a certain time to meet a certain person!"

Lizzie was instructing him all the way through and we afforded ourselves some excitement. He texted, 'tell my wife I love her' to Lizzie's phone, igniting her determination too. She had new energy, where mine had become jaded. But it showed I wasn't imagining his state, she was convinced of it herself. My friend of over 25 years was a great judge of character and I didn't need to persuade her at all, quite the contrary.

We arrived at the boat with our belongings and at this point I casually mentioned perhaps we'd like to pick someone up from Israel and bring them back. The pilot smelt a rat and became very afraid. Babbling in Greek, he refused to take us and even refused to refund the money. Within minutes, from a glass of wine and nibbles, we were sitting on a bench on the marina. Lizzie was in shock, she had checked out completely at a loss and that's when all my experience of a crisis came in. Immediately I jumped to action and we were helped by a kind stranger, who provided with us with somewhere to stay.

This adventure cannot be told completely to protect those who helped us. We stayed a week in Cyprus, with potential on a knife edge. It was possible but would take more money, more time and a whole lot of courage from the people involved. But we came back empty handed. I did leave some money with a contact there, just in case they could manage to create the window of opportunity for Ilan to come. He just wasn't prepared to take any chances, his hopes had been dashed over and over again and he had no inner strength or resources alone. So close, yet so far.

I had to get home as I'd finally got a job, a real one, first time in over 20 years of self-employment. I hoped I could handle it.

After my return I endeavored to concentrate on my new job. Only a month had passed, when I received a call from Ilan saying he was in hospital with a suspected heart attack. He was very distressed, rambling on I wasn't there to take care of him. I didn't hesitate. I booked a flight to Israel and left within hours. I knew deep down it wasn't true, not really. But I went through the motions of going to help him. I wasn't enjoying my work at all and the look on the face of the owner when I said I was flying to Tel Aviv told me I would have some big problems when I returned.

Alan and his wife knew I was there, it was just before their major holiday of Yom Kippur, and they were concerned for me. Using the money I'd left In Cyprus I'd hired Alan again when I returned, which had brought some temporary sanity to Ilan but temporary really was the operative word.

I don't like Septembers, two in a row where we had been thwarted by efforts to get him out by sea. After two failed attempts, I pledged not to take that route again. Alan had told me he was confident of being able to help Ilan even with a year of no legal activity. But there was a problem.

Ilan wouldn't read any documents, said he couldn't concentrate and was being unreliable to the point Alan told me in one conversation he thought Ilan had developed some kind of multiple personality disorder. I listened with such pain and disappointment to Alan's frustrations and concerns. Ilan was clearly sabotaging all efforts to help him. It was such a contrast from 2005 when Ilan and I had been united in our efforts.

I went to the apartment he was renting and waited. Yet again, pulled into the stupor of being in Israel, this seemed like a crazy act. But I sat outside. His landlord let me in, so I showered and made myself look just as irresistible as I could. Ilan called, saying he'd 'felt' me being here, but it took hours before he finally arrived. You know, I just wasn't connecting the dots, he hadn't picked me up from airport, but why would he if he was so sick?! It was all so ambiguous; I guess I knew he hadn't been in hospital, or not in the way he'd described

I wondered exactly which planet Ilan was on. I was angry with him. He seemed to have no empathy or connection to the huge efforts being made for him. I'd risked everything to bring him home and he was turning down all reasonable help. What really angered me was the irrelevance of coming to England or not. He needed to finish his problems with Matty no matter what. There was no freedom for him until it was resolved.

I think in those hours waiting for him, I knew I was losing him. I believed he had lost himself in the trauma of the betrayal just after our wedding the previous year.

Eventually, Ilan turned up. I'd made an effort to look my absolute best and as he entered the room, on seeing me he collapsed in a faint, crashing to the floor of his small kitchen. This wasn't the greeting I'd expected. I'd played a lot of scenarios in my mind and this wasn't one of them. I knelt over him as he hyperventilated. I have never had this reaction to being so well dressed! I tried to revive him and as he stood up, he started to punch the wall with hands and his head saying 'no, no, no' loudly and repetitively. He was hurting himself and hyperventilating. It was so distressing.

I was transfixed, unable to stop him. He sat down and I tried to hug him and he began self-harming again. This was beyond anything I could imagine. I didn't recognise this man, not the gentle loving partner I knew and was fighting for but a stranger who was totally out of control. Of course I should have taken him to hospital there and then but everyone who knew us was hostile to me. They wanted to keep Ilan and his mother had already refused to believe me. Ilan was suffering was some kind of Stockholm Syndrome. He was afraid to confront them for if hope failed he would be left with his family and feared retribution. He couldn't handle seeing me at all. He went to work and in the evenings he went out with Eitan.

I could say at this point it was one of the worst and most distressing visits of my life there but there would be more. Eitan was constantly calling and Ilan whispering to him. On my first evening he declared he was going out bowling and just left me there alone! He wouldn't give me any lifts to the town; the apartment was a 45 minute walk but actually half that I as I learned that Ilan wouldn't even show me the short cut. I couldn't bear it.

Sure, I seduced him, and it was then I knew for certain he had been with another woman; his touch was different, pleasing another woman's body. I didn't recognise this lover. We had a terrible time. It was just hours before Yom Kippur. He had a deadline to deliver a subpoena to Matty and almost everything was closed. But somehow he mustered up more determination and tenacity than I'd seen for ages, travelling from village to village to find a post office and a courier and in fact achieved the objective. There would be a 24 hour curfew on communication by technology and Ilan knew Matty would be out of control. It was the equivalent of taking a child's presents on Christmas day. It was regarded as very inappropriate behaviour with lots of intakes of breath at his audacity.

The day of the fast came and as the evening approached, yet again Ilan left me alone and went to his family for dinner. I cannot believe I even tolerated this. That evening his son visited. As he heard the knock on the door, he went into a major panic and tried to make me hide in the bathroom! I wouldn't of course, and the night went peacefully. After his son left, Ilan was screaming hysterically at me. I was making him choose. There was no sense from him.

He went to work, and I hunted around the apartment for clues. I found an astrology compatibility chart, which I learned much later was someone very important; a receipt for two double rooms spent over a weekend in Eilat with Eitan, which Ilan claimed was a work thing. Absolute rubbish, there was never a professional connection between them. My first real fears of another woman were becoming founded. Of course, anything secret or illicit would be with Eitan's full knowledge and by this time I was being kept away from his family.

Things were bitter, but I wanted to try so on request Ilan said I should visit his parents. When I arrived Naomi instantly called Ilan to check if he had endorsed this visit. I was really in some kind of unreality. I tried to explain to them all the tough times I was enduring.

"How many times do I need to tell you that Ilan is not well?" I began. "I'm staying with him in his apartment."

"He hasn't got an apartment, I don't know what you are talking about." said Naomi.

I couldn't believe what I was hearing. Whether things were good or bad between Ilan and I, the fact I was staying in his apartment couldn't be denied. In that moment I realised they were either in major denial or lying was just a normal activity. I grieved for a moment, recalling the many occasions I had sat with her and told her everything when Ilan had not wanted to talk. My own mother in law was bare faced lying.

"Well, your crockery and various things from your home are in his room." I insisted.

"I don't think so, I don't know where he lives." She repeated.

His father showed no interest in me, they just carried on preparing for their lunch as if I was nobody. I couldn't understand why.

"I've just paid £1000 for Alan to look at his case, and I paid £600 to the court this week for another file." I explained.

"What court? It's all nonsense. Ilan isn't doing anything in the courts." His father said abruptly.

"Please listen to me, help him, help us. I am in a financial crisis in England. I've lost my home, had a lump in my breast, and I've just spent my rent money to progress the legal things. Ilan is in despair. He can't continue like this. He is emotionally broken."

"Listen to us. Ilan left you plenty of money in England for any eventualities. He told us, he'd left you a fortune. So don't come here complaining." His father, Amir declared.

I recall Ilan declaring in some mad moment, he'd hidden £100,000 under the pillow for me before his departure from England. He'd told his parents a total lie in a moment of madness, and for some reason they preferred to believe this nonsense. I remembered an occasion when his father had told me I was a 'diamond', the best thing that had ever happened to Ilan. He'd also done plenty of direct nagging to me to leave Ilan and make him stay in Israel to keep working. Perhaps the apple didn't fall far from the tree. The only difference was Ilan was a trapped man, and his parents were in their normal environment.

I began to cry. They were unmoved. Their behaviour was stupid. I needed to keep my mental focus.

"You are using our son as a bank, well there is no money left in his bank. You cannot keep bleeding him for more. Just go home. He's fine. We are not interested in him, you, courts… nothing. Have a bowl of soup before you go."

If it wasn't so real I would have laughed at the absurdity. I'd received nothing from Ilan but here I was, sitting in my in-laws house facing incredible animosity, and yes, with a bowl of soup thrown in. Never forget Jewish hospitality. They were having none of it, their perfect son being used and abused by me. Oh the abuse, it was right there in the kitchen and not by me. They were rude and showed no care. It was my week from hell.

I stumbled outside blinded by tears and coincidentally saw my ex's mother. She opened her arms to me and hugged me tight as I surrendered to my grief.

Ilan's parents exited their house and saw us. His father waved and said.

"Do you want a lift back to Ilan's place? Come with us, we'll take you!"

The term 'Hutzpah' comes to mind. In English the best translation is audacity. They clearly didn't want to give the impression that they had hurt me. Turning on the image like a light switch and in the same breath mentioning Ilan's apartment, the very thing they'd denied just minutes before! My ex mother in law held me and calmed me down. She said Ilan was a good man, his family was rotten, and I was a wonderful woman. She'd always been sad about my divorce with her son. She wasn't fooled, she knew me well, and had always known me to be an honest woman.

After the visit, Ilan tried to get me to stay in a hotel. I felt like some secret mistress with none of the fringe benefits and I refused. Then finally he said he'd met someone, a casual date, but was going to end the 'relationship'. In my head there were warning bells and alarms going off. The word relationship could only be used if it was true. I gave him my wedding ring back telling him when he was ready to be committed then I'd take it back.

On the last day he opened his heart. His life was unbearable and he couldn't talk to anyone. He begged me to write an email to his sister to explain what he was going through. Of course I did but it went unanswered until I'd gone, by which time Ilan was back in denial.

Why wasn't I strong enough? I'd given him my ring, whilst simultaneously paying for a lawyer and his case. Everywhere in the world I could think straight but here my mind was either in slow motion or reacting to some urgent panic or drama. Ilan had been right about one thing, there was no way I would be able to function normally in Israel, especially in Nahariyya with its small town gossip and primitive mentality. On the day of my departure Ilan fell to his knees sobbing uncontrollably. He told me he needed a doctor or a counselor and begged me for help. I was powerless. I couldn't stay in Israel under the circumstances and knew once I'd left he would sink back into denial and emptiness.

I needed to get him out of Israel for treatment in the UK. It was the only option. If I could get him home, I knew I could get him well. Ilan was terrified of his own family and Matty. I'd asked Alan about an evaluation of his stress but he didn't want to go into this, preferring to believe Ilan was playing games. That made less sense than the truth of Ilan's disintegration. He hadn't played games before and I could see he was falling apart emotionally, which was having a devastating effect on his mental processes.

I'd sent a text to my employers during my stay in Israel regarding their commitment to me as I was contemplating giving up the job and staying to help Ilan. They'd assured me that I was important to them and wanted me back urgently.

When I went back to work, I was fired within 48 hours. I was asked if there was a watershed moment and this was it. It was massive.

"If I can't have England, then I don't want you." Ilan said when he called me one day.

The bombshell assaulted my senses one morning on one of my relentless quests to stop the separation. I would have lived in Timbuktu in a tent but Ilan was focused on his freedom first, in his mind forgetting that this story was also mine. He wasn't seeing my descent, that I had no work and had finally succumbed to benefits. I'd held out on a mistaken belief that he wouldn't be allowed back to me if I claimed benefits but I had no choice. I was borrowing money from everywhere to live and eat, focused on getting Ilan home.

The visits dwindled as my air miles ran out and he got busier and busier in Israel, becoming afraid of everything and trusting no one anymore. He started to keep me a secret and my infrequent trips resulted in us staying in hotels. One particular time we were in Tel Aviv, and his parents called, the usual stereo call. The first voice would be his mum with questions and banal stuff. Then it would be his Dad, with exactly the same questions. Ilan used to dread those daily calls and do everything to cut them short. Nudging him to tell them I was there, he finally told them and I spoke to Naomi. I got a strong impression then that Ilan wasn't letting them know I'd been so many times and that perhaps they felt I was avoiding them. Who knows, it seemed Ilan had all the cards. I didn't want to make an effort with them since their rudeness to me.

What an incongruent situation but yet again it was all moment to moment stuff. Who was this man?

Chapter 14

2010

Shaman – inner wisdom from an external source

I cast my mind back to the call Matty had made one day early morning when Ilan and I were living together in England. She told him she'd put a spell on him and he'd be back very soon. He laughed so hard at her, telling her she was speaking nonsense. I remember telling him,

"Ilan, don't joke about these things, because it doesn't require you to believe in it for it to be true."

I'd lived a life delving into spirituality; meditation and various new age things all my life and I believed that *she* believed. I'd had a conversation or two with her and she'd said more than once to me until he was dead by his own hand, insane or in hospital, she hadn't finished. She'd said the same to him many times too. It was anger, but deep down it was more than that.

She hated me, hated what we had and it had gone way beyond normality. It seemed deep, personal and I was truly afraid of her hatred, her power and her capabilities. Perhaps it was my imagination. But I spoke endlessly to people from various organisations; religious, spiritual, friends, non-believers, and ended up with the same feeling. Perhaps it was my own psyche, taken in and doing it to myself. I don't know but it seemed that whatever we tried to do, every single door was closed and even by the law of averages this was extreme. I shared these calls with friends and family immediately and to this day Ilan regrets his dismissal of her threats.

I turned to the spiritual world because it had never let me down. I recalled when Ilan was days from being closed in Israel, a good friend had foretold it and on that trust I'd booked indirect flights to get him out. I trusted this realm more than most. It was always 'right' in the moment, with insights which came here and there, and then 'right' in the next moment and it was good enough for me.

Call me crazy, it's no big deal, I probably am. But I had turned to various media to get help to get the problem solved and whilst everybody had sympathy there was no real action. The doors were closed and yet every time I gave up and wanted to walk away, the universe threw Israel back into my life, from business or other sources and the money flowed each time I needed it to renew my vigour but the money didn't come for dresses or indulgences for myself and others I cared for.

So In 2010 I was exhausted, couldn't do anymore and gave up. Ilan and I barely spoke and I was ready for the sake of my friends if nothing else, to let go and move on. They'd had enough of listening to my nonstop monologues. Jan was suffering watching my pain, my 'obsession' or compulsion to finish this by getting Ilan out initially but now trying just to touch his heart or head in some way. She begged me to pull away for a while. For her sake I said I would, for I realised how much I was hurting those who loved me. She actually bribed me with Mars Bars, a symbolic instruction and I kept my word.

I decided I needed a break so I searched for something appropriate; a spa, a healing weekend, but nothing felt appropriate. I'd always had in the back of my psyche something shamanic. But something pulled me to a website advertising a one-to-one healing week with ayahuasca , the healing herb made famous in South America. I booked to stay for five days, with instructions to cleanse my body of various things such as salts, alcohol, spices, etc. I wasn't entirely comfortable, quite the opposite in fact. I booked to see a local shaman just to get a taste of what I might experience. She was nice, but told me basically that there was no bad energy on me and it was pretty much in my imagination. I felt a bit stupid and wasn't sure whether to make the trip. But I'd prepared myself, bought the white sheets and various natural gifts, flowers and fruit and off I went. By this time I was living in a sort of fugue and was so traumatised myself I just did things day by day. I knew I wasn't functioning as well as usual, which was the main reason I was prepared to try anything. I needed to feel like myself again.

I only told a couple of people I was going. What had made me go? Well, anyone who had said they would directly help me with Ilan's situation was adversely affected almost immediately. It became far more than co incidence, and although my rational mind wanted to discount events, I knew inside that perhaps something more malevolent was occurring. So I put my trust in the instinct that had helped me all my life and I set off.

I have never known fear like it up to that point in my life. I'd faced challenges and fears over and over but this was something else. I was terrified the nearer I got to my destination. I was telling myself to turn back and go home but another part of me knew it wasn't ME saying it. So when I arrived I was almost a nervous wreck. Given all my past experience of taking on new experiences with gusto, this new feeling of fear was very unusual but I felt I had to still go through it. I met with the most beautiful woman I'd ever seen; her skin smooth as a 16 year old but in fact she was over double that age. She glowed; she was powerful, kind and in control. She turned out to be an amazing human being.

When I arrived, I entered a sanctuary; a beautiful room full of flowers, fruits and candles. The essence of incense filled the room taking me back home to my spiritual core. There was a kitchen and shower; it was a serene and fully contained space. It felt exactly like a sanctuary. Almost immediately the woman lit some candles and some tobacco and blew smoke over me.

"I might have made a mistake in coming here. It's all in my imagination. I'm fine. I spoke to another Shaman counselor who told me it's probably stress." I said.

She looked at me and, told me, "You need to be here, there is some major work to be done."

I did not go in there with some naïve belief in this. I was actually very scared, but I knew myself well enough to know that the fear was being somehow put into me, it wasn't mine. I had against advice researched ayahuasca and what happened to people who took it. I'd watched The Tribe with Bruce Parry on TV and seen the powerful effect it had on him and others and was truly intimidated by what I was going to do. I'd never taken drugs and didn't like the idea of not being in control, a funny thought given my actual life didn't appear to be in any control.

I was about to go through one of the most powerful life changing events of my life which I was embracing with some genuine fear and skepticism. Don't imagine I was a 'new age' addict at this point. She knew immediately that 'something' was controlling my life. She read into my heart and my mind and saw my life in an instant.

"We've work to do." She repeated. "You need a good night's sleep, and you won't need your sleeping pills anymore."

I had been on strong sleeping pills for years since Ilan left and she knew just by looking at me. I hadn't told her a thing. That night I slept without them and I was amazed. I'd tried cold turkey before and had spent over 48 hours awake before succumbing to the pills again so this was in itself my first miracle.

The first ritual I had to do was to drink pints and pints of some tree bark designed to make me vomit any negativity. It felt like I was someone else but I had vowed to do exactly as I was told and did it. A deep part of me knew this was the right thing to do and I'd been so long separated from myself that I told my fearful side to butt out and go with the flow. Normally I couldn't drink pints of normal water in succession, and the warm drink did its job. I threw up over and over, the warm bitter sweet liquid refusing to settle in my body for more than a minute or two. It wasn't like being sick from a dodgy meal, more akin to the experience of drinking the liquid which swirled around me and then emptied me of the anger and misery inside me. I did feel so much better afterwards. I felt cleansed of many negative thoughts, but it hadn't settled my anxiety.

The night approached. I followed the instructions to the letter and was prepared. She turned up, candles were lit and strong earth music played in the background as she prepared the Ayahuasca. I have never taken hallucinatory drugs before and was literally holding myself quite terrified. I had never liked to 'lose control', though some might doubt that who'd seen me over the years with a few drinks too many, or emotionally bereft at times, but I knew what I meant. There was no going back.

I drank the glass and waited. She had a much bigger amount than me and explained as it was a natural drink we would be connected through nature: me, her and the natural world.

We were going to be joined in the world of the shaman. Their belief was in the spiritual power of plants, trees, animals, the elements and actually, surprisingly to me, God. The closest I can describe the work of a shaman is from the movie Paul. The movie when the alien takes the pain of others into itself to cure them.

Was I going to start seeing things? Would I stagger around, on a 'trip'? I had no idea, but the drink was in my system and that was it. There was no going back, my trust now given to this wonderful woman. If I didn't believe in God before I went I certainly did when I left.

Whilst considering myself more spiritual than religious, what I experienced I believe was true. She sang like a true angel, something beyond human. It was incredible. I had somewhere to lie down as did she. This was supposed to last all through the night. It turned out that my total physical, mental and emotional exhaustion was to win over that intention. I couldn't endure the whole night in the manner it was meant to be done but it didn't detract a fraction from the enormity of what would happen.

"I'm certain you have some kind of bad entity around you." She said.

Then she proceeded to describe my life all about Ilan, my life before him. She left no stone unturned. I hadn't said a word and from then I had no doubts and trusted her fully. It was like a scene from the movie Avatar, she could see me, right into me.

That night she cleared me, not from being possessed myself, as she told me I'd been strong and had good protection but it was something that would affect innocent well-meaning people around me. I was in a haze; I don't feel it would be right to say exactly what occurred because it is very private for the shaman. It was both terrifying and healing for me.

After a while I lay down to rest. I was told this would be recurrent throughout the night as staying still too long wasn't good with ayahuasca. I felt the music go through my nerves, sinews, my whole being. It sounded like 'tree' music and I let myself go just becoming at one with nature. I 'heard' a voice in my head, wooing me, telling me to *come up, up, up, tocome and all would be well*. I answered that I was held by a cord and the voice said, *no, cut, cutand come, it will be fine.* Another part of me resisted. I was afraid. I cried silently in my mind to my shaman to help me, help me. Literally in the same second she jumped from her bed and starting to sing and chant, forcing me to sit up. I felt sick, tired and dizzy but she was relentless. I later told her what had happened but she knew already, saying that was the ayahuasca connecting us completely both as one.

I don't doubt for a minute looking back that I was being tempted to step away and I'd always heard and believed in this 'cord', just like an umbilical, keeping us alive. I remembered people telling stories about not being actually able to die in your dreams, always waking just before. These were things I'd picked up along my life path and had never agreed or disagreed with the stories.

The next day she was exhausted. She had taken so much of my baggage into herself to release me. This is what a shaman does. To take fear, pain and sorrow into themselves then transmute it leaving their client free again. What a gift. I felt fresh and new.

I had to relax and wait for a couple of days before the next event. She came to see me and we talked but mostly I played relaxation music, spending most of my time in solitude. I rested and went for short walks in the village. But this time with what I thought was less fear. If only I knew. I prepared again as instructed for our second ceremony and this time drank with less hesitation. I was in a bubble, safe and away from everyone, with not even a mobile phone signal.

That night she performed in a similar way, singing and chanting but then told me to curl up with my head down and NOT look up. She carried out certain actions and I kept my head down starting to tremble. Really tremble until it became so strong I was wobbling like a jelly, terrified to my core. The tears were streaming down my face and in the smallest voice I said.

"I'm scared."

Everything stopped as she told me to look at her and said,

"Now you are being truly honest. I've just taken all your fear out of you. Fear you've denied, ignored and pushed away, unrecognized."

I'd been scared always but had faced up to it or denied it and carried on. She'd vacuumed all the repressed fear out of me. I was like a new born baby. That night we carried on with more rituals and with every last ounce of strength I completed the requirements. Did I hallucinate? Who cares! I looked 10 years younger the next day.

She told me to call Ilan and anyone else who mattered. The people who had helped me, who didn't know where I was told me they'd been sick, had headaches and strange nights on the two occasions of my ceremonies. Later their lives picked up and the difference was remarkable.

I called Ilan, who also said he'd been sick for days but sounded like a man coming out of a hangover; calm, not raging with resident animosity or anger, just saying he hoped it would all be alright. I returned home and met with Jan, who grabbed my hands, held them, looked in my eyes and said "wow". She was one of only two people who knew where I had been and she saw a transformation before her own eyes.

But I needed to hold on to this, to work at being this person and of course events would eventually pull me back but writing this reminds me that I really offered myself in every way to fight the good fight against the evil and ignorance which had been prevalent even though invisible. It's still difficult for me to believe that I undertook 5 days of personal challenge. The main thing I grasped was that alcohol or drugs can cause a lack of control, and I'd gone willingly into something I had no self-control over. The change in me was noticed immediately by family and friends. I looked younger and emitted a sense of calm that even through meditation I'd never achieved. The result was tangible, and I'd faced all my fears to achieve it.

Chapter 15

2011

It was May and a couple of days had passed since our wedding anniversary without a conversation. My heart was heavy. I had no more energy. At lunchtime Manny called.

"I've just had your husband on the phone to me, he's coming home!"

I'd been busy and saw there were several missed calls from Ilan. He called again and we talked for nearly 2 hours, him sounding just like the man I knew.

"I've got the order to sell the house. I'm certain my portion of the equity will be enough to deposit so I can leave Israel." He said.

It's always about money up front, not the present but the future. Ilan was regarded as a bad father. He had become in their eyes a man who would avoid paying if he lived outside Israel. Matty demanded huge sums of money, constantly expressing her fear of him not paying. The courts had listened. The outrageous, illegal and immoral demands had been accepted.

We'd always known that his half of the house could be signed as equity in principle but finding a lawyer or getting it heard in court was like finding hen's teeth. Ilan had always believed and depended upon the house being sold and finally after years of wrangling, the court had ordered the sale.

He was so excited, spilling his heart with hope and expectation, like a normal person.

"I think I will be home for your mum's birthday in July. It's nearly over. How are you? How's everyone? Can Manny start looking for work for me again? "

Questions spilled from him. You cannot begin to imagine what it's like to listen to a human being without any hope, it's robotic and just tortuous, but here he was full of life again. I knew he had situational depression, it had already been diagnosed that he was suffering depression but like a lot of men he thought he could cope without therapy or medical help. He'd believed that once this battle was over and he was home he'd be right as rain.

His self-awareness peaked during the next few weeks, aware that he'd been horrible, cruel and cold, and he was full of remorse. But here we were again planning a future and even able to talk about normal things. I was hesitant, not daring to really open up, but little by little I couldn't help it. We reached early July and suddenly one day he was angry, withdrawn and secretive.

"Hi Ilan, how are you this morning?" I asked.

"I don't want to talk." He said coldly. Oh please, not again I thought. Something had gone wrong but he wouldn't open up about it.

"Talk to me, don't run away again. Just tell me and we can find a way through it together. Is it about the No Exit Order?" I asked.

"It's worse, much worse." He said.

"There is nothing worse than losing your freedom. Is it family, is someone ill?"

"No, nothing like that. I've been betrayed. It's tax, it's the house. I'll talk to you later." he said, then disconnected.

He'd reacted to some bad news yet again. I couldn't imagine what it was. If not the block on his freedom or a family illness, I had no idea what could have sent him spinning back into the black hole he inhabited so regularly.

I called and called. He didn't answer his phone. I emailed relentlessly and yet again went into a frantic phase. Didn't he know in these manic depressive phases that there was a 'me' here? What could I do? I called Abe, who told me,

"Ilan's gone. He's a low life and unreliable. He's not the same man anymore. He's worthless and I don't care where he is."

This was his former partner talking as though Ilan was some kind of errant worker, forgetting they'd built the business together for over a decade and he should have been grateful for Ilan's loyalty to him. But despite my mistrust of him he did often say things with a grain of truth.

I'd been saving for years and finally had enough money to go on holiday and had already booked a week's cruise to Norway for August. It was our first holiday since Ilan had left. I tried to stay present and enjoy myself but my mind was constantly pulled back to Ilan. Where was he, what had happened? He had rambled something about tax, the house, being betrayed yet again but it hadn't made any sense. All I knew was he had become consumed with anger and I was yet again the victim of his moods.

On my return, Jan urged me to go back to Israel.

"You need to get yourself over there. You need to find out once and for all what is really going on. I'll come with you. Maybe he has another woman, and he's prevaricating between Plan A and Plan B. Who knows which plan you are? I can't stand back and watch you suffer like this. You are disappearing as a person."

"He sounded like my husband but something is occupying his soul." I said. "He's been hopeful for weeks, we've talked so much. It doesn't make sense anymore."

Ilan and I were both lost in our own way to his captivity. He'd responded a few times to my emails, saying *he'd call, 'don't worry, his house had been 'stolen' from him, he was in bad shape '*. It was as if normal service of his awful behaviour had resumed overnight. I knew he was unstable but Jan saw it in a different way and wanted the truth. She was afraid of flying yet overcame that to be with me. She hated the place, her body disagreed with it. We were not tourists; we had come to uncover the truth. Our first port of call was the bailiff and I asked to see papers as his wife, showing my marriage certificate and yet again trying to recall my Hebrew to make some kind of sense. They showed me the paperwork, which had a debt of 19,000 shekels, about £3000, which was a dramatic reduction in the previously alleged debt.

In Israel an alleged debt can be filed and whilst defending it, interest is mounting. Defending in Israel is a really tough call. It is always better to be the plaintiff. It is almost impossible for people outside of Israel to understand the judicial system, because winning a case does not mean that the judgment will necessarily be enforced. So with my trusted friend beside me, we pored over the papers and she concluded Ilan had been telling the truth.

Jan had always been a protective, fiery woman. Coming from Glasgow, she had the energy to defend her family and friends to the death. So the bailiff was done and next we went to the mortgage company. I remembered where it was and again went as his wife with papers. They told me the house had not been sold. Ilan had told me it had been, to a guy who was paying in stage payments. They assured me over and over that I was mistaken. This was breaking news and I didn't understand it at all.

Our next call was the civil/family court and our contact there told me all files had been closed as everything was over. He knew me from the countless times Ilan and I had practically lived in the court and the file could fill a supermarket trolley.

Then we went to the rabbinate to discover that we had a date for a divorce within a few days. The chief secretary told me Ilan had been nagging and persistent to come in and sign the divorce and I didn't even know about it!

I didn't believe him, telling him that Ilan's number was no longer his and he wasn't answering. The secretary immediately called the number and Ilan answered. We were sitting there listening as he confirmed the date with Ilan, who said he couldn't make it as he had a doctor's appointment. At this moment I was crumbling with shock. Ilan had indeed been telling the whole truth about his cases and battles but this, what was this about? He had become a Jekyll and Hyde character, one moment talking of coming home, and the next filing secretly for divorce. I wish I'd had the hindsight, or even the foresight to have dealt with his illness differently.

We were armed with some truth and a terrible situation in which I was about to be divorced without my knowledge. We needed to find Ilan and talk to him. Jan was incredible. She went to Matty's house. Matty was away in Barcelona and her sons answered the door. Jan observed immediately a latent anger and defensiveness in them and her heart bled. She's a mother to everyone.

Her next step was to go to the factory. She met with Abe, who was incensed with rage, as she went in a professional financial advisor capacity, ,stating we had a right to know the financial background of the company and money trail because I knew Ilan was still a partner on paper there.

Finally we decided to go to his parents. What a crazy time. I had brought a wig knowing everyone in the street would recognise me. I was in disguise as we parked a little further on from the house. She told me to sit tight and walked to his parents.

Telling them she was from the UK doing a financial investigation, she gave the hotel details and asked them to notify Ilan with the intention of making a quick retreat. I was like a kitten on hot coals in the car, with people I knew walking past. I began to nod my head back and forth as if in prayer, causing some raised eyebrows. This was a hotbed of gossip, and I was shaking like a leaf. Jan came back to the car.

"They've called Ilan and said he's on his way, only minutes away. I can't just leave now, I said I was getting some papers from the car, and you, you keep your bloody head down!"

She was thinking on her feet and I was a mess. Within a couple of minutes Ilan pulled up in his car. She got out and went to talk to him, across the road from his parents who never stopped looking and straining to hear them. I was a nervous wreck, hiding in a wig in a car from my own husband. Ridiculous, but you had to be there to understand.

My heart was pounding and I kept glimpsing over the passenger seat. Ilan looked good and he and Jan talked for at least 15-20 minutes. What was she going to tell me? What was going on? Was this real? What had I been reduced to? I was writhing and squirming, wishing every minute she would hurry up and come back but simultaneously dreading what she would tell me. Finally she came back, started the car, warning me to keep down as everyone was looking and that when we were clear she'd talk. We got back to the hotel, a few minutes away.

"You need a very large drink." She said as she ordered me a Gin and Tonic. "Ilan is well. He is sick of you; he doesn't want to know you. He said he is happy in Israel. He wants you to stop harassing him. I'm so sorry."

 The story went on and on and I gulped my drink as the tears started. She was incredible, just sitting in the space, whilst I cried a river of tears and drank myself rigid.

"It can't be, it just can't." I sobbed. "We'd talked so well together. There must be a reason for this. You saw yourself he'd been telling me the truth.

Something has caused this. His parents were listening. You saw for yourself."

"We need a night off from all this drama. Let's go back to the rabbinate tomorrow and from there we will decide what to do." She said.

I was in shock. The emails saying he was in despair and not well did not match what I'd seen and what she'd heard. Was this the end of my marriage without even a face to face? I needed to speak to him.

The morning after, at the rabbinate we were given the name of a good lawyer or two and told to get some advice. Poor Jan was trying to drive, needing constant navigation and my head was nowhere. But summoning my inner reserves we made it to the car park and went in search of advice. I met a wonderful lawyer. They always are wonderful in the beginning, as they want the whole fee up front, promising they will stick with their client to the end.

He believed things would be quick and I knew it meant the firm was looking for a profit. There is no lawyer who will charge monthly for time like they might in the UK. He was young, passionate and action orientated. He reassured me so much I paid £800 straight away and he commenced with cancelling the divorce file. He also began a search for the deeds on Ilan's home. It seemed Ilan hadn't been lying but hadn't been honest. Of course, it depended upon which personality was in charge.

The house was still in his name on the deeds, so the lawyer immediately put a charge on the property, closed the divorce file and opened a new one instantaneously so Ilan couldn't do a quickie for free with no accountability. Plus I had protected his interests by stopping Matty from selling the house should she wish.

The next day we went to Jerusalem. I wanted Jan to experience Israel outside of this drama and just be a tourist. It was beautiful and we wandered around the old city, stopping for coffees and cigarettes on a regular basis. During that afternoon on one break, Jan was disturbed.

"I really don't want to say what I'm about to say. I don't know if I'll ever forgive myself. But I can't stay quiet either." She said.

"What are you talking about? I know you've been pensive today. Tell it like it is." I said.

"When I was talking to Ilan, I couldn't put my finger on it but since then I have tried to work out what bothered me so much. Then today, it hit me. It's his eyes. They are dead. He's just not right. He was so cold, so brittle and he 'performed' really well. But he didn't ask me how I was and we are friends. It even took him five minutes to recognise me. Something was not genuine in his behaviour. We have made a mistake." With those words, she sat back and I saw her completely relax with the relief of following her instincts.

I recognised the look. I knew more than anyone what it felt to trust an instinct. I knew she trusted herself.

She had been in agony waiting to telling me this as she'd watched me purge myself for 36 hours trying to come to terms with events.

"I have to let it go." I replied. "But I need to say goodbye to him myself."

"If that's your decision, I'll support you." Jan murmured. "But I think we need to help him."

The next morning we went back to the factory. Private detectives we weren't! A conspicuous hire car, not the usual white but black was sticking out like a sore thumb. Ilan's factory was set back from the road accessed by a driveway with a DIY store, small buildings at the front, and at the rear covered with trees was his factory.

The trees had grown so much since I'd lived in the room next to it for 3 months so long ago. My feelings were so mixed up. I think I was on automatic pilot still not quite believing we were trying to hide and spy on a place I'd walked into regularly. We were behaving in a crazy way in a crazy country.

We parked behind a bamboo fence finding the perfect spot adjacent to the driveway believing we were well hidden. We were, until someone came and closed the fence, leaving us totally exposed. In our absurd situation we laughed so much, giving us huge release from the tension. Two mature business women doing this! If only people could see us now we thought. It was a memory that could never be translated as it really was. Finally Ilan drove in. My heart was thumping trying to break out of my chest. Jan started the car and drove around to the factory blocking Ilan's car from exiting.

"Don't lose it. Stay calm. She instructed as she got out of the car to approach Ilan. I followed her. Ilan barely acknowledged me but he was exceptionally nervous. He was unloading his car and concentrated on it as if it was a Mastermind exercise.

I said, "hi, we need to talk."

"Sure." He replied.

"Don't even consider making a dash through the back exit. If you do, I'll go to your parents." I said coldly.

It hit the spot, and he mumbled that he wouldn't. We stood, waited and watched. Jan whispered, "This is not the cool cucumber who I met the other day. He's discombobulating in front of us."

I saw the stranger in front of me, the man I knew better than he knew himself, and noticed how composed he looked. I knew he was literally terrified. I could see it.

We walked around the corner to a coffee bar and started to talk. I recorded everything. We had the documents in our hand, the charge on the property which had been ratified that morning. I interrogated him ruthlessly as there was so much I needed to get off my chest and so much I wanted to know but I was hardly able to hold my tongue to hear the answers. In retrospect I wished I'd talked less and listened more.

"So Ilan, you are trying to divorce me without my knowledge?" I challenged.

"No Mar, I don't know what you are talking about. I have not been near the rabbinate since we married." Ilan responded.

Jan and I looked at each other. He seemed genuinely surprised at this news but we'd heard him ourselves on the telephone. We had to concede he'd been trying to extricate himself from the appointment but it did leave us wondering if we were sitting with a split personality.

"We have been to the bailiff, mortgage company and the court. Your house has not been sold. You lied to me." I continued.

"It was sold but the guy pulled out as Matty was making things too difficult. She took the house from me. She bought it. The court forced me to give it to her. "

"Come on Ilan, you can do better than that. I've seen the deeds and your name is still on the property. I've flown yet again to get to the truth and you are still talking nonsense." Cold and hardened by two days of crying and then Jan's turnaround, I was in no mood for cryptic conversations.

Jan was listening intently. "Ilan, we have got all the papers. You've been telling the truth about a lot of things but it doesn't explain your behaviour. This is your wife. She has sacrificed everything to help you. Stop playing games and just tell the truth."

The traffic was rushing by as we sat outside a roadside café. I was recording the conversation on my mobile phone. I didn't want to rely just on my memory. Ilan was rigid in his chair. His body language was nonexistent and he couldn't make eye contact with me.

"Look at me Ilan." I demanded. "Look me in the eyes. You cannot lie to me when you look in my eyes. Maybe you can fob everyone else off with your indifference but not me."

Ilan looked up at me. He started to swallow hard as his emotions showed and his eyes filled with tears. Each time he looked away, I pulled his face toward me to maintain eye contact.

"Mar, don't tell him about yesterday." Jan warned me. She was referring to the papers we had received putting a charge on his property to stop his name being removed.

"Don't worry, I won't." I assured her. She was concerned as Ilan was both my strength and my Achilles Heel. If he truly opened up she was afraid I would be lost again. She also knew she had instigated this meeting from her own doubts of Ilan's wellbeing. I needed her more than I ever had before as we sat together.

"So where are you living Ilan?" Jan questioned him.

"I don't know, here and there." He replied.

"So where are your clothes? There is no way you have clothes dotted around the neighbourhood. There must be another woman." She pressed.

"No, there isn't. I am working on myself. I want to be left alone." He answered in a monotone.

As the conversation progressed Ilan varied from fear to opening up. It was a staccato conversation. After almost 2 hours Jan was showing him family photos and urging him to let us help him to leave Israel with the promise of not letting him down. But I tried to stand firm.

"This needs to be goodbye as I can't keep doing this. You have until tomorrow to decide as we are leaving Israel and I won't come back again if you keep up this crazy behaviour."

He was choking with emotion as he said "I can't end the connection with you Mar, I can't." It was a mess as we were enmeshed again in another stalemate of our soul connection.

"You have 24 hours to come to us and we will go and provide what is necessary for you to come home. We can get the £3000 and any guarantors needed." said Jan.

It was time to leave as the conversation wasn't getting us anywhere. Ilan was not really present to us or himself. As we walked away he pulled me to him and told me it couldn't be over between us.

On our last final day we did as we'd promised but Ilan never showed up. He was on the phone constantly, warming up again, becoming who we knew but not showing up either in person or truly as himself. He directed us to our destinations and yet again swore his undying love but sadly was too afraid to hope again.

I met him alone before we left in a petrol service station for a coffee. He called my mum and my sister and started to break down.

"I can't afford hope." he told me, "but I'll try one last time and if it doesn't work, that's it forever".

He cried so much as we kissed and hugged. I was his wife, his friend, but here I was in the most surreal situation imaginable.

We headed for home and Jan needed weeks to recover from the trip. Just like Lizzie she had found it deeply disturbing, turgid and very dark. It wasn't my imagination after all. But would Ilan hold up his end of the bargain and try once more?

Well he did. Surprisingly he did. He called regularly and renewed with vigor I put my effort into finding some money. If only I'd ever been able to find money like this for myself, I wondered if the Universe would have provided so quickly. Ilan put in a request to the bailiff to lift the order offering about 18 months to two years of money ahead, something we'd always been told was a norm. We'd got him out with a year's money for 3 children before so 2 years money for only one child seemed similar. He stipulated that we had NO guarantor, just the money and if the guarantor was required to please tell us immediately. He'd offered 45,000 shekels, and the response from the bailiff was '*give us 50,000*'. There was no mention of a guarantor and I knew I could find the money somehow. Ilan was elated and again started to talk with hope and normality.

"The buyer pulled out from the house, because Matty made things too difficult for him." Ilan explained during one of our many calls. "My name is still on the house I know. She has to prove she can pay the mortgage without the child support being taken into account. I'm the guarantor of my own house now!"

"Why didn't you tell me all of this?" I asked

"It wasn't just that. I had a huge VAT bill. Which I thought was a company one. It seems it wasn't. It was a personal bill."

"It's not possible, you worked in a limited company. More games from Abe?" I enquired.

"Games? This is the big one. I found a document in July. It was witnessed by a few people; a lawyer, an accountant and the bank. It was apparently signed by me, signing over my company to Abe as a gift. Do you remember we called Abe on 8th December to say we were coming?"

"How can I ever forget the date? It was the worst day of my life Ilan. It was the day we made the biggest mistake of our lives. Of course I remember. We landed at 3am the next morning."

"That's right. But this document I signed was dated 8th December, at 3pm."

"What are you telling me?" I reeled as the words sunk in.

"He stole my company. Matty went to court the same week offering to buy my half of the house. In exchange for my freedom she would clear the alleged debts and I could go. I agreed. Better to come to you with nothing than not see you again. I couldn't fight anymore. But in the court she took over the house and put the debt in the bailiff as a weapon. I didn't owe anything, if it was zero, I could leave. By putting the figure in the bailiff, she'd asked for a guarantee that I would pay regularly, and if so the 19,000 shekels would be removed when she felt comfortable. I refused. She got the house by the court ordering a power of attorney to take it from me."

"Oh my God!" I exclaimed. "Just as you thought you could come and were excited, they must have seen your change and betrayed you again." My heart broke for him. How much betrayal could one man take from the people he expected to support him?

"I couldn't talk. I ran away again. Seeing you in Israel turned me inside out. You came all the way back again for me. I have to get justice. Maybe Abe will give me the bailiff money in exchange for me not prosecuting him." He said.

"Don't hold your breath. It takes an age in court and judgments are worthless." I warned.

I continued to try and raise the money with yet more loans and also some commission, plus an advance from my contract company and I prepared to return to

Israel. This time I booked a ticket for a 24 hour turnaround, taking nothing with me. We had the decision. It was in black and white. There would be no need to stay longer than the time it would take to deposit the money and return to the airport. Deep inside me I feared that Matty would demand a king's ransom and calculated about £20,000 as a possible demand. Yes we had the decision, she hadn't responded to it, but it didn't stop me worrying.

I was prepared to give anything at this point for I couldn't lose him or allow him to lose himself again.

I gave him the flight number and asked him to pick me up. I didn't get a confirmation from him but off I went making sure Jan texted him too. All I took was the money and my own English mobile phone and my debit card. I flew on Saturday, expecting to return with him by Sunday evening.

How can I begin to describe the events of those 24 hours, which turned into seven days? Every time I say a visit was the most awful, there is another one to top it and this was the one.

Arriving at Ben Gurion Airport in Tel Aviv with almost £9000 in cash, I was praying and hoping that Ilan would be there to pick me up. But he wasn't. I waited, again remembering the times he'd been rushing from the waiting crowd with flowers, kisses and tears. But as the last straggler came out and an hour had passed, I had to accept that he wasn't coming. Yet again the country pulled me into a stupor of no common sense. I stayed restlessly in the airport, clutching my bag of money hoping against hope that he'd show up. I wonder why I didn't just turn around and catch a flight straight back home but I didn't.

After barely closing my eyes all night, when morning came I hired a car and went to the bailiff with my bag of money to pay what they had asked for. They told me that without him I couldn't do it for it was his case. I drove to Nahariyya feeling exhausted and disheveled with little time left to me.

I arrived at the factory full of defiance to face Abe. It wasn't pleasant. The landlord of the building sat down with me and the police were called. This is Israel. If someone doesn't like an action they call the police. It is a military state and this was intended to intimidate me. Abe saw the cash and laughed at me, telling me that Ilan was living with another woman. Abe said she'd been there with him, kissing and cuddling whilst I'd been calling Ilan insistently to file the papers. I absolutely refused to believe this, telling Abe that Ilan was desperate and I didn't trust Abe's words and something was just all 'rotten in Denmark'. They both told me if I gave this money to Ilan, I'd never see it again and it was all a scam. I couldn't believe the lengths Abe would go to.

But Ilan was nowhere to be seen. What was I to do? My return flight was approaching and all I had was the clothes I was wearing, the money and my phone. Finally I was told to creep through an alleyway because Ilan had arrived in the factory from the back entrance. In a dream state I complied and there he was. When I saw him, he cowered in a doorway, trembling and shaking. I didn't know what to do. I reached out to touch him and he retracted as if I'd singed him with a hot iron, crying and shaking. It was awful; could someone actually pretend to do this? In all my life experience, I couldn't believe that was possible. He was in a terrible state. I told him I had the money and had been to bailiff but they needed his presence.

I'd known him for over 25 years. He'd only been like this since his No Exit Order. My instincts were nudging me, trust him, trust him. He's showing up, good or bad to ME. He told me to wait which I did. Waiting in my rental car, he came to me. He had one leg inside the car and one outside. If I said it was 20 minutes I think I underestimated it. His physical uncertainty showed his mental torture.

"We need to talk. Let's go to your parents. We can explain why I'm here. Tell them about the bailiff. We have to go and deposit the money. Wake up Ilan." I urged.

It was agonising. His body displayed his mind, which was split in half. I'd never seen anything like it. But he was my husband and whilst half of me was compassionate, the other half was angry that I couldn't take control of the situation. Eventually, he told me he'd drive his car, and I'd follow him.

We set off and half way there he pulled over. He stumbled into my car unable to breathe; panting, heaving, sweating, banging his head on the dashboard and moaning over and over,

"The pressure, the pressure."

I held him tight, willing him to calm down, not fully understanding this crazy behaviour but feeling I had to keep him together.

He finally said, "I can't go to my parents with you, I just can't. Trust me please. I'll meet you later tonight."

I had no choice but to agree. I drove to Haifa and found a really cheap hotel. Once there, I took a double room based on his promise of coming to me. I was so confused. I knew our history and the betrayals he'd endured but was there enough time for my influence? I just didn't know. I waited and waited, sitting on the balcony, writing a diary to pass the time. The rollercoaster of his behaviour was always linked to bad news or his hopes being dashed. It was a pattern. I realised that I wasn't really qualified to deal with someone in this state but prayed that his love for me would awaken him to a rational state.

Finally he called. "Listen Mar, I'll meet you first thing In the morning at the Bailiff, I promise."

So I endured a night with no brain, no logic, no common sense, lost in hope, fearing the worst and imagining all would be well tomorrow. Somehow my sense of myself was still back in the UK and I was being sucked into the lies and madness.

I arrived at the bailiff court at 8am and he was at the entrance. In the queue to enter the bailiff, he started to sweat, shake and shiver. I was later to learn about something called Legal Abuse Syndrome which is when a person almost becomes allergic to court and I was to learn he fitted the bill completely. But I didn't know then and I was engrossed in my own determination and desperation.

The administration office told us to *"pay the 50,000 first and you will get your decision after"*. This was not like before where we had the decision and order first. Ilan was nervous and demanded an alternative but they stood firm *"pay first, decision later"*. He was back in a building of authority and was more than uncomfortable. We checked with lawyers passing through and they all asserted that our decision looked watertight. So I went to the post office to change currency. It took almost an hour. Another deadline and under pressure with me praying Ilan wouldn't lose his nerve.

I returned with the cash. It took an age and I was trying to hurry the clerk. Come on, come on, he could run away again. My worries were dominating me. Ilan was really scared unhappy about the process but I pressed to deposit the money. The head of the administration office was arrogant and cocky, assuming Ilan was a waster, a term they use in Israel, and ignored the fact I'd come from England with a return flight. The £9000 was paid to the cashier and all we could do was to wait.

Ilan had never been good at waiting but I was. I'd sat outside courts many times for hours on end, prohibited from going inside with him so I'd become accustomed to having patience. He wasn't. We sat, talked, paced and went inside and out of the building several times. He just couldn't sit still. Matty had not responded to his request so we dared to hope it would be successful. I failed to notice that Ilan was not physically prepared with a bag or his passport and we only had hours before I was due to leave. Either he didn't believe in the possibility or he had no intention of leaving. I was never to know which it was for years.

"I've tried to live without you. But I can't. My mind permeates with thoughts of you nonstop. It's in my conscious and probably unconscious thoughts. You are just there, inside me, all the time. I can't make it go away." He told me.

I knew exactly what he meant. We hugged and talked from 8am until at least 11 hours later. Neither of us knew what would transpire. Pacing the floor; popping our heads in for news, we were turned away over and over.

Ilan grabbed my hands, asking, "Will people forgive my madness and my abuse Mar? I'm all over the place. But I'm so scared. I don't know what to do. I'm frightened to come as people will hate me for what I've put you through."

I reassured him over and over. "It will be ok. Everyone knows you have been a prisoner. No one here has helped. I understand completely you have forgotten how to feel normal."

He started to believe telling me, "I'll pick up my passport and tell everyone what I think of them if we get the release paper. There is so much I want to say, but only when I'm free."

He was behaving erratically; shaking and having what looked like panic attacks. I felt I should have got a doctor but just held him as he held me, whilst we waited with familiar anxiety for a decision to hopefully change our lives for the better. We refused to leave the building at 4pm as it was closing to the public.

"They're just playing with us. Making us wait until the bitter end." He said, biting his nails with ferocity.

"It's going to be fine. They don't like to lose. We wouldn't be here all day if it was going to be rejected. They told us already. Put the money in. We've done what they said. No guarantors. Don't worry." I was trying to reassure us both.

Finally at about 6pm the decision was returned. *'We accept the bond, but we'd like a guarantor as well'*. It was the very thing he'd stipulated we couldn't and wouldn't do. How stupid could these people be? They hadn't read his request at all. But they had my money and Ilan had no freedom. They had allowed us to suffer for almost eight hours, and I was in no doubt they knew exactly what they were doing.

I was incensed and demanded to see the head of the Bailiff.

"How dare you treat us like this? I've flown from England to give you the money on a decision you made. What is wrong with you people? You behave with breathtaking audacity. This is a man's life you are playing with."

The Head of the Bailiff court responded, all behind closed doors.

"This man cannot be allowed to breathe any air outside Israel without paying over double this money at least. He can live here, and not even pay but he cannot live outside with even 5 years ahead. Give us another 100,000 and I will buy him the ticket myself. This is life. Fathers pay by staying in Israel. If you don't like this, go to the court and appeal."

"Then give me my money back this instant. You deceived us. You gave us a decision, you knew our offer. How can you suddenly change this after you have my money? I am a British citizen and you are nothing but thieves." I exploded.

"No, you can't just have your money back. It doesn't work like this. Go to the family court and make an appeal if you want it. The matter is closed, go away."

Ilan couldn't breathe, couldn't translate and the office manager wouldn't either. She was arrogant and rude. These people didn't understand the concept of captivity. They'd got the money and that was business concluded for them.

Ilan stormed from the building and we went back to my hotel. He was out of his body and out of his mind. Not again. Here we go again.

We held each other and he told me, "This time I won't run. This time we will face it together. I can't handle this alone Mar. They are breaking my hope again but I'll try. Let me go and get a change of clothes and I will be back later to prepare the appeal with you. We will fight this together."

But for Ilan it was a dejavous and I felt the same. Could I summon enough energy for this when we were barely a couple?

I waited and spent the night researching reciprocal laws between UK and Israel. There were plenty, one being that a separated man could live in England and be obliged to pay child support through English Law. I had known it a long time, yet no lawyer was prepared to discuss international law in the family court for us. I wrote a defense and appeal whilst calling Ilan constantly but there was no reply. In fact I was not to see him again. His promises to not run away were forgotten.

The next morning I drove to the civil court to place an appeal. They didn't want to know. *He* had to be there. I told them he wasn't well, and couldn't cope, but shoulders were shrugged and I faced plenty of backs as people turned away from me. I called him over and over and eventually he replied saying he was on his way.

I went to a translation company and had my appeal translated to Hebrew. I was running out of time. Ilan still didn't come. I cried relentlessly and didn't know what to do or who to turn to. My flight had gone and so had my money. Jan was in constant contact and I was oblivious during this time to phone charges using my UK mobile. I had no support network in Israel. I collapsed in the street in tears and desperation and finally by chance a wonderful lawyer came back to the bailiff with me and wrote a request for my money to be returned. Within an hour the judgment was received agreeing that I could have it returned. This was New Year's Eve in Israel, September, how I hated September. Everything was closing early to enable people to be with their families but I was bereft, alone and not knowing whether to stay or leave.

Ilan ignored my calls from then and my texts. I was alone in a country I'd known for 24 years without a friend in sight. I returned to the factory the next morning and found the landlord of the factory. I was hungry, tired and dirty. He gave me some bread to eat and told me I was a fool. He claimed Ilan had actually travelled outside the country in August with his girlfriend and plenty of people knew. I was torn in two. I had to remember what people had done to him and the things they'd said to me. I remember Abe once on the phone telling me

"He just won't quit on you. The price he pays for trying to leave us here to manage is that he will never leave

Israel. We've almost broken him but you, you are the person he holds on for. Just leave him alone."

I recalled these words and those of his family and how Ilan had upset Eitan telling him

"I'd rather have a Stop Order and my wife in England, than live with freedom without her and have the superficial life you have."

Those words had cut his brother to the core and he would tell Lizzie more than once that there was no love lost between siblings. I remembered someone once telling me that it took on average 20 months for a person to break down from this enforced captivity and knew that Ilan had held on for much longer because of my love for him. But none of these memories changed the fact that Ilan had abandoned me.

I waited and Ilan arrived. He saw me, reversed like a Formula 1 driver and disappeared. My desolation was complete. Jan was desperately concerned for me and I was prevaricating. I couldn't decide whether to stay and wait for the money to be returned, or leave and fight for it from England. I actually stayed for 5 more days but learned that the refund of my money would be 14 days after their holidays, a month in total. I couldn't think. I went to Abe again. I had no choice.

He told me "When you and Ilan were in the bailiff, I'd been calling him all day. He told me he was in the rabbinate divorcing you. So I don't believe you were in the bailiff. No way does Ilan want to leave here."

"Look, Abe, look." I said desperately. "Here are the receipts for the money. Here is his request. Here are documents he signed yesterday. It's all true. I'm not the liar here."

I flung the papers down in front of him. He looked at them carefully, and believed me. I was angry with the idea I had to justify anything to this wretched man.

He called Ilan's parents to say I'd been telling the truth. This was the problem for me. The truth was always there but Ilan's behaviour was erratic. He was lying to them, not to me, but the lies had split his personality. Abe told me Ilan's parents were shocked, and armed with my truth I naively believed they would welcome a visit from me to get all the information.

I visited Ilan's parents with my proof.

"Go away, you are not welcome here." His father said, trying to usher me out of their front garden.

"I'm begging you. I have papers here from the bailiff. Look at them. Here are receipts for the 50,000 shekels I've paid for Ilan." I sobbed. I tried to push the papers into his hands.

"I'm not interested. If you put those papers near me I will tear them to pieces. I don't care about you. I don't care about Ilan. I don't care if he is alive or dead. I'm sick of you." His father retorted, and then spat on me, It was the highest of insults.

"If you don't get off our premises, I will call the police. Now go away."

"Ilan told me I could come to you for food. I'm on the street, I have nothing."

"Just go away, or we will have the police here to arrest you. It's not our problem if you are desperate."

Again, his parents treated me like a cur. This was my lowest point. I was a vagrant on New Year's Eve in a foreign land.

I wandered aimlessly around the vicinity for days until Jan put her foot down and booked me a flight home. When I arrived back in civilisation I was 7 kilo's lighter and filthy. I fell into Jan's arms at the airport, collapsing with grief and relief. She didn't know what to do for me. It was overwhelming to be back in normality.

Chapter 16

Returning home – rebirth

Returning home like a battle weary warrior and not really knowing who I had been fighting against, all I wanted was to recover, rest and sleep. I was desperately worried about the money. Ilan had been outrageous by running away and abandoning me but I reflected it was not really a surprise, given that he hadn't turned up at the airport even to collect me. I felt abused and used. Recalling the events in the Bailiff, I knew Ilan had done everything he could to get some kind of paperwork before the money had been deposited. I knew beyond doubt that he was seriously disturbed but that wasn't helping me to manage the terrible way I had been treated.

September had been another fiasco and my £9,000 was still being held by the bailiff in what they called a safe bond, all I wanted was my money back. I was not really taking in the bitter experience of yet another September disaster. It was becoming an annual event. Abandoned within minutes of the bailiff reneging on their judgment for Ilan to come home, I wondered how I'd even got to this. I was browsing the internet for an English speaking lawyer in Israel, just to ask when the endless holidays would be over so the cheques from the bailiff could be issued, and then returned via Ilan to me. The lawyer was curious and asked questions but I was in no mood to revisit this Groundhog Day situation.

Ilan had no idea which part of the world I was in. He'd refused to answer calls and had become indifferent yet again. The lawyer was intrigued by events and very kindly offered to meet Ilan to look at his file and made an appointment. I was barely speaking to Ilan at this point. But Ilan agreed to see the man, he was making noises again about his hope, and perhaps we could still be able to make a go of things. I loved him so much, and knew deep down that his behaviour was circumstantial, and if he wasn't there in Israel maybe things would indeed work out. But he didn't attend, his excuse being he'd been in a car crash and was being cut out of the vehicle. He was so far out of touch with reality I couldn't be bothered to react. He made the second appointment taking his files and his story.

The lawyer was staggered. The injustice was beyond his experience. He was sure he could get all the decisions overturned. In a click of a finger Ilan became human again, and I was reeled back in. One final push, like the last labour pain, and we could give birth to a new life.

My unconditional love had carried me this far and as a determined woman, I knew one more effort could take us over the line. He revived so quickly and another round of conversations began, it was almost like the beginning. We were advised to increase the offer by another 20,000 Shekels. I had no doubt although it was much more than required by the court, Matty would demand at least double, continuing to extort us and the bailiff would accept whatever she wanted. By now I understood Ilan's hopelessness in the face of kangaroo courts. Either she had very strong connections in the system, or as the evidence was growing from stories, the system was set up for this abuse.

When we finally talked again he was a different person. He was terribly upset about what had happened but didn't want to really discuss it immediately. I was like a broken record only wanting my money. Deeply hurt and barely recovering from the ordeal, I wasn't ready to listen to a single word from anyone over there except the date and time for my money being returned.

Over a three month period he talked more and more, the maximum in one week alone was almost 40 hours of conversation. I was compelled to talk too. I wanted explanations and answers for his shocking behaviour. My brain rationalised that he couldn't fake that much and my heart was melting again desperate for this horrific problem to end, which in my view was his removal from Israel.

I was in financial hardship and eventually Ilan received the cheques from the Bailiff. He called me and asked what to do so I emailed simultaneously to the lawyer for advice. It was all in real time and I was embroiled again. The lawyer was too busy to see Ilan, so he held on to the cheques. He couldn't cash them as Matty had prevented him from having a bank account.

Time passed. Ilan was burning his bridges with a vengeance, ready to take on anyone who would block his path. He sounded stronger and we had a lot of conversations about normal things; politics, news, books, jokes, plans and we were both happier, being more relaxed and hopeful for the future. We increased the offer to Matty to 70,000 shekels. The 50,000 was still in the bailiff.

I had decided to throw caution to the wind and give her whatever she wanted. I knew she'd demand more than that, probably double and made the decision that I'd find this money and buy him out once and for all. Ilan was fragile and gaining his self-awareness, able to see his own behaviour for which he was remorseful. He became hopeful again. He was my

Ilan once more - my friend and my husband - returning to his old self. He called all hours of the day and night, seven days a week and it felt right.

Turning to the Universe for help, my prayers were answered when I received a letter out of the blue regarding a dormant pension I had. On checking, I learned I could transfer it to a self-managed fund, and get some commission for doing it, which would be enough not only for the offer, but any significant increase she might want. I'd done the maths, and decided I'd cover the child support for the full duration ahead. I told him to hang on tight as the money was assured and in a few weeks the cash would be available. Her demand was to be 110,000 Shekels, and I was fully expecting it, and was prepared to pay.

He asked me to renew our wedding vows, planning it for my upcoming birthday the next February. It was a couple of weeks before Christmas and I started to believe this was it, it was finally over and he could come home. He agreed with the lawyer that he needed a psychiatric evaluation and I found him numbers, wrote to some of them myself, and heard him on the phone trying to make appointments. He insisted that any help must be in England, but the legal advice was he needed a report to show he couldn't handle his affairs and was depressed and burned out. This was the man I'd known for over 20 years talking to me.

It took a lot of courage for him to admit he was unwell. He said it was me who kept him going, my love and determination which kept saving him.

Finally I hoped I was getting some sense. But my next action was to be so unexpected, that no-one could have predicted it, least of all me. I was beginning to sink into the same fatigue and trauma as my husband. I wasn't going to know that then, or even recognise it or admit it.

We judge others for their behaviour and still can't look in the mirror for the reflection of our own. I was going to be sinking fast. I ranted so much about Ilan's denial but was in full blown denial too. Of course our marriage hadn't fallen apart I reasoned with myself. It was all going to be alright. Of course this blip in bad behaviour was situational. How could it be anything else? This turmoil of deception lies and corruption that I could see so clearly was beginning rapidly to tar me with the same brush of rollercoaster emotions.

But nothing I'd gone through was to prepare me for events of the next 12 months. I wish I could have foreseen them, but in my wildest imagination I couldn't have known. The following year was to almost break me completely.

Chapter 17

The United Nations

Ilan's galvanised energy brought me back to the bigger picture. The hundreds if not thousands of men, women and children languishing in Israel from the Stop Order/No Exit Order and maybe many other expressions for it, for example 'ex parte' order in legal terms. It all boils down to the same result which is an impingement of movement of citizens, dual nationals and in some cases outright foreigners to Israel. I'd connected with a few in my research for a solution. A wonderful man called Dr. E, who was a French Doctor and had his own fight. His daughter had been abducted from France, and was hidden in Jerusalem, and he'd spent many years trying to find her.

At the same time a No Exit Order was placed upon him too. He was very vocal in his disapproval of the system, and what he called abuse of fathers, which led him to talking to people in France at the highest levels. He got the same answers as me when I approached the government here who said it's a domestic issue, can't get involved. The press gagged us all, everyone who had a story to tell. This tool of captivity was so commonly used in Israel. People regularly were prevented from leaving the country. I had read and also heard that tens of thousands of children had these no exit orders placed on their behalf before the age of 18. Lifting these orders was a license to print money for the Israeli courts.

What person had a house to bond abroad, or up to $100,000 bond to be paid? What person in Israel would be a guarantor, exchanging their own freedom of movement, and being liable for alleged debts, or future security for another? It was ridiculous. It was so contrary to British or European culture, and I was to learn more and more about this destructive legal weapon. No psychological safeguards were set up to measure the damage to the psyche of individuals suddenly held hostage. I can remember being asked many times in various official places, would I like to place a No Exit order, as commonplace as ordering fries with a burger in a fast food restaurant. At this time, it was common practice in a divorce for fathers to be separated from their children aged 6 or under, then require a psychological evaluation to be carried out to assess their parental ability. This was part of a law encompassing The Tender Years Clause. Can you imagine the devastation to families embroiled in bitter divorces? This could often result in fathers not seeing their children for years.

Dr. E was determined to highlight this, and I wanted to talk about the damage to a soul in emotional captivity. Meanwhile, Ilan was renewed, determined to fight Abe for the loss of his company, and invigorated by my actions which would secure his freedom at last. Hook, line and sinker, that was me. I opened up more and more. I was falling in love all over again. We actually managed to talk, about politics, books, our day, TV, jokes, and Ilan said it was the happiest he had been since he'd been trapped there.

The more I learned, coupled with my own experience, the more my eyes opened. Israel uses freedom as a gift or punishment with impunity as a weapon of choice. Ilan and countless others were being held by a moneymaking system, backed with their paranoia of needing iron clad guarantees of any eventualities in the future. I pitied Israel.

By no means can I be described as anti-Semitic; I married not one but two Israelis with half my life connected to Israel in good times and bad. I've also experienced a myriad of cultures in over 40 countries and see people as different in language and location, but all wanting the same things; peace, love and a secure life. Those needs cross all cultural divides.

Israel is a chameleon and a contradiction. There a hundreds if not thousands of books available to read on the policies and politics of Israel. I am not a political animal but I know the truth needed to be exposed.

To distract myself from thinking only of Ilan, I started to research. I wondered if there was some connection between the behaviour of Israel to their own people, and how they treated their near neighbours. Israel promotes itself as the only democracy in the Middle East. That would imply that freedom of movement and freedom of speech would be the minim expectation. But it wasn't happening. I found a website, named 'Breaking the Silence'. It was of Israeli Defence Force (IDF) soldiers who had been brave enough to talk about their experience in national service. They weren't in the army as heroes, saving the population from real war or terror. They were serving time disrupting the ordinary lives of Palestinians, by fear and humiliation.

I learned that the suicide rate in young soldiers was very high and statistically off the norm, though spokespeople claimed there was no evidence of PTSD, they hadn't been in a war. Maybe these soldiers just couldn't live with the things they saw or were expected to do. Post-Traumatic Stress Disorder isn't just from a war; it can also arise from prolonged exposure to atrocities, or like Ilan, prolonged captivity.

I found another group – Machsom Watch – a group of women in Israel who go to the checkpoints to ensure that Palestinians entering Israel for work are treated with humanity. It is written on their website that a woman wasn't allowed through the checkpoint, whilst in labour with twins; gave birth to the first baby which died, and was still refused help, and lost her second baby. For a principle? These people are not terrorists, nor a major nuclear power. They just want a normal life. It was clear again that freedom is used as a weapon to tragic effect. I wondered if the soldiers in question have clear consciences.

Maybe those with strong views of Israel's need for security could justify the daily mistreatment of normal people, and why they would need to express the same abuse to their own people, perhaps in a more insidious or invisible way, but the same in principle.

I've read of many holocaust survivors who are dead against the current policies of Israel, and how turning Palestinian territory into a Ghetto had some disturbing similarities to the past. I read in Israeli newspapers that these survivors are not as well cared for as they should be, almost an embarrassment now compared with Israel's might of today.

It's said there are always two sides to a story. It doesn't mean that both stories are calm and reasonable. Whatever the history, which can be read in thousands of books on Israel; and whatever the fears are, whether real or imagined, I see no reason to crack a nut with a sledgehammer.

I was being given many stories; of foreign nationals who couldn't travel from Israel without huge constraints and conditions, mostly financial. I learned of children who cannot travel to see extended families, for they had No Exit Orders themselves, done by a parent. I even learned of young teenagers who had gone to court to try and set themselves free before their eighteenth birthday.

After watching the historic moment when the Berlin Wall came down, it is a tragedy that Israel has built a wall of their own, much bigger than Berlin. When completed it will be almost 700 kilometres long, as of 2012, over 400 kilometres had been erected. In 2004, the International Court of Justice declared, "Israel cannot rely on a right of self-defence or on a state of necessity in order to preclude the wrongfulness of the construction of the wall". The Court asserted that "the construction of the wall, and its associated régime, are contrary to international law".

Sounds reasonable, but despite the statement Israel went ahead anyway, causing families to be separated, towns and villages divided and yet more misery for the majority of law abiding Palestinian people.

I believe all people should have the right to freedom of movement. It is not the case in Israel. As shocking or as defensible as some people may find the policies with the West Bank and Gaza, it was plain to me in a simplistic way. If they could hold innocent people of their own, and even some foreigners, for no crime or suspicion, and it was normal for them, then their behaviour externally is just that – normal. I think most people in Israel will know someone who has had the experience of No Exit Orders, or heard of people, probably heaving a sigh of relief that it isn't them.

What I couldn't grasp was how Ilan's family could be complicit in such a destruction of their own flesh and blood, and what was their motive to trap a grown man?

There had to be something else I could do, and Dr. E would point the way.

Often when driving, I would play imaginary scenes or imaginary conversations in which I would take every role in turn. It's said talking to oneself is the first sign of madness but for me it meant I could imagine every permutation, so if and when it became real I would be prepared. It worked a treat when planning ahead for sales meetings as I would think through various potential objections or create the scene I wanted, knowing the part I would need to play to get a successful outcome.

My hidden thought had always been in the periphery of my mind, never in full Technicolor, more a wisp of an idea. I had no frame of reference to create the scene, until now.

With a small overnight bag by my side, I was en route to meet Dr. E. We'd emailed and talked many times, yet never met. I couldn't conceive how I was expected to recognise him without any description. I waited at our rendevouz point, starting intently at every passer-by, *is this him, could that be the one?* The airport was unfamiliar to me, and totally dependent on the appearance of my colleague I began to worry if I'd got my instructions wrong. Finally, an hour after the appointed time, Dr.E turned up. He knew me straight away.

"Marianne?" he asked briskly.

"Yes, we meet at last." I responded with relief.

From all our conversations, he was not what I was expecting, from his voice I'd been searching for a tall wiry man. Short in stature, portly with thinning hair and glasses, I was faced with a focussed whirlwind in a small package. His English was excellent, laced with an incredibly heavy French accent.

"There is no time to waste, viens." He instructed.

I was trying to recall a character from a movie 'make haste, no time to waste', it was on the tip of my tongue as I walked hurriedly after him. That's it! Alice in Wonderland's white rabbit!

I towered over him, instinctively trying to shrink. I'd brought the wrong footwear and by the time we'd walked – far too quickly for my liking – my toes were pinching so it was with huge relief we finally arrive at a local Hostel.

"We'll share a room." He declared. "Don't worry, I'm in a relationship."

I observed how full his mind seemed as he bustled and hurriedly made a reservation, handling everything with barely a glance at me. Regretting I'd not brought enough clothes, being a woman who always packed too sparsely, my dominant wish was to have brought comfier shoes. These boots I'd chosen were smart and fashionable, but there is nothing worse than blisters for breaking ones' concentration.

After the flurry of activity to check in and leave our belongings, we found a nearby restaurant and I gratefully sank into my seat.

Dr.E was a godsend. My French hovered between rusty to none, so he handled the waiter with aplomb in his native language. My mind was a blur.

"OK, Marianne. Tonight we prepare, and tomorrow we begin."

It was plain for me to see Dr.E was suffering his own trauma. His daughter had been kidnapped from his home in Paris almost five years before and secreted somewhere in Jerusalem by the mother. On arrival to search for her he too had a No Exit Order placed upon him. Talking quicker in English than me, with barely a pause, he deluged me with stories, particularly of French Nationals trapped in Israel. Combined with the torment of no freedom, these people had been faced with terrible court decisions, extortionate financial demands; many were homeless and hopeless, sleeping for months on the beaches.

"The big issue is the Tender Years Assumption in family law. Do you know of it?" he asked.

"I've no idea…" were all the words I could edge into his monologue of pain.

"It is the assumption that all children 6 and under are given automatically to the mother in divorce." He explained. "It is irrelevant if she is fit or not for the job, it's automatic. Fathers are removed from contact with their children and have to battle in the courts for their rights. They cannot leave Israel; if foreign they cannot get work permits either. It is impossible. There are some terrible statistics. Tomorrow we will show a report to explain this."

Tomorrow! In the morning we would be going to the UN. Not the giant one seen on the news, but an offshoot. The Human Rights Committee, known as the UNHRC.

"You are a woman." He continued. "So your presence will add weight. People think we just complain, but your husband, he is trapped, you are a reasonable European and your words should have influence."

"Have you been before?" I asked

"No, but don't worry." He said, as he turned his concentration to his meal.

It's the blind leading the blind I thought.

It was unbelievable that his daughter had been taken from France, and despite all efforts to see her, he himself had a No Exit Order. He wasn't intending to return to Israel, as he knew he would be imprisoned on landing. My heart broke for him as well as myself. He told me of dozens of people who were facing ruin and destruction, both from No Exit Orders and the barbaric law known as the Tender Years Clause.

That evening as Dr E selected the papers he wanted to distribute, I was redundant, so I laying on my bed distracting myself with a book, I realised I had nothing with me, no papers, only myself and my own story. But it was the UN, a real place with really important people who could be unbiased and who could actually listen.

Dr.E turned off the lights and went to sleep immediately. I hugged myself in the dark. *Geneva. I'm actually in Geneva.* I repeated silently. I felt less isolated with Dr E's myriad of examples and documented real stories. It was possible we could tell the world. I was nervous and excited, and whilst being happy with Ilan's current though fragile state, I knew this whole thing was much bigger than our story.

As I drifted to sleep from an eventful day, my last thought as usual was there would be one less person in Israel when I awoke. Saddened by the knowledge of the high suicide rate, I also said a prayer for Ilan. I imagined the families and the grief of another suicide. Perhaps they hadn't seen how far down their loved ones had gone and I doubted they would. Image is everything. I didn't believe those suicidal people would admit to their depths of despair, and felt no one would listen anyway. Who had heard my own cries for help, or even cared that Ilan's identity was eroding. The problem is that by the time a person can understand their predicament, they are so broken or defeated, and there is no other recourse than to accept their fate.

When I woke, Dr.E was showered, dressed and ready for action. He mused out loud, checklists ticked off, chattering constantly as he prepared his papers. With a limited wardrobe I got ready quickly, pulling on the tortuous boots, and prayed for a taxi.

"It's only a block away." Dr. E announced. "We'll walk."

Like a walker in an Olympic event he sped off, with me rushing to catch up. Normally I'd out walk anyone, but not today. I'd barely a chance to take in my surroundings. It was only my second trip to Geneva, the first as a guest speaker for an event – collected, chauffeured and cossetted. It was in a former life I thought sadly. The one when I was in demand, confident and professional. Now I was a pariah in

Israel, unanchored at home and almost penniless. My inner warrior challenged me. 'You are still the same woman'. I listened to my inner voice and fresh determination surged through me. How dare they do this to me, well, no more. 'I am the same woman, indeed I am.' I agreed with my warrior.

We passed by Lake Geneva, and whilst Dr.E was chattering and concentrating on finding our location, I took a moment to pause and take in the beautiful fountain in the middle. For me it was the symbol of Switzerland. Neutrality and reason is my concept of Switzerland. Where better to have a UN building.

As we walked, Dr. E explained to me that every two years member countries had to present to the Committee on various issues. The topics were listed under articles. The main one of interest to us was Article 10, family matters. . The country presenting would renew and refresh previous pledges or requirements and the HRC would question to see if the particular country was truly endeavoring for improvement in basic social issues. This week it was the turn of Israel.

 "No one in Israel could make it." He was grumbling. "Everyone was too busy or making excuses. All talk and no commitment as usual. They've got a chance to tell it like it is, and suddenly everyone is busy, or scared. I know you have passion, and we will need it."

He was right. Second to food and money, complaining was a huge part of the culture. There are so many words for difficult, bad, terrible. But it's hard to hear the positives. I recalled someone once said the word 'Ne-hedar' (pronounced nay hedar in Hebrew), which means great. In almost twenty years I'd never encountered it, they said it was hardly used.

I'd better summon up some passion, I thought to myself as mercifully we had arrived at our destination.

As Dr. E burst into a torrent of French in order to gain our entry to the building, I gazed around me, and spared one last thought for my husband before going in.

Ilan was so proud of me and humbled by my intention to speak for him. Our love was renewed, and hope had sprung up again. He was more reliable and consistent, and I was overjoyed that he was coming back to being himself. It was a honeymoon period for us compared to a few short months ago. Ilan finally met the lawyer, who had immediately seen Ilan's need for a psychiatric assessment, and Ilan had readily agreed to it. Our long daily conversations had given him insight and he knew he urgently needed some help. I heard him on the phone trying to make appointments, and he choked on his request, as he admitted he was in deep emotional turmoil and trauma.

Yet again, it was me he had turned to, hoping I could forgive his erratic behaviour. He had his own Everest to climb, and it was all the more difficult as he was such a proud man. So whilst he was concentrating on his own affairs at last, I was financially melting down.

My money was still locked in Israel and I was ready and fired up to find a miracle in Switzerland.

Dr. E was chattering to me again bringing me swiftly back to the present. "I'm not sure of the agenda, but I'm sure we'll get a chance to speak from the public arena."

We entered into a beautiful old building, nothing like the outside, with a sweeping staircase in front of us, marble floors and pillars, and walked down a corridor into a very modern room. We arrived whilst they were in session to a room full to bursting point. On the left were rows of seats for the public and on our right were three rows of seats for UN members, headed by a top table of the UNHRC chairman and a number of the Israeli delegation.

There was no space for us in the public seating area, so we were ushered to a couple of spare seats along the UN committee row. Prime viewing! Headphones were provided, and as I turned and looked upwards, I could see above me boxes behind glass, with each of the main country's interpreters. You could flick a switch and hear any one of numerous languages.

It was amazing, and for a few short minutes, I played with the headphones switching from language to language being translated so quickly. Here I believed that real decisions would be made, and were being made.

Dr. E had thought this day was the day the public could speak, but it had actually been the day before.

As this realization dawned on us, we decided we had to do something.

He was sitting opposite me, continually writing me notes and passing them across the enormous desk. Feeling disconcerted, I wrote back, *what are we supposed to do now?* His reply, *don't worry, we'll arrange something in the coffee break.*

Dr. E took dozens of copies of the report he had brought during the break. Somehow he had managed to persuade the secretary to use the photocopier. I was learning quickly from him. Look efficient, look in control and all will be well.

But I had only myself, and my life experience. How were we to even get heard? There were several breaks, and during those, we sought out UN committee members. Dr. E handed documents out to everyone, and I was handpicking individuals to approach, based on instinct. The universe did look after us, and even if I didn't get what I wanted, perhaps on a bigger scale something really good did happen.

All I could think was how to summarise my life to a stranger, and get the attention and credibility needed in a few short minutes of intruding on their coffee break. I was getting a crash course in lobbying. At this point in time, a soldier held in Lebanon had just been returned to Israel after they had negotiated his release by freeing terrorists. Coming from the Thatcher era, and our British mantra of never doing this, the thought just popped into my head. I caught the attention of the head of the Israeli Delegation, a Mr. Arthur Lenke, and struck up a conversation.

"I understand you've negotiated your soldier's freedom." My icebreaker was innocuous. I looked calm, but inside I was a mixture of trepidation and bravery.

"Yes, we are very pleased." he replied, showing a politician's smile.

"In Britain, we would never exchange terrorists for a soldier." I challenged him.

"We are prepared to take our chances for our soldiers in Israel." His tone didn't change, and the smile stayed pasted on his face.

"That's interesting; I can tell you of another Israeli, who has been a captive for 5 years, who was a great soldier for your country. He also has ransom demands and they want 3 people in exchange for his freedom." I pushed harder. My heart was thumping, and I only had another minute before he would walk on.

"Really, tell me, where is he?" Mr. Lenke enquired. He seemed to show some interest in this news.

I was ready. "In your country! He is my husband, and is being held to ransom for child support for 30 years ahead, with a No Exit order. He is guilty of only being a father, and I want him back. You have stolen our lives for mistrust and money."

I'd said it. The truth was out. My pain and frustration was expressed in every word, showing outer composure whilst inside me a little warrior was cheering me on.

His demeanor changed instantly. The politician's smile had faded, and he was at a loss for words, looking very disconcerted. He whispered to his party to find out who I was. I looked straight at him, knowing he understood exactly what I was talking about. I heard them in Hebrew, and my anger spilled. As my heart pounded I spoke in Hebrew.

"Just ask me directly MrLenke, I have had to learn your language because of all this."

I will never forget this moment. He didn't brush me off with customary political niceties, or say he'd look into this later. He simply walked away. I knew immediately I'd hit a nerve and this was a political time bomb.

There was no doubt in my mind Ilan was not someone who'd slipped through the net, or was a one off, this was surely every day practice.

I had only one other opportunity to speak with an Israeli delegate before Dr E. and I became pariahs. It was one of the delegates of the IDF (Israeli Defense Force). He'd admitted he was aware of this primitive law, as his own father had divorced and seemingly paid a small fortune to leave the country. Another man who had been a good father up to the moment of separation had suffered.

Dr. E and I had been mining, and we'd struck gold. The committee members had listened, and almost all of them were to bombard the delegations with questions. This was real juice, I felt, as the main discussion was always of the tired old conflict and now they had something new; Israel's internal affairs towards their own people. I could feel a buzz in the air, and energy as the committee was to move on from the disparity discussions between Jews, Arabs and Bedouins.

"How many people did you talk to Marianne?" asked Dr. E.

"Not as many as you, but I think I handpicked some influential ones, by their body language." I replied.

"I've covered them all, and given them all the reports. I don't have any hope, I've been disappointed too many times regarding Israel, but we can only try."

Within the reports Dr. E had distributed was some explosive information. The risk of suicide in divorcing men was much higher than rest of the population. I'd told individual members of the committee of the scandal of Israeli courts demanding exorbitant child payments for the future. They were aghast at the fact of over 30,000 children having No Exit orders on them under the age of 18. Dr. E had educated his lobbied members well and they were preparing questions on the draconian ways of handling family law, and the victimization of men.

There were two things I didn't know until then; one was contact centre visits being the highest quantity in the world, and the other being the use of Ritalin in children almost the highest in the world. If it was so clear to the people, when did politicians lose their humanity I thought. They must listen. They have to.

I was excited with their belief in us. After all we'd travelled far to give the information. When the moment came for Article 10 and questions on family matters, there were questions from every single committee member. It was amazing to see. The energy was high and the Israeli Delegation was shell-shocked at the sudden deluge. The questions weren't just pointed, they were asked at times with derision and disgust.

I recall one member saying how pleased he was not to live in such a primitive and barbaric country if they had such ransom demands of their own citizens to enable freedom of movement. I learned that all questions tabled in the conference had to be addressed. The Israelis were furiously taking notes, looking more than a little disconcerted. I could see from their body language that they would rather be anywhere else but in the room. They did scramble some answers together between several breaks to research and check their data.

They tried to explain that men and women complained of victimization so it was balanced. So it's alright then, I chuckled inside. If all people complain it doesn't make our information less valid, quite the opposite. They claimed their court system endeavoured all the time to find solutions as children were the absolute priority. I could barely stay seated.

How could they even try to say it when the 'Tender Years Clause' in family law was breaking families? In my eyes the connection was clear. Children were removed from their fathers, many of whom were broken by no freedom and ridiculous financial demands often more than their income. That would explain the contact centres and high Ritalin use. It didn't take a rocket scientist to join the dots.

They acknowledged the suicide rate but thought surely not all the men committing suicide were divorcing. They admitted they had issued 10,000 No Exit Orders this year, but refused to give exact numbers and details, just stating not all were issued to divorcing people. They wouldn't reply to the number of children trapped in Israel, and would only say people were mostly stopped from leaving Israel from debt, but never for up front child support demands. So much of this was blatant lying.

They were out of their comfort zone. No conversations this time about Arabs or national security excuses to hide facts. This was purely about their own treatment of their own people. They had nowhere to hide. Continuing with speeches of how marvelous their family courts and judges were, they tried to convince the delegation that matters were concluded in a positive way all the time.

It was shocking. Only a few hours before, they'd been discussing the fact that 25% of Jews in Israel live below the poverty line, their explanation being because Orthodox had such big families and brought the statistics of poverty to such an unacceptable level. The statistic of 50% of Arabs being below the poverty line was not explained.

The statement which had me almost jumping out of my chair to challenge was their view of having no need of a Human Rights Commission in Israel, because of their basic law of no restriction on liberty and freedom and that Israeli values of the dignity of people were more than enough. Wriggling around in my chair, I was bursting to stand and denounce their words.

As the session was coming to a close, with polite thanks and complimentary comments, the Israeli Delegation claimed they had to rush to the airport for a night flight to Tel Aviv and leave immediately.

As they were going, I dashed to see the IDF leader, who was suddenly unable to help or point me in the right direction for a solution. A woman who headed the PR department in the government refused to speak with either myself or Dr. E.

I was euphoric. Finally a light had been shone on the internal affairs in Israel, and they had been found wanting. We had sown the seeds to the international community of some of the awful truths of life in Israel, not so squeaky clean in terms of how they treat their own people especially in the event of marriage breakdown.

What struck me most was their lack of humility. I knew that justifying a position is to be expected in a political arena, but not to admit to any flaws or even listen showed how little they cared. Well, apart from the infamous image of course. There is pride, and there is ego. I doubted Israel would look in the mirror at their own behaviour when their defense is the hostile environment surrounding them. There was no indication of investigation into the abuse.

I was on a major high. It felt fantastic. I was no one of importance, yet between Dr. E and me we had stirred up a hornets nest. I talked to a few of the members and implored them to send a mission to Israel to establish the truth and investigate the restrictions of freedom of expression and movement.

Returning to the airport in Geneva, hugging myself with the joy of accomplishment, I looked at the departures board, and saw there were no flights to Tel Aviv that evening!

Chapter 18

The turning point

Ten days before Christmas he called for over 3 hours. He had told his family everything. The offer of 70,000 SHEKELS hadn't been accepted. Matty was writing with a counter demand. Even with this news he seemed sure of himself.

"I've told them I'm coming home." He said, "You have been my love and my savior and have never given up on me. I want to be a man first and foremost. Then I can be a husband, father and provider when my head is clearer. I told them Mar, about everything; Abe and Matty and all the court cases. I told them you had been to the UN for me. I love you so much and can't live here anymore."

I listened in tears and felt so proud of him but alarm bells were clanging. He'd spoken too soon, I was sure of it. His family had been dropped a bombshell. They'd been unaware of most of this and I sensed they wouldn't exactly take this sitting down and give him a pat on the back.

I told him. "'Listen, I need to come. I know you don't want to run away, but *this* is the time to run. You've got to get away from your family. They'll play with your mind and could turn you inside out. You should wait until the decision from the court before you tell them these things. Ilan, I'm worried sick about you. I know the money isn't here yet but this is far more critical. I'm really afraid for you."

"No more running, Mar, I have to stand still and do what is right. It's all the running and avoiding that's messed me up and hurt you. I have to see it through."

This was amazing insight and courage given his fragile state and despite my concern I was proud to hear him.

I was also very proud of myself. Dr. E and I received news. The UNHRC had decided to send in a mission to Israel to investigate freedom of speech and freedom of movement. What a groundbreaking result we had achieved. Even if no one really gave us the credit or recognition for being there and working so hard, we both knew we'd done very well. It hadn't given our own agendas any satisfaction but spiritually I think it was a good thing for all those children and fathers. Perhaps that was all that would come out of my decade of despair. It was also to be a time when Israel broke relations with the UNHRC, which they wouldn't resume until October 2013.

The Committee made the strongest recommendation to Israel to revoke the Tender Years Assumption. What a result ! I hoped the children of the future would have both a mum and a dad, it was exhilarating to know Dr. E and I had played a small role in bringing awareness and potential change.

But by the time this law relating to the Tender Years Assumption had been ordered to be revoked, my fears for Ilan had been realised.

Only days after our beautiful conversation Ilan made a choice. He wanted to die, and I didn't see it coming.

Only days before he'd been full of hope. It was a couple of weeks before Christmas and I had started to believe this was it, it was finally over and he could come home. He agreed with the lawyer that he needed a psychiatric evaluation and I found him numbers, wrote to some myself and heard him on the phone trying to make appointments. He insisted that any help must be in England, but the legal advice was to prove he couldn't handle his affairs and was depressed and burned out. This was the man I'd known for over 20 years talking to me. He was so brave to admit his problems.

Ten days before Christmas he called for over 3 hours. He had told his family everything. The offer of 70,000 Shekels hadn't been acknowledged but he seemed sure of himself. However Matty eventually replied with a demand for 110,000 shekels.

Matty's demands had overwhelmed him and he broke. The family had pressured him with fear, threats and emotional blackmail, any of it, all of it. He told me. As soon as he'd told his family he was leaving Israel they had begun in earnest to dissuade him. He'd burned his bridges and thought he was strong. The offer of 70,000 was in the bailiff and I was assuring him that no matter what Matty thought she wanted or would get, we'd find the money one last time. I was afraid that he was premature in his announcement to his family. He'd told his brother first, which had had brought about the fateful family powwow.

I was stuck in England waiting for the pension transfer to be finalised so I could bring the money and get him home. The very time I wanted to travel. He needed me and said so. But he repeated he'd had enough of running and avoiding. I told him the pressure from his family was going to be powerful. He wanted to prove he could withstand everything, and finally be the man.

Just a day after his proud speech he stopped talking to me. My heart sank and I worried incessantly. We were less than a week from receiving a decision from the court and Ilan was in bad shape again.

"Help me Mar, they are messing with my head. Eitan won't leave me alone. He's filling me with so much rubbish."

I sent Eitan an email immediately imploring him for empathy and understanding. He might have been Ilan's brother but as his wife I knew him better. I begged him to help Ilan to lift the Stop Order so he could make decisions from freedom. I never received an answer.

We'd talked a lot about his children, two were grown up and he was still barely able to see his daughter, Matty had done a good job. I was so terribly afraid for him. I'd told the UN only the month before of my fears of Ilan becoming a statistic rather than a human being with absolutely no clue of his impending actions. I was very afraid.

"Calm down Ilan, stand above the hysteria. Your family must have heard you talking from your heart.

Surely they can't be so cruel as to take your life and dreams." I encouraged him but I had a sense of it being a major turning point. His family had no idea that we'd been in contact for quite some time.

So, did he get their instant blessing to be free, to make his own choices? Absolutely not! He called me the next day in a complete state of terror, literal terror. It was palpable down the telephone line. I couldn't get any sense out of him but I felt it through and through. I felt it from my head to my toes emanating from his voice. He told me he was being brainwashed, emotionally tortured and then he dropped the bombshell.

"Mar, I can't come." He said

One week before Christmas with presents ready and my money almost in my hands. My stomach knew first. But the shock, the complete and utter shock; it paralysed me totally. He refused to tell me who had said what. The email to Eitan at Ilan's request to beg for his blessing and support was still unanswered. So from planning to renew our wedding vows on my birthday in the coming February, suddenly I was faced with an unexplained goodbye.

I can still feel that shock reverberating through me as I write these words now. It was suddenly all over in just one call. But that was only the first shock. He instantly turned cruel and aggressive and demanded a divorce. He was like an animal reneging on all our conversations, telling me they were all lies and he hadn't meant a word he'd said. He was twisting the knife, a knife I didn't even know had existed and he'd only at that point plunged it skin deep as I was yet to find out more.

Of course his family was shocked by his sudden declaration and news of his endeavours to leave and learning about all the court cases, plus my efforts. They wouldn't have expected their puppet to start thinking and it was going to be my fault. It worked, the emotional blackmail, whatever had been said. He was terrified and told people there that his children's lives were at risk. He told lawyers and I heard this second hand, not directly, which made it all the more believable.

He was erratic, still contacting me, first threatening then numb and empty, swinging from one mood to the next. I had no means of even finding him if I travelled as he was so desperate and in truth I was afraid to confront his family after September.

On THE day, he called relentlessly to all my phone numbers. I didn't want to answer, hoping not to inflame him and hoping he would calm down from whatever drama had befallen him. I was sitting on Skype talking to Dr. E. In came another call and before I answered, I asked Dr. E to be my witness, took the call and put it on the loudspeaker. All my dreams were about to come crashing down on me.

"You finally answered the phone." he said. "I just want to let you know that I don't want a divorce from you."

I held my breath and waited.

"I won't be here for a divorce. They've destroyed my life, and I won't be here in the morning. It's better for everyone if my life was over."

"Ilan, where are you?" I knew from the sound of his voice that it was no idle threat.

"My favourite place and soon everything will be ended. I can't go on anymore." He responded in an empty yet despairing voice.

"What about your children? Think of them. You are a father." I said, trying to stay calm when every fibre of my being was feeling pain and anguish.

"They'll see me in another life. I want to leave this world and stop everything." He murmured.

I asked over and over if he'd taken anything.

"I'm tired Mar, really tired and it won't take long now." He mumbled.

I'd been a counselor on phone help lines and I knew I had to keep him talking. Dr. E was listening to the call and was dumbstruck.

"Ilan, listen, stay awake. Is there anything you want me to say to the children?" I asked.

"No Mar. It's better not to tell them anything. I have no plans, and no future. It's better for us all, you will be a widow. Everyone here has stolen my life and my chance. I just want it over now. I don't care what happens anymore and want to end it all."

I was rigid with fear. My husband thousands of miles from me could die and there was nothing I could do about it. I had only one choice which was to text Eitan. I wrote that his brother was taking his life and he needed to find him and rescue him.

"Please Ilan, don't do this. It will destroy your children for the rest of their lives. Don't do this." I begged.

"I'll see them from the stars at night." he told me. "They won't let me leave and I can't live like this so it's better this way. Don't worry and be happy."

After almost half an hour he had disconnected. I was frantic and helpless. I couldn't call his family. They were responsible for his state though they blamed me. I had a vital witness to the call in Dr. E but had no idea if Ilan was going to live or die.

Dr.E tried to calm me.

"Marianne, I have a very deep understanding of what a Stop Order can do to someone in Israel. You know I've been in that state myself, and remember what we told the UN." He reminded me.

"I know, but the pressure he's been under this week from his family has tipped him over the edge. I don't know what to do. How could they take him to this black hole?" I sobbed.

I waited all night for some news. Surely Eitan would have gone to his aid? Surely he would have a modicum of human kindness to let me know if my husband was alive or dead.

Not a chance of it. I barely slept, calling Ilan's number over and over to no reply. It was during that night when I realised it was possible to really hate people. I railed and ranted to the four walls of my bedroom, pacing the floor and praying for some news. It was a night of cruelty which his brother inflicted upon me. Less than 72 hours before, I'd had a dozen emails from Ilan describing his excitement and hope at the idea of finally returning home, then this sudden U turn of horrendous proportions.

The irony was I'd arranged a counsellor to visit Ilan the very same morning, who'd reported back to me that Ilan was a time bomb waiting to go off, veering from calm to numb to desperation. He'd reported that Ilan was an imminent risk of suicide. I'd no idea Ilan had sunk to such depths in a matter of a few hours. In truth he'd been heading in this direction for a long time. I needed to hear something but no one was answering my prayer.

I skyped to Dr. E. I needed to talk.

"I cannot say with certainty as a professional at a distance whether he is actually committing suicide. But it is a definite cry for help. He is in a terrible condition; his mental and emotional state means he could die."

I couldn't bear to hear what he was saying.

"He doesn't care about his own life, to such a degree he isn't thinking about his children at all. He is in great danger. I am so sorry for you, I know how much you've been trying to help him. I know how close you were to getting him home. But I don't feel the system will help you ever."

What a great family. I didn't hear anything all night. Can it touch one's imagination to understand what it's like to be planning a future, full of love and finally hope, to being at the mercy of these people who had clearly said enough to take Ilan to a place he didn't want to be alive?

The indifference of his family continued. It was over 18 hours later after constantly calling his number he eventually answered. I was a wreck. I can't remember a night like it. My nerves were frayed, my composure gone and anxiety off the Richter scale. My hopeful, fragile gentle man had gone, he was numb and void of emotion. It was like talking in an arid desert with nothing and no person in there. This was a pivotal moment. Throughout this whole nightmare, deep down I never thought in one REAL moment that we wouldn't make it.

I was crumbling, my purpose gone, my identity shattered. He just didn't want to be alive, but he was, well he was breathing anyway. The trauma for me was just beginning.

When he responded to my call, I inanely asked "So you are alive then?"

"So they say." His voice was devoid of emotion.

"Did Eitan find you?" I wanted to know.

"Yes."

"Ilan, did he help you? Did he take you to a doctor? What happened last night?" I deluged him with questions.

"He did his best." Was all he could say.

"Please, tell me what's going on? You didn't want to live yesterday." I tried to stay calm in my state of fear and need to know.

"It doesn't matter anymore. I talked with Eitan, and I have to stay for my kids. I can't come and be a 'donkey' working for your demands." All said in a deadpan tone yet laced with venom. They were not his words, they belonged to his brother.

Then suddenly he reiterated his demand for a divorce, and even though in a full state of shock and a daze I agreed.

He refused to discuss that night or give me any explanation just that he had to stay for his kids.

"Ilan, they are all grown up now. It's not what you said last week."

"I don't love you Mar, I never did. I just said those things to make you happy. The plans could never be real. I wanted them to be, but they can't be. Everything is in the past."

"So you lied to me? Proposing to me again was a game?" I was blown away by his words.

"No I didn't lie. I meant every word of it. It wasn't a game. I just can't, I can't. Don't you get it? It's not allowed. It doesn't matter anymore. I have no choice and no freedom so I'm making a choice." He talked but made no sense. He was incoherent, yet deadpan.

I couldn't get any answers. We did talk a few more times before the New Year. He was flat and I was broken. My purpose had been stolen and all my dreams had been shattered. It was if he'd died and at times I wished he had. At least my memories would have been better than ones which were coming.

Chapter 19

2012

I needed yet another lawyer and fast but this time for myself. My saviour turned up in the form of Dr. Yoram Fay, a talented attorney who was Israeli/Hungarian and fluent in English and brimming over with empathy and compassion. He came to England and we talked. He read everything and we immediately filed for guardianship of Ilan. Ilans family? They closed ranks, claiming they had no idea where he was, so we declared him homeless.

The money was still in the bailiff and I desperately needed it back. After all I wasn't going to allow his family to keep the man *and* the money. My mind worked overtime. It was relentless. Turning and turning with conversations running through my head. Had it all been a game? I just didn't know for sure as Ilan had turned off as quick as a light switch. I was sure this suicide attempt had been genuine, for Dr. E and I talked about it and as a medical doctor he had been convinced Ilan's life was in danger that night and he'd no concern of the consequences if he had died. If there was ever a time Ilan needed psychiatric help it was surely now.

I hated his family. I was his wife and they'd ignored me. He'd told them of his plans and hopes and in days they had reduced him to a vegetative state. I was left just with myself and all my thoughts and it was a terrible plight to live in. They had won. All I could think was that they had won. They had a living and breathing body trapped in Israel and had murdered his hope and his spirit. What an empty victory.

Despite emails to all his family they didn't respond. Silence is a deadly weapon and they were using it to great effect. I was in huge debt with an uncertain future looming and unaware that I was deep in trauma. I'd been so busy keeping Ilan afloat I'd lost myself. I didn't care about anything anymore. It was of course about losing my husband. But he was more than just a partner. He had been my mission and my cause. I'd unearthed so much information about Israel and their barbaric treatments and at this point I'd lost the will to care. It was going to take a lot of time before I would hit rock bottom and find my own courage. I genuinely believed I already had hit a zenith.

My own life was breaking down totally. I was suffering from heartbreak with no closure and no answers.

The pension company I'd moved to were closed down and my future security had gone. It didn't even touch me. The commission of £9000 was languishing in Israel, or so I thought and my old age was of no concern to me anyway. I could barely make it through each day.

I got bronchial pneumonia and I didn't care. I laid on my bed or sofa shivering with cold and just didn't care. I emailed Ilan over and over to put me out of my misery and do the divorce and send me my money back. I veered from desolation to rage and grief.

Manny had a massive stroke in early February. It was gargantuan they said. It gave me something to concentrate on and I visited him every single day in the hospital. I was feeling such loss. He was critical for a while and would lose the use of his left arm forever. He was my link to Ilan in some perverse way. I kept thinking Ilan would wake up, come home and at least help his best friend. I emailed him with the news and asked for his help. He said yes but did nothing.

I was in a fugue. Somehow I galvanised myself to prepare papers for the Israeli court. We had the evidence of Ilan's suicide attempt and I blindly continued on some level with my mission. It was a futile mission really. He'd made his decision. I felt patronized and marginalized. So much for telling people I was his savior. He'd stabbed me in the back, front and sides. I was the last on his list of people to consider and I hated him.

My sister, my beautiful soul, was diagnosed with breast cancer the same month as Manny's stroke. I couldn't take it in. The news was catastrophic. She was to be diagnosed with a tumour on her bowel the week she finished 8 months chemotherapy. That would be further bad news.

I was less than 8 weeks into the year and it was bad news from every direction. Due to my illness I fell one month behind in my rent and was given an eviction notice, even though I'd paid regularly for almost four years but nothing touched me and nothing could hurt me anymore. I was in a waking nightmare. This was trauma.

Four months passed, I emailed constantly, veering from mood to mood, desperate for an explanation or answers or at least the divorce. The date in the religious court had been set for 5th February – my birthday – the day we'd planned to renew our wedding vows. Ouch, ouch. But he hadn't turned up. He told my lawyer his children were going to be murdered and was crying and screaming, a testimony which Yoram still has. In the words of the lawyer *he was roaring like a tiger and then crying like a kitten, claiming people's lives were at risk.* In the UK I would have had him straight to a doctor, but no, not in Israel.

The country doesn't recognise mental illness. Even a suicide attempt wasn't classed as a risk. I'd written countless letters over the years to their Social Services and taken him to the 'TakhanatBriut (healthcentre). I had proof of him trying to make appointments with a psychiatrist, and had his doctors' notes saying he was clinically depressed and at one point a suicide risk, but hey this is Israel, as long as you don't harm another you can be as crazy as you like! But what harm to me? His wife? The harm was enormous. I was deep in trauma. All the years I saw it in Ilan and once in it myself I had no will to recover. I didn't even think about it. Just like him.

The thoughts tumbled through my head day and night. I was back on my sleeping pills, the healing from my Shamanic experience long gone. He'd been cruel and selfish. He'd not considered me in his equation at all. I imagined all sorts of things but the financial situation weighed me down more heavily than anything else. I had to survive and find somewhere else to live.

Finally in April I received an email from him. He was 'working on himself' and didn't want to talk to anybody. Working on himself! Oh sure he is, and I saw red. This was abnormal. It was still all about him. What about me? What about me? I had not received my bond and there were no answers forthcoming. How I managed to work I'll never know. Everything was automatic and going to the hospital every day to see Manny was a blessing for me. I felt selfish with this thought as Manny was to lose everything which was dear to him.

One idle day I searched Ilan's Facebook page. He never used it but something prompted me to look. I'd never done it before, that's how sure I was of his indolence to social networking. I found myself looking at his page and there he was with a woman with quotes underneath ' me, me, me ..and my true love'. What was this, staring at me? Who was she? The rush of betrayal that struck the core of my being was immeasurable. My soul howled in pain. This was no ordinary betrayal. I messaged him; I wasn't even his 'friend' on Facebook as we'd never used it to communicate. I was dazed, stepping into yet another realm of the surreal. Facebook. I poured rage at him using capital letters, the only way to shout.

I visited Manny in hospital with the photo and cried on him all night, some Florence Nightingale I was. Ilan called that night three times but left no message. I didn't have my phone and wouldn't have answered anyway. My heart was breaking so much I felt I needed a hospital bed of my own.

The next day I got down to the detective work. Was I a woman scorned, would hell have no fury? The photos came with 2 likes, and one comment. I felt sick to my stomach. By using the photo and those people, I eventually traced the fish tank behind them, an innocuous thing, but distinctive. Finally I found a name, Elvira Agami from Baku. I spent days looking at friends of friends, Elvira and Ilan, cute couple kayaking, camping, parties, holidays, right back to the beginning of 2010! I'd been right in my fears. He had been with someone. I thought also of all the times I'd spent with Manny. Birthdays, football matches, concerts, days out. If someone had looked at those photos they might have drawn the same conclusion. Photos don't give the whole picture but it was enough for me. My detective work had discovered one 'like' had been from Elvira's daughter, and when looking at her page, all her photos started with 'me,me,me....' I knew her daughter had put the photo on his page. She'd also commented about her own birthday on Christmas Day. It had been done deliberately, and taken nearly 3 months for me to see. There was no end to the plan to hurt me.

So who was I now? I'd been planning our future and his homecoming but he'd been with her throughout. My memories were all linking together from 2009 when he'd done the astrology. Fury, hurt, pride and my refusal to believe rushed through me in a torrent and I couldn't stay with one emotion. They all washed over and over me relentlessly, my own traumas here trumped by this one. I was confused beyond reason. Nothing was adding up.

His behaviour hadn't really indicated such duplicity. The truths Jan and I had unearthed didn't prove any games. I knew he was ill and leading a double life. I remembered one time we'd decided to play the game of breaking up. We'd hoped everyone would calm down and he could leave Israel if they thought we weren't together. We'd kept it up for a month or so and he'd told me he didn't enjoy it at all. It felt like two lives for him. The one inside him and the life others expected of him. But this betrayal was enormous. I didn't care what problems he might have for there was no excuse in my mind for what he'd done. We were individually careering from one disaster to another.

I continued trawling and trawling and then discovered a photo of Ilan's NEW business, and a few days after this I received the news that all my money had been removed from the bailiff, all of it but by whom? Rumours were that Matty had taken a large proportion. Within that same week he had a new business. The business had been incorporated and in the name of Eitan the week after my money had been stolen in January. AchoutNirosta, the name of his new venture. Eitan was the front man, the helpful brother who'd told Ilan not to come in his hour of desperation. I hated him from that moment.

So with Yoram's help we added a case to sue both Matty and Ilan for the money alongside the guardianship lawsuit to keep all our options open.

I was losing it. Yoram stayed calm, trying to support me, patient always with my rants and excruciating pain. Ilan's personality might have split, but so had mine. Finally out of the blue in June Ilan called me. He was like a dead man talking. He had no content, no concept of reality and no explanation at this point for the money. I still hadn't got the final truth.

Matty had responded to our case immediately, citing Ilan had been settled with Elvira for years. Matty was the innocent party, could she please be excused from attending the court. Ilan? He didn't reply and we needed to serve papers. On receiving translations of her papers I exploded with rage. She had been to the bailiff to demand the money, claiming she didn't know it was mine. The paperwork she attached as proof had MY name on it, with the declaration it was my money. She was fully aware, or perhaps she just couldn't read.

He called a week later but this time with violent language, rude, obnoxious and aggressive, saying he was sick of listening to my problems and his girlfriend was private and personal business. The knife was twisting into my gut. Pre suicide Ilan had died, now post suicide and not counseled Ilan was a monster. He knew about the papers. "Matty is breaking my head." he said.

So I had no choice but to sit still and wait for our court case in October. I bombarded him with emails, wanting answers, wanting to know about the money, needing closure, a divorce and an agreement.

I didn't want to but I had to have something to give me a pointer and a future. But there was no response to my hope, just disjointed responses about his total fear, his promises to call and desires to talk, but not one clear sentence. He had plenty of self-pity, harking back to a past of such beauty and love but never saying goodbye and no answers to my questions. The questions burned through me about my husband, his lover, my truth, his lies, my fight but his surrender.

The week before I was due to fly in October was a year that I had staggered through, lurching from one trauma to another like a ball in a pinball machine, the flippers pushing me in any random direction with no respite. The noises stayed in my head whilst I spent hours replaying and listening to his recorded calls yet understanding absolutely nothing. But that week he was finally interviewed by a social worker which we'd ordered and got. Well more appropriately let's say the real Ilan never showed, but a good impression of a Ghandi like figure did. He was calm, un-manipulated, handling life's ups and downs in a normal healthy way, the report said. He'd apparently been trying to divorce me for four years and I'd been blackmailing him to that very day!

Oh, brownie points to you Ilan. He told them after he'd returned to Israel; he'd taken a few pills and within a few WEEKS, decided to build his life. It was impossible, for we'd married 18 months after his entrapment. What about my life I thought as the words sliced through my heart. The report bore no resemblance to the facts.

The knife continued to twist and turn in its journey to remove all sensation from my organs. It was a long knife, cutting my throat, squishing my lungs, writhing through my stomach and my jaw had been clenched as if in a vice. So the social report conclusion? Well, he seemed fine. Perhaps there might be a few issues with his wife on future direction and finances. As far as his psychological and emotional state, we are not qualified to answer!

I howled to Yoram on the phone to release me from the pain. I begged him. What is THIS, it's not my reality. Yoram had talked a few times to Ilan or should I say to many versions of Ilan; an arrogant Ilan, a scared and desperate Ilan, the indifferent, rude and verbally aggressive one, and eventually he and Ilan met. I'd played and manipulated to his greed, or Eitan's, by emailing his brother constantly, going as far as to say I'd back off and not claim against the new company. It worked as he had finally visited my lawyer. He'd emailed to say he would be taking Eitan, so I emailed a vitriolic reply indicating Eitan must be the gatekeeper of his mind and life and was probably aiming to control the meeting. Ilan went alone and as luck would have it Yoram served the papers with only a couple of days to spare.

But Ilan had no answers, no purpose and not a single intention or action. Yoram was perplexed and I believed he was out of his depth in handling mentally disturbed people.

With days to go all I could think of was would Ilan show up in the court? This couldn't be happening. I'm going to have to stand in court against my own husband and he and Matty would have to sit together as defendants! This was sick. I flew overnight, my brain scrambling to get into the Hebrew language again, something I rarely used and now needed again for something so vital.

Matty was waiting with her mother when we arrived. The old feelings of fear and intimidation reared up in me. I felt sick. She didn't have a lawyer. She looked at me with hatred and disdain.

"He's not coming." she told us.

"Yes, he is" Yoram replied. "I've just spoken to him. He's on his way."

She didn't look pleased and dialed Ilan's number. She had his number! I hadn't had the number for months, yet she did. They talked for a minute, and she disconnected.

"I told you he was coming." Yoram repeated.

It felt like a miracle that he turned up. He sat behind me. I was furious that his incompetence had brought me here again. I turned to him and told him to be honest. He wouldn't return my gaze and became more withdrawn as I begged him to tell the truth. He'd always wanted his day in court and this was it, please just tell the truth.

He answered the questions. I don't believe he told a word of truth.

"I don't even really know her... she's a woman from the UK with a good heart, who gave me money with kindness, no strings and no commitment. How much? I don't know... about £500 altogether... the emails? No, not from me, must have been written by somebody else. I never sent her anything... The phone calls? I don't recall them. I made no promises and I had NO intention then and have no future intention now".

I could barely take this in. My Hebrew was rusty and I was later to see this testimony in black and white which was not so different from the social services report.

She loved it. I'm sure she did. Her work was done. She'd achieved her objective, and had a front row seat to see the final destruction she'd spent so many years toiling for. She looked at me victoriously.

The judge decided she could keep the third of the money she had received from my bond. In fact it was also judged I should pay her for the inconvenience of her attendance.

In the judgment, it was agreed that Ilan was unclear and uncertain of his statements. But the criteria for mental well-being were his ability to dress himself and drive. I couldn't find the words to express myself.

The judge ignored Yoram's insistence that they look at the evidence. I had brought the communications and reports. They wanted me out, and they treated me with no respect. I felt just as abused by the court as I did by Ilan and Matty.

As the case ended, Matty left with a smug satisfied smile, and Ilan whispered. "We'll talk outside."

Outside the court, he sat and talked with Yoram and myself. I needed Yoram to witness what rubbish or excuses he would come up with.

"So you were ordered to pay me 35,000 shekels and somehow decided I gave you about £500 since we met?" I demanded. It was becoming too much for me to handle. I was already exhausted from yet another overnight flight. "You have 60 days to pay me."

Ilan stared at the table. The only way to describe him was zombie like.

"I made things serious with Elvira just over a year ago. August I think." he said.

I was furiously backtracking in my mind. This was the month he'd disappeared from contact. The same month Abe had said he'd been in Bulgaria with her. The same month I'd agonized over his wellbeing.

"So you were with her in September when I came with Jan and then two weeks later when I came with all the money?" I spat. "You were calling me from then until nearly Christmas until you tried to commit suicide? What kind of sick bastard are you?"

"I didn't want to meet you here, not in a court." He replied. His voice was empty. His body frozen to the chair, he was still avoiding eye contact.

"Where the hell did you expect to meet me after stealing all my money, and setting me up?" I demanded. I was furious now. "What happened to your demand of getting a divorce?"

"I can't. I won't. I don't want a divorce Mar. I wanted to tell the truth just now, but I couldn't. They didn't ask me the specific questions. I just say what I'm told to say." He was robotic, devoid of emotion.

"Ilan, what are you talking about? You are making no sense at all."

"I don't understand anything. I never said I don't want to be with you." He said

I wanted to explode but needed calm to get my answers.

"You just told the judge I'm some woman in the UK, some charity for you."

"I tried to call you all this year, but I couldn't do it." was all he said.

"You told the judge you gave up a few weeks after arriving in 2006" I exploded. "What does that make me? Some kind of meal ticket, some kind of idiot? Then why did you marry me in 2008? I can't stand this."

I looked at Yoram in disbelief. Ilan was like a robot, on automatic. Yoram shook his head sadly saying it was shocking. We discussed Ilan's behaviour in front of him. He sat with no response or recognition of anything.

"I just do what I'm told." He repeated.

"Ilan, you've stolen, lied and cheated on me. What makes you think I can possibly want to be married to you anymore? Can't you understand this?"

"No." he replied. "I don't understand why we can't be married."

I was exasperated. But this was no ordinary conversation. Ilan wasn't even present. It was frightening, and Yoram said we needed to get him some help.

"Apart from her, where is the rest of my money? Who took it?" I asked.

"Some went on my VAT bill. The rest? I don't remember. Elvira and Eitan sorted everything between them." He said.

What a revelation! I hadn't been a meal ticket for Ilan. He'd never taken my money. It had always gone to courts or lawyers, never his own hands. I was a meal ticket for everyone else playing on my desperation.

"How do you live?" I wanted to know.

"Elvira pays everything. I have no future with her. I didn't do the Facebook picture. You know I don't know how to do those things." These statements were not said at once, just comments, pauses and more comments.

Sitting outside the small court on a busy street in Ramat Gan, feeling like I'd been transported into an asylum, I looked to Yoram for guidance. Ilan looked terrible. The worst I'd ever seen him.

"Look at me." I said. It always worked. When he looked into my eyes he couldn't stay in control.

"Mar, don't. Don't look at me. When I look at you....it makes me want to cry. Don't. I don't want these feelings." He'd started to cry. His façade was crumbling, thank God.

"I did try to end my life. You were right. I've got nothing here. Work isn't going the way I thought it would. Eitan controls everything. My life is no good." He cried more.

I was moved yet wanted to stay untouched.

"Ilan." Yoram said. "Give us the guardianship. Let us handle your financial problems. Marianne needs her money. The one piece of good news from the court today is that Matty did not have the right to take your house. Let me handle everything."

"How does it work?" Ilan asked.

"We will write a letter now, in which you agree to pass your legal affairs to me. I'll take it into the judge right now. Your life will continue as normal. You will be free from any court ever again. If you don't like it, we can rescind this at any time." explained Yoram.

"Ok, yes please." Ilan replied.

Yoram wrote the letter and passed it over to Ilan for his signature. Ilan read the document and took the pen. His hand started to tremble and then he put the pen down.

"I need some advice first." He said. "I can't make the decision."

My heart sank. We'd been so close. If I had the guardianship, I knew I could restore everything. It was a naïve thought, given the corruption of the courts but I had to hope.

"I'll ask someone first." He reiterated, folding up the letter and putting it in his pocket.

"In that case, just get the hell away from me." I stormed. "Go away."

"I will. I am programmed to do as instructed." He replied. It was terrifying.

He turned and walked away. After a few steps, he stopped and asked permission to come back.

Weirdly I gave it, and he gave me a big hug telling me he wasn't prepared to lose me, ever.

It had been surreal and horrible. Things had happened so fast, one thing tumbling into the next. Yoram and I went for lunch.

"He performed for a few minutes in front of the judge." Yoram observed. "But he has no rational thinking, and no connection to reality. But the serious thing here is there has been a premeditated decision by some people to keep your money. Perhaps we need to look at filing a complaint to the police for fraud."

Stirring the ice in my Gin and Tonic, trying to be calm and make sense of the day, I hadn't the time to process anything.

"He is definitely ill." Yoram continued. "He showed no signs of pleasure, or games, or skill in his words. But he passed muster with the impatient judge."

"So, what do I do now?" I asked

"I don't know. I think we have to wait 60 days to see if the money comes, and if not, then we continue with the courts to get it. After 60 days, we'll talk about going to the police." He advised.

As I was leaving Yorams car following our lunch Ilan called Yoram to ask to speak to me. I agreed to take the call.

"You said I didn't communicate enough. So I'm calling now. Is that enough for us to stay married?" he begged in the voice of a child.

"Ilan, thank you, but it's not enough." I knew better than to make this complicated. He was so mentally disturbed.

"I've no one to talk to. You are my life. Please don't leave me here. I'll prove it to you. See, I've just called, it's a first step isn't it? I am not with Elvira. It's not what you think."

"You have another wife now Ilan, go and talk to her. You've all stolen my money and lied. You have abused me over and over."

"Don't use naughty words like that." He begged. He sounded like a young child. "I'm trying my best."

It was like talking to an alien….he had no connection whatsoever to anything normal.

"I can't let you go. I'll do the guardianship."

"I can't handle this Ilan. You need professional help. I can't talk anymore." I passed the phone back to Yoram, giving my thanks and exited the car.

Before I flew home, I called Yoram.

Yoram told me "We talked for hours, going round in constant circles with no satisfactory outcome. Ilan was incapable of making any decisions, and told me he would call next week. But he insisted that he didn't want divorce, and no matter what I explained, he didn't connect this at all to any of today's events"

"I can't leave him like this. I just can't." I replied.

He said "Today is closure for you and it is your chance to start again without this abuse in your life from now. I can see Ilan's cruelty was breathtaking, but his enjoyment of it seemed to be zero. He is disjointed and beyond help or redemption."

Within a week of flying home to deal with the shock, my brother's wife died suddenly, completing the worst year of my life. It was going to take all I had to pull myself together or accept help for my traumatised state.

Chapter 20

Dying from the inside out – what once was a man

I was beginning to lose control of myself.

I'd watched him die from the inside every day, taking a part of me with him each time. I had to hearing him cold and controlled. How could he be, when I was falling apart at the seams trying to keep HIM sane. It was madness in itself. How could a stop order on his body become the stop order of my life, how could fighting for his freedom lose me my own? To have my hope snatched almost at the last moment when I knew it was all within our grasp, with no explanation at all. I knew nothing, just listening to a cold distant cruel voice telling me that I am nothing, nobody at all and he was more than ok.

His denial, it's beneath my contempt. I hate the condition. It's supposed to be a protection, not a weapon. Denial kills empathy, compassion and all positive human contact. I read somewhere on the internet about carer's burnout – carer's burnout? That's a laugh. The victim of the trauma gets to do denial, go to sleep, not be responsible, and the carer? Well they can see, hear, feel and experience this nonsense and cannot break through all those walls.

I was tired and helpless, helpless in watching hopelessness, in despair of his despair, and most of all being blamed when I tried to 'touch' carefully on the issue. Then of course I took the brunt of his wonderful denial. If he would just wake up for one second, put himself in my shoes for one second, he wouldn't do this, but compassion – such a dangerous emotion – it had brought me right back to the beginning.

Perhaps I should have said things differently, walked around eggshells more carefully and should have gone along with his self-deception. I should have talked more about the weather or the results of Saturday's football and then maybe I could have managed. But I wanted the issue discussed and really seen.

I had wanted to fix it and I jumped so quickly into the deep conversations then all I received was his trusty denial right back at me. It was the cruelty, the seemingly intentional cruelty, the black and white of it all. How could Ilan be such a Jekyll and Hyde and could he really hide behind amnesia, convenient forgetfulness and denial? So I read some more and heard the same stories, until I was yet again back to square one.

I felt as if I was a game of snakes and ladders. One dice roll taking me up the ladder and events had taken me from the penultimate square of victory to sliding down to the bottom. I was thrown into desperation to try and find a key, a final solution but now realised that his free will had gone. I didn't want to be the reasonable one. Everyone else had taken a piece of him, but it had taken all of me to keep him together.

I saved his life he said. If I'd known it was so he could wander round in life narcotised, taking each moment as it came, with no responsibility or even action, I might have thought twice. I'm all for living in the present. Present centredness – the art of meditation - staying in the moment. The real deal is to be aware of it, not asleep in it.

Sometimes I could kill him myself. If he only knew what I'd been through, falling from one trauma to another, but there had been so many they just became events, or incidents barely touching the sides. I was almost immune to what might happen to me, but I was so affected by what was happening to others. I was wondering how it could even happenand if I had been living in the same bubble. Every time I tried to push the predominant thoughts away, I would scream 'denial' in my head, no, no, no. I couldn't avoid thoughts, I needed to face them and look at where this denial of his had got us to.

I couldn't distinguish anymore the difference between avoidance, distraction and just taking a plain bloody break from it all. How could I, I was still in a catch 22 of someone else's making, which had made my life bounce all over the place like an ping pong ball struck by an amateur. So I tried to think logically and tried to feel, to reach the spirit or heart of me but nothing seemed to be aligned. I was jealous of him. I envied him. He was sleepwalking through life, waiting for things to happen, even with warnings that events to come were going to be traumatic. I told him over and over to not let it get there and had been astounded by his stupidity.

So we were all in prison, and I was imprisoned because I loved him and others hated what we had. But when he talked he seemed so much in control, so calm, seemingly so put together and I felt myself disintegrating and questioning myself so much more. Maybe it was me after all, he'd told me so many times I needed a shrink and I had a vivid imagination. I started to record our calls, hardly registering that this was a crazy thing to do, totally not normal, but I needed to be sure I wasn't imagining things.

When I heard them back, I could hear him running, avoiding, angry, defensive, then I heard this calm rational loving voice of mine, saying 'how much do you hate yourself that you can even utter these words to me.'

I realised it was not personal, but still it felt so desperately personal. I was so hung up on the past, and he was too. But not the same view of it. I saw how good it was as did he. We were not wrong; the proof was in the damage around us, of people trying to prevent it. It was good. I wanted it again.

I knew I was jumping a chasm of problems to see that vision, but I saw it. I'd been fighting for it. He saw a good past too and yearned for it but could not imagine it again. But amidst all those thoughts and feelings he couldn't disconnect from me. His future was vague, his today was his distraction. But we both agreed on our past, our memories were accurate, and we were connected at a soul level which we could not break willingly. Somehow it just wouldn't go. I was furious with the knowledge of other people choosing how I lived my life, determined that I should be destroyed and broken by others deciding who my husband should be, where we should live, and with permission.

How dare he give up on ME? How dare he give up and live a useless life and existence because of his weakness! His trauma was so disabling. I had been traumatised over and over again, and had still got up and kept on going, trying to find a final solution to this wretched daily hell. If I could, then I mused as to why he couldn't. He was immune to my suffering. I walked in a parallel dimension, smiling, saying hi to people and functioned at the most basic level. I tried to work, smiled for people and even at times pretended to enjoy life. I was grateful for what I had, but so angry and empty at what had been stolen.

My whole life was stolen and I didn't know who to blame. All the players in this game are to blame. Most of all the system which helped Matty get her revenge. I saw one foul action, like a bad apple could poison a barrel full of lives and as the perpetrator she had moved on, seemingly aware of the damage, and perhaps even celebrating there would be no consequences for her.

I felt as if I was swimming up a waterfall, and thought each time, that this time will be THE time, and this would finally end well somehow. The crazy things I thought, he's living with another woman; wouldn't that be enough to finish a marriage in itself? But then I rationalized – no - because he is not living. He is in a bubble; living in some bi polar existence, so disconnected from himself that it couldn't be classed as genuine infidelity because he wasn't the same person.

The whole picture was too enormous to be broken by something presented as a bit on the side. He was a bastard, a thoughtless heartless bastard. Yet all his words and behaviours were not synonymous with classic love rat behaviours either. I was certain he'd been so hopeless that he was making the most of trying to restart his life. Life in a prison isn't real. Israel was his open prison.

 I voraciously read about captives, hostages, Stockholm syndrome, greedily taking in all the information I could find. It was not just for the knowledge of his condition, for I started to read about victims. I read about people like me. I'd finally arrived at the point I knew I was the victim too. I'd never considered it before. I'd arrived. There was a 'me' in all of this. I'd been so caught up in the fight for freedom I'd ignored myself. I didn't want to be a victim, it was such a helpless position and despite resonating with the information, I concluded it was still just a battle.

It was a battle of the soul; for Ilan and any other person to have the right to remember that they can choose their own direction. But the paradox was it had been so easy to lose myself in Ilan's loss of himself. Trauma and the mental and emotional instability that came with it had nothing to do with love.

He talked of survival; dreamt of days gone by, remembered the best time of his life ever and talked as if it was an unattainable goal, to get on a plane and live it again. But he could not actually 'live' where he is, and least of all how could he live in his own head? I could barely manage to live in my own. I wondered how such an intelligent man had become so stupid. The answer came quickly.

It was subjective as many people had thought I was stupid to relentlessly not give up. I didn't know who was the smartest, the man who had stopped living and hoping and planning, or the woman who was tortured by her promises and her whole moral fibre to do what was right. Was it right to leave him in that state?

There were many more beside Ilan stuck in hell. So many people do shut down from a traumatic experience, and 'move on', or put 'closure' on it. They all seem like great words, but the damage is to the soul. It's an injury to the soul. The soul is screaming inside, 'don't do this to me, I wasn't born for this. This isn't MY destiny. I came into your body because I had a purpose, listen to me, not your head.' The soul is crying for help, and the mind is the jailor, silencing it over and over with stupid logic. Our world is built on the power of the mind, but I didn't believe it was a reliable organ. Not when it is disconnected from its soul.

I was doing plenty of soul searching, pondering on how I had got to this point. I had willingly, freely surrendered all my worldly possessions for the freedom I envisioned. Round and round my mind went. Filled with thoughts, I played conversations back, remembered so many events, and couldn't determine if he was a criminal, or was sick. I questioned myself. Perhaps I was the fool but I came to the conclusion that I must still be correct. I hadn't been mistaken and I needed justice and truth to prevail. It would be a mountain to climb to get to the truth for it was well and truly hidden. So far, it had been hidden by ignorance, jealousy, greed, power and control.

He looked haunted. I saw a photo of him yesterday and he looked so haunted, so vacant in his eyes and the saddest thing of all is that I saw a photo of him two years ago and thought the same thing, and the year before and the year before. It's all by degrees, until I realised it was a condition, a state and it had become his norm. He couldn't bear a cross word in the beginning, then outbursts of frustration started, with days of apologies and tears for his behaviour, then as that line got crossed, I didn't draw it deep enough, because my compassion was my downfall.

I allowed him, allowed myself to have these conversations until they were so abusive to me I couldn't catch my breath. All that hate, frustration and anger was all pointed at ME. Now, here I sit, only a few months from a potential divorce, potential police charges, and me actually closing his life down to a point even those who hated him could only dream of. I couldn't grasp it and wished with all my heart that I wasn't awake to this.

How did we get to this place? To believe so much and lose all the time, when I knew I was telling the truth.

Chapter 21

The beginning of the end

My life was stolen, literally. By whom? That is the question. It's been taken, piece by piece, until the memory of who I am, what I had, what I'd achieved, is just that, a memory.

But today I had decided to get it back. I was not sure if it was like an insurance claim, where you get new for old, as surely you can never get it back as it was. But whatever it would look like, I knew that I would have to start to get something. I wanted to see the colours, feel feelings again, have plans, thoughts and hope for the future. I couldn't sit and let my life be controlled by people anymore.

Falling in love had started this. It had been life changing. If I'd known what was involved, I had asked myself over and over if I would repeat the last 10 years of my life. It had become a movie, B rated or blockbuster, perhaps the final outcome would decide or maybe I would fade away into the background of a life lived certainly, but not with the satisfaction of the fulfilment that drove me, pressed me and wouldn't let me go. There were other people crying out for help and if Ilan didn't want to save himself, I was certain I was going to save myself and expose the truth for others.

I was a Gold Medalist at tenacity. I never quite knew when to quit. That's what they said, the people who knew me best. 'She's amazing, wow, strong, resilient, will always bounce back.' I couldn't find one person in the world who had experienced anything similar and I felt so lonely. I just didn't know how to stop. A Gold Medalist in dealing with trauma, that's what I was.

I learned the meaning of unconditional love. The kind where you really would throw yourself under a bus for the one you love. The love we dream of, watch on TV and sigh over. The one which we wish we had and settle for something less because we believe it's all Hollywood. But I knew it wasn't Hollywood. It really existed. So much so that people couldn't bear it. They had done everything they could to destroy it and the worst revenge of all was to break Ilan until he broke me. Which was worse, to betray the one you love in a fugue, or to be the betrayed one? I tried to imagine it both ways. Well, it didn't need much imagination for my side of the coin. I was the innocent victim. I really was. Ilan was an innocent victim too. But the abused had become the abuser, and I had allowed it.

So what is trauma then? I think it comes at us in a few ways, the mental – someone messing with our head, saying stuff that makes us doubt ourselves. The physical – someone hurting us, and I've had that, I think it's almost the easiest to get over sometimes. The emotional – when our heart is broken, the trust smashed and we are personally rejected. That's a common one until someone else turns up to fix it, or we mend slowly. And then there's the soul – when our hope is taken, our spirit, our essence has been destroyed to the point we can't recognise anything.

At this point, all the other traumas are just stuff, just stuff. I knew it totally. Once the soul trauma has occurred, the rest that comes just doesn't really touch us. I have lived it and I'd watched Ilan slowly lurch from disaster to disaster. At first, with each setback, we had cried, hugged, and regrouped, ready to try and fight our problem with different tactics, different help, telling our story over and over until we were sick of it, but getting better each time at telling it. A bit shorter, a bit less emotional content, until eventually it was just a matter of fact statement, 'my husband has no freedom of movement, he is an invisible hostage damaged by people who wanted to hurt him, twisting his head confusing him, playing the game of false hope, the roller coaster of hope and despair, until his body and mind cannot take it anymore, and he has given up.

He denies it matters, 'it's just life. No holidays, no travel, no working abroad, nothing, no rights to choose.' In a nutshell, our story became a few lines, sometimes a couple of paragraphs. The replies to the simple fact of a human being's destruction were 'this is life, stuff happens.' Ilan had wanted to wait and tread water to avoid dealing with the consequences. Because Ilan started to create his own disasters, so entrenched in being the victim, it had become the excuse for all his behaviour.

Like someone with a disease, the disease is the excuse for all bad behaviour, bad days, cross words, selfishness, and abuse. 'It's not me, it's the 'disease'. People say. For Ilan, 'it's not me, it's the stop order. I can't leave the country.' Now, it's 'I won't, won't, won't even consider this, as past disappointments teach me that it's doomed to fail.'

I could hear his soul, the other half of mine. His soul screamed through his eyes. 'I can't live, I can't breathe. I'm crying and he won't release me. The only control he has in his life of no control is to crush me, trap me and imprison me, just like people have imprisoned him. He wants to be the master of his own misery and unhappiness. He mistakenly believes he is in control.' Oh his soul was definitely crying.

Ilan was waging a battle with his own soul. His thoughts were his weakness and he wasn't listening. His trauma had finally become my own.

The pain for me, as the person outside looking in, was how he couldn't seem to remember his cruel words and had lost his moral compass. He was capable of such cruelty. I knew him, I could see in his eyes how haunted he was, how vacant. What I couldn't understand was how no one else in Israel could see.

Because they didn't care. Our friends in England saw in an instant. It was not my imagination and I didn't understand why the obvious wasn't obvious to everyone else. They could just get on with their lives when such a tragedy was unfolding. If a person can suffer such abuse of their human rights until they have no brain left to choose, why can't everyone else see it? What made it so wrong is that I knew they could see and hear but it wasn't happening to them. It was impossible with all the information and evidence that people in Israel were ignorant. They knew exactly what they were doing and many seemed to enjoy it.

He refused to see, limiting himself to the identity of victim. He couldn't and wouldn't look any further. He refused to think beyond his victim mentality. Just for a second today, he listened, and I thought maybe, maybe I'd got through to him. But of course my impatience let me down again.

Chapter 22

2013

With huge reluctance I'd decided to go to the police in January and press charges for the loss of all my money. Ilan's crazy confession outside the court had some ring of truth about it. It was a very short day trip. I wanted to go, file the complaint and get out as quickly as possible. It had taken me three months to come to terms with the revelations of the court case, and despite a court order to pay me back by December, I'd received nothing.

Again my frustrations rose with the system in Israel. What is the point of getting a judgment and a court order if no one bothered to adhere to it? The mighty money making machine of Israel played a hand in this. If the order was ignored, then go to the bailiff. Pay more money to try and get repaid. Open another file, pay a lawyer more. By the time that was completed, it could cost more money than the debt itself. Unless one was an insider and I was an outsider. Money wasn't going to leave Israel, I knew it. I wasn't wrong.

I found my way to Yoram's office. He had told me everything would be fine and I needed to be there in person to put in the complaint. We would be going to the Fraud Department.

I flew on his reassurances. As we entered the building he said.

"This isn't going to be easy. I just want you to know."

"You tell me this now! After flying overnight? Why didn't you say something before?" I responded in disbelief.

"Didn't want you to be worrying about it." He said.

Entering the huge building, we were led to a room in the fraud department.

We pressed on with our claim for over two hours and eventually the officer gave me some forms to sign.

"You have it." said Yoram. "They've accepted your claim. Usually they'd class it as domestic and not bother, but we have a result."

The paperwork was very reassuring. Not that I could read it. The highlights for me were we had a case number and passwords to go onto the computer to see how our claim was progressing. There were pages declaring their commitment to me as a plaintiff. In essence the paperwork promised me they would investigate, feed information back and keep us involved every step of the way. They even went as far as saying we should send them half a dozen questions we felt they should ask. I named Ilan, Elvira and Eitan in the complaint as they were the names Ilan had blurted out in distress in October.

As we left the building, Yoram received a phone call which he cleared very quickly. He turned to me and asked.

"Did anyone know you were coming today?"

"Only a couple of friends at home." I replied.

"What about here in Israel. Did you tell anyone?"

"Of course not. Who would I tell?" I asked.

"That was Abe on the phone. He knew you were here. Not only that, his call came within a minute of us leaving the office we've been in for over two hours. I don't like this at all. I didn't confirm I was with you, but he asked for you."

Stunned with his words, I couldn't take it in. How anyone could know I was here was not just a mystery, it made me feel a little afraid.

We called Ilan from a number he didn't recognise. He was shocked to hear my voice from a local number. "When did you come? What are you doing here?" he asked.

"Why don't you ask Abe" I responded angrily.

We argued for over an hour, until Yoram nudged me to leave. I almost missed my flight home and despite my concerns I was pleased we had a police file which was not in Nahariyya.

I tried to follow up on the police computer. The password was declined. I called Yoram repeatedly to follow up. He didn't. I asked a friend in England who spoke Hebrew to get me the right number so I could do it myself.

The file had been moved to Nahariyya. It was my worst outcome. As if this wasn't bad enough, when I finally got through to speak to someone I was told the file had disappeared. I was asked for my name. When I gave it, the officer became very defensive and refused to say anything more. I tried several times and was fobbed off or passed around.

"Probably someone crossed someone else's palm with silver." concluded Yoram with no concern.

I was supposed to just accept it. I had been thwarted yet again and was outraged. How did these people get away with it? Of course if I didn't agree, I could open a file. It was a disgrace that every promise and protocol in my file had been disregarded. But the point was people had known I was there, and I was unsettled.

'Back off Israel, or you might have another Spanish experience'. An anonymous call had been made to me. I didn't recognise the voice but of course I wouldn't. Two weeks ago, I was found bruised and unconscious in a hotel in Spain whilst on a business trip. I didn't believe for one second it was anything to do with Israel. But my terror was real. I didn't know how anyone in Israel could have known my movements and made such a connection as to threaten me. I couldn't accept even the slightest possibility. I had been warned since the UN to be careful, and received a few threats in previous years but this was something else. That really would be a movie. Not possible is it? I would like to be declared crazy today by someone who would explain it all. Boy, I would like to be crazy, really.it would be much easier.

It had only been 8 weeks since my visit to the police and I also received a text to my work phone, in

HEBREW, formally saying I would be contacted soonest, from Ilan's phone. I was sure he didn't have the number as he'd only called or texted to my personal phone and always in English. He swore he didn't text me in Hebrew, and the text was one minute after the threatening call. Please tell me I'm not mad, I silently prayed. I called my lawyer immediately, my friend saw me soon after and I was very shaken up.

No one in Israel could have known where I was. Perhaps I was making some dangerous enemies. I logged a complaint with police here and they came to see me. Unlike Israel, they were very efficient. I called Ilan who swore he hadn't texted me. He was very angry and abusive (another usual) and disconnected. I started to believe that someone was really playing with my head. What happened in Spain was irrelevant, it had been an accident, but it was Israel/Spain in one threatening call that had scared me. Somebody knew I'd been away and had decided to play mind games with me.

After 3 weeks off work, black eyed, and bruised, I decided I needed trauma counselling.

"If I can't access that part of my life, I will avoid all contact with those who remind me." A very good friend told me today.

Suddenly it's like seeing a red mini and then they are everywhere. I can sense and feel people more than ever. Now I pick up on other peoples' traumas everywhere I go. I was blessed with the gift of being able to channel the truth to people, not mine, but THE truth. It's both a privilege and a curse. My friend's words were embedded in me already. But I listened and understood. I'm different I realised. I don't avoid contact with reminders, I do the opposite. I search for reminders to fuel the need for justice.

The compulsion for truth and justice keeps me going when others may give up. Today, as Ilan's wife, I sit here in England whilst he prepares for a minor operation, very small in the scheme of things. March 2013. My mum is back in hospital, my sister still battling with her cancer, others I know with grave problems. I've been to see them, prayed, supported and loved them with all my heart.

But I can't do that for Ilan. The last time he had a procedure for tendon problems in his wrist, I was there. He was so afraid of doctors. He needed to see the children's doctor and never has managed. In his 'other' life someone else will be there for him I suppose, probably the other woman who fills his space. The one he doesn't have real feelings for, not in his heart. She will be there. I wonder if she knows how scared he is. Does she know how to make him laugh at the right time, to get his thinking right? I doubt it.

Or maybe he is so closed down that he doesn't care anyway. He still loves me but he can't access that part of his life, and just like my pal he's trying to avoid reminders. But his heart and soul can't quite close the door. This crime of separation has been committed by others, not us. Today I feel frustrated, a mixture of emotions: angry, powerless, helpless, distracted, obsessive, the list goes on. My doubt creeps in again, can I achieve this goal of somehow making an assessment a condition of our divorce. I'm thinking that my best outcome is a financial concession on all the money lost and owed in exchange for him seeing a trauma specialist.

That would make a good point in the religious court when we go. From his sporadic conversations this past month which have been a deluge compared to last year, he is ebbing away again. I think because he knows and believes that somewhere in the dark shadows there are people who want me to just disappear. He has avoided me since I told him. I had a little monologue on the phone a few days back, one of those calls, when I just talked and talked in the hope something would reach him.

I've always been the one who reaches him. I described this feeling of waking up in the morning, and just for a few seconds, it's just that, waking up. Then the realisation crashes in again as my first thought is like a hammer smashing my brain, another day, another shock to my system. It's like this every single day. Years ago, it lasted all day, as we searched together for support and answers. Now it's just a moment in the morning. I describe the motions of life, of getting up, hoping with all one's heart that the good intentions of the night before will bear fruit.

That the energy planned the night before will bubble over, the joy will be found in the new day. The truth is too much, the pain wins over good intentions, and the day turns into a grinding plod. Sometimes it is almost possible to forget 'the situation', distracted by work, people and sometimes there are real pleasures and great fun. Then it hits, sometimes in a crowd, or driving, or drifting, life is not this. It's not being lived. There is no colour and it's hard work to keep painting the colour in life. The good times become bitter sweet, the bad ones are just too awful, but either way it takes energy, tons of it, to stay normal. I get angry I said, at the whole injustice, but a big hole just stays there and never gets filled.

"So, you have decided to analyse my day." he said

"No Ilan. It's not your day, it's mine." I had been talking about me. But I knew it was his day too.

I'm so blessed. I have a great family, wonderful friends and I think I'm more aware, continuing to have brutal determination. He is not as blessed, as being asleep is less painful but less joyful too. He claimed he buried his life, there is no future, no plans, just the now, just an existence. This was not even as fulfilling as being a plant, or a vegetable growing, because their purpose is to be just that, and it's done wholly in synch with nature. Ilan is human and with no hope, there is nothing.

He's angry, very, because he is afraid for me as he believes I've risked too much. He is angry because he could not protect or take care of me. So the carer in me fights on finally understanding what it feels like. I don't know how to get tough. I understand the abused women, who can't leave, and no one gets why. Or the mother who gives her child money for drugs and no one gets why.

I believe sometimes the words therapy and counseling should be renamed. The words create a stigma because they put people off. Instead we turn to well-meaning friends who have too many differing opinions rendering the advice useless. I think about self-help groups. It makes me smile, because trauma has an ally, a best friend – denial. Maybe we should form a group full of people who refuse to believe, in the face of captivity, and get them together!

I Spoke to Ilan again today. He was so cold, detached and unbearable. Nothing I said which was good or bad news touched any part of him, nothing. I just didn't know how to handle it. He said he is not in a hurry to divorce, and offered to pay me £500 per month. I didn't believe a word; I'd heard it all before. He was indifferent, irresponsible, angry and no empathy. As if I didn't exist on the planet, yet he is still not prepared to face the situation. I cried last night, remembering.

"Come on Ilan, don't be afraid, it's just a simple hand operation, quick local anesthetic, and it's done." He was so scared.

The physiotherapist couldn't handle his fears. I knew that Matty was planning to close Ilan's freedom. I knew it so had booked an indirect flight to UK, for just a day after the operation. Ilan had no doubt about my word, nothing. His trust was full and he left Israel with his hand strapped up to come home. This time there would be no plans for a better life, just a bandage on a wound.

I asked him "how long are you going to keep up this nonsense dream state with no reply, or just your 'usual' 'I don't know' response? Is it really ok for all my money to have gone, whilst you earn 5,000 shekels a month, and claim to live for free?"

There was no reply.

I continued. "Are you sorry, do you have any feelings? Do you have any gratitude at all for everything I tried to do for you?"

"Sure." A one word answer was all I received.

He was probably sick of hearing me trying to get my closure, my answers, desperate for a chink in his armour, a moment when he might pour out all his true feelings. It wasn't a stupid hope, because we'd been here many times over the years. And eventually he'd pulled himself up just enough for the real him to show up. I'd seized those moments, satiated by the truth, hearing it, knowing it, until some crisis shut him down again. The attempt to end his life was the biggest one and something died in him from that moment. His shadow, his friend Denial stepped in saying 'me? Suicide, don't be crazy, as if!' He had become cold, hard, shut down and cruel.

It's almost impossible to describe how it felt to hear my partner not want to live anymore. Unless someone has experienced it, it's impossible to understand. My stomach caved in like a punch from Mohammed Ali, the breath sucked out of me. It was not happening. He'd seemed ok; yes there was pressure, of course there was, but he had tried to be strong before the time was right.

Now a big tough unfeeling person had taken over. I went into many forms of denial myself. He was a fake; it was all a game, no big deal. What's the fuss?

So was he a calculating, manipulative criminal mastermind, or was he not? On the surface, without insight, I might go for the first but the circumstances were unique and quite extraordinary. The revenge of an ex was a dish served very hot like a madras curry. She was like a Duracell battery, just never-ending and with no respite, to this day in fact. Hell hath no fury like a woman scorned they say. She wasn't even scorned – she had someone else – it was in her testimony. This was a dog in the manger act which went into folklore and legend and became someone's truth.

There were many players wanting a piece of us. They had so many agendas, all there if examined closely enough. So clear, and as I think of the story of his captivity and my adventures to change it, it was no wonder I thought I was the crazy one. I didn't like having unconditional love, set in a country with no exit, a country in fear for its existence and not at all 'touchy feely'. Israel is the ultimate Alcatraz.

The system abuse which takes limitation of freedom of movement for granted was worse than I had imagined. In Hebrew, they cannot say 'I am', only 'I was', or 'will be'. If asked to say 'I am', an Israeli can only say 'I'. That's an indictment and also a glimpse into a culture that cannot just *be*, always in a state of past or future. I know that from my studies in the history of language. No words to just 'be'. How informative it is. It's not entirely their fault. They hold on to the past and want assurances for the future. I've stopped hating them for that but it took a long time. Nevertheless it doesn't excuse this whatsoever, and he's not the only one who has got lost in the system and lost their sense of identity.

Chapter 23

The start of the fight, for justice, for truth, for love.

I'm an invisible woman. I can't get closure. Dumped, ignored, betrayed and almost bankrupted and I can't get closure.

Is it that I am desperate for instant replies? Perhaps. It comes from being endlessly ignored, cast aside as if I'm yesterday's newspaper. But I'm still here, I'm still me, and living in it. Is it avoidance, people being busy, or just plain fun? You see I could get paranoid. My value system just doesn't get it. Everyone is just going to get away with this? It seems so. Hey it's only your life's work, your identity, your family's money, no big deal.

I'm trying to move on, really I am, trying to let go of a bad feeling. I'm already history for those who did this, so I have to make it all history for me. I feel so small, so pointless.

I used to be a person once, a long time ago. It hurts so much all of this. I rack my brains for the answers, the understanding, a grown up conversation, someone to tell me why I was used, abused and then trashed.

It's not about love; it's about respect and human decency. Ilan has none left. I'm just a name from the past, whilst he builds his life with no compunction or conscience. Living it up, full of money, his children stable, the new life he claimed all due to me not giving up on him. So, not even sorry, thanks, goodbye, nothing. I'm invisible. Standing in the UN, fighting for his rights, he'd already used them without any notification to me. Not even telling me it was a useless battle. He'd made his life with Elvira and lied to me all through this.

A fool for love? Understatement of the year! Writing thousands of emails and letters to anyone in the world who might even listen; going to the UN, borrowing against his word? Now that's a total fool because I truly believed in this cause. It hadn't just been him; I'd seen and heard about the others, so many others, who'd suffered beyond measure. It was for them too. I'd been compelled to publicise this atrocity of denying emotional freedom, imprisoning people mentally and emotionally for money, for demands no human being could deliver, leaving them damaged and giving up.

But did he? Or had he chosen already and used me for years? I don't have that answer and it seems from all well-meaning advice that losing a lifetime is no big deal. I can't find another one of me, someone who tried so hard, to even go to the United Nations like I did. Is there someone else out there, are you there? Who did this to you? Let me know. Tell me I wasn't the only one.

Does he cuddle up with his lover and laugh at my stupidity? Does his family care that I'm left with nothing and have to rebuild not just my life in terms of a heartbreak, but needing intensive therapy to deal with death threats and a useless man who defrauded me with their blessing? They have ignored every single letter I've written, begging on my knees for answers and closure. I am just a dead person, a nothing, a nobody. Is this real?

I'm so angry. This isn't normal. Ilan's family are in full awareness of what's happening and still they ignore it, colluding in this breathtaking abuse of me. Ilan is avoiding me big time, I just want my life.

How could it get to this? Let's get to the crux. Matty used a system to keep us apart, and he uses the same system to stop my freedom too. It's not just them, it was all the heart breaking stories I read. A website resource I had has disappeared, .my police file in Israel has been closed with NO notification to me or my lawyer even with all the evidence. The twilight zone, that's where I am.

Today after chasing my lawyer for months, I decided to follow up the police file myself. I'd flown to Israel in February to open a file to press charges against Ilan for fraud. That wasn't exactly easy, being questioned for hours. Eventually we won the golden ticket and got a crime number and a lovely print out of the police charter, with their promises of delivery. A month later, a letter saying the file had moved to the fraud division, then nothing. More empty waiting time.

The alien from UK, actually believing that even in that country the police would honour their promises. Despite requesting follow up, I eventually did it myself and well well, the case was moved to his home town and then closed. No notification, nothing, just closed. Just like that, no idea of the date, or what happened, it's just closed. Just like my life closed. Yoram was shocked to hear it. I was beside myself with fury. Yet again, who are you Marianne, a human being with rights, complaints, horrendous injustice and theft against you? No, you're nobody, a file against our citizen, lip service? Who knows, but the flight, the cost, the emotional enormity of the decision I'd made to even take this step, and there it was, in the bin.

I'm supposed to believe there's no corruption? Please, let's wake up and smell the coffee. You see the players might change, but the stage remains the same, the ingredients for abuse of another person all laid out to be used by perpetrators and not the innocent. I've been told my husband is bigamously married. He denied knowing me then admitted to taking the child support money to get himself out of debt, and starting a business. I've a judgment to have money back, which in Israel I'm told "hey it's only tens of thousands, no big deal, don't waste your time." I cannot get divorced, can't move on, with a complete instinct telling me so loud it's all designed to make me give up, and they're doing a great job.

I have met people who fought and fought the system until they were broken and just gave up, some strong and courageous people who had to withdraw for their own health and well-being. I was told that everybody has a breaking point but the system will always win, it's just how long you want to fight it for because there is no justice. So many people, they start with gusto, enthusiasm, like contestants in a game show or a test of endurance, convinced they will be the ones to get the victory and share it with those who went before.

But one by one they fall by the wayside, just too weary, too exhausted to try again. Even a Duracell battery runs out eventually. Perhaps I lasted longer than most and if it was just about walking away from Ilan and moving on, then I have had many times and moments in which that was the decision I wanted, and did indeed make on occasion. But what about now? The same man holds me, hurts me, abuses me, lies, cheats and steals from me and how many times I beg for mercy, for release, my pleas fall on deaf ears.

Even in Israel, the process is *supposed* to be similar to UK. A complaint is filed with the police and they ask questions. If they feel there are no grounds they inform you, and give 30 days' notice to close the case, or in that time for you to add any further information you might want, and then, only then is the file closed. Yoram, my lawyer, says this is "normal" in a way, and that it happens frequently, but nonetheless is not ok. It's all about delaying tactics, making time pass, so the other person gives up. That's what Ilan had done to him, now it's being done to me. Israeli mentality, to break the other person by just delaying until they can't cope anymore and life moves them on.

It's so simple, yet can be made complicated and also depends upon who you know, which judge you get on the day, as there appears to be no precedents set across the country on laws. The mood of the judge can be the determining factor and even if you win a case it doesn't mean that judgment will be enforced! What a crazy place. So now Ilan uses avoidance, as he's been taught well and knows it broke him, so why not join the club?!

I hate him now; I hate him for doing this to me, for keeping my money, pretending he didn't steal it and keeping me married to a bigamous cheat. He knows my lifetime upbringing and values need closure, I need to be free to live as a single woman and make my choices from that position.

Yet he ignores my pleas, ignores my calls, somehow like a vampire sucking off the energy of my despair. In every pathetic conversation, he claims no responsibility, no accountability, just lost in a haze of confusion, angry, changing minute by minute in his temperament. Telling me I'm crazy? Making me believe that, I am trying to start again, pull away and live the 'normal' life he clearly lives, and I have to force myself into it with never ending difficulty. He's working, earning, laughing and playing, photos show that, and I'm stuck, in his view because 'he lives there, and I live here' and that's his only answer.

I wonder one thing, I tell this story and I'm almost sure others are living a similar nightmare and there isn't anyone who will support my efforts to get closure on this in Israel. Right now I'm in a really bad place. I want it over but my worst nightmare is that it is over, I know it is. But it's not sealed and signed - the defeat. The victory belongs to the people who decided for us, the taste of success is in their mouths, they won. Call it what you like, they won. I understand the whole being there for your kids deal. But Ilan left them, lived with me, married me, and then reneged and didn't want me there because he was unable to cope with the emotional nonsense.

OK, it's over and I get that, so why isn't it finished? I can feel myself slipping backwards again, so fragile, wanting everything just to progress and I can't see beyond myself right now. Isn't it a terrible place, when your feelings and thoughts are so dominant, you barely know what else there is?

Chapter 24

The end of the dream – a marriage destroyed - two futures in tatters.

Why can't I just live my life in full? I want to be busy and productive with positive plans. I yearn for it but the lethargy in me just wins the day every day. Every productive and positive thing, like cleaning the house, making some calls, earning some money, it all seems to be the last thing I want to do. I remember hearing a word – narcotization – I thought it might be something to do with taking narcotics! It does, but I also learned it means to 'shut off the juice', to deny your own energy. Suck it out of yourself with meaningless activities. I suppose it means breaking off from your own life force.

It's so weird, knowing in my mind that there are things I can do which will make me feel so much better about myself, knowing it and still somehow being unable to summon the right energy to do those things. I am stuck in some kind of sleepwalking. The effort is so huge but when I do take it, I know I feel better, in fact I do. It's like a semi trance, just wanting to sit and waste my time. But when I do, the memories drift in, and I don't want them anymore.

I feel good today, why? Because the only thing that keeps me sane, keeps me going and stops my mind from being in turmoil, is speaking to him. When I hear his voice, I am reassured, very reassured that he is not getting any better. In fact, probably worse, I am counting on this.

What kind of a wife and partner am I, who depends on my husband's depression to continue? To need him to stay in that state, or regress even further? Well, it's keeping me going, because I know for certain that what I personally know IS the truth. I have to keep remembering, not just me or him, but the hundreds, if not thousands of people suffering, not just in Israel, but all over the world, not being free. It's burning a hole in me. I can't be bothered most of the time and then I drag myself to write, because I know if I keep my discipline maybe these words will reach the right ears and eyes and hopefully no one will have to endure this living nightmare in the future.

Today was a good day, spending time with friends, listening to their everyday lives, fully in the moment on one hand but constantly making comparisons, feeling the edge of something that has become a total part of my identity, my existence. I fight off the guilt of feeling good by imagining him having a good life, a good time too. Then it eats me up as I need to believe he isn't. What a mess. I got my 'fix' yesterday, talking to my zombie husband. He's not good, he's very 'tired' of it all, and I realise he mixes up 'can't' with 'won't'. He doesn't want to talk, because he can't leave. Really, or is it that he doesn't want to leave and can't talk about it? No, my mind is twisting again. Stay in the moment. I know it's going to be alright, whatever alright is.

But my heart is relentless. It cannot give up hope entirely. Damn hope. Why does it stay? I know he has a flicker of it too, not in his actual waking mind, but in his soul. Or why are we not divorced today? He told me yesterday, he's not in a hurry to divorce, madness in itself. I tell him yet again, we are facing divorce courts and legal action for his stupid actions, and it is like its news, an eternally endless day starting over the same each morning.

He doesn't seem to realise this is going to be real. I am taking the ultimate gamble and I fear my own mind right now. I claim the sanity in this situation, claim that I am awake, aware and full of ideas, but maybe, just maybe I will have to face the ultimate reality soon. The one we both avoid. The one in which these people win. I think they may have already won.

My faith is being tested to the limit. Can I hold on, and keep faith? I'm just not sure.

Today I woke up and it didn't hurt. What a new sensation. It didn't last long. I can't seem to stay in that space. I'm so angry. He *can* leave Israel. Not with a magic wand but with a bit of paperwork and he doesn't have to do it himself. I can arrange it, having that dubious honour of being his wife and next of kin. Nothing makes any sense to me. There he is today; bold as brass, having a picnic, with lover and entourage in tow, including his brother, his thinker.

I can see the photos on Facebook. From one conversation telling me he wants to come to visit my sister who is ill, he answers the phone this morning in a quiet, dangerous rage. He was very cold again;

sarcastic, rude, refusing to discuss the potential visit and then happily picnicking. All my anger, resentment and bitterness flies into me at once. I have examined deeply, is it jealousy? Should I be jealous of him, or her having him? Elvira, is his long-time lover for almost 4 years now. I've been informed by pictures, but never from his own mouth. They were visible to me a year ago just so I could be humiliated on the world stage through social networking. But, prodding my mind, I only seem contented when I hear his wretched miserable voice, not because I actually want his unhappiness but because it vindicates all I have done.

I remember my dream. The recurring dream I had for a week after we were first torn asunder. It was horrible, a nightmare. It had barely been a week, we were still thinking at that time he'd be home for Christmas like before it was a storm in a teacup. Throw some money at it and we'd get our lives back on track. But this dream, it came every day. I saw Ilan in a room, a stark room with a window, a bed with a pastel blanket on it, a chair by the bed, cabinet and small wardrobe, with a very thin window. I walked into the room and he was staring vacantly at the wall. I whispered to him, "Hi love, it's time for me to take you home." But there was no response. I repeated this over and over and then he grabbed my wrist and said, "Please take me home." And then I woke up. It came every day, the worst dream, in the worst situation.

I only remembered it last year, and realised that to be free, both of us, probably meant I would actually need to lose the love of my life. Events had finally taught me I have to set both of us free but not in the way I wished for.

I need to know deep down that none of this was a waste, a game or a pointless exercise. I was a successful woman, a great judge of character and I couldn't be this wrong. Sometimes I just feel like I'm going crazy and Ilan does have a way of telling me I have a wild imagination, especially when I repeat his own words back to him. It's like he's hearing them for the first time, all news to him, and then he loses his patience and lets me know in a way that I am unreasonable or mad for wanting MY money back,

MY life, MY freedom. All I get is 'I don't know' to every request I make. I'm astounded at myself.

How did we get here? Were we already here? Was my life real, is it real now? I will get the answers eventually but it doesn't stop the questions pouring into my mind. When something so massively life-changing happens it makes me feel as if there is a before and after. Just like the term BC. For me it was Before Captivity. Before the event when life was normal with the usual ups and downs, some not so good, and then after the event, the AD – After Destruction - when I yearn for the normal ups and downs which sound so pointless when I hear about them from others. It's unfair to others and I feel ashamed that I hold the ace cards in hard times as if that is something to be so proud of. My badge of honour, look at me. You see it's all circumstantial, he wouldn't be like this if he was here at home with me. So many people interfering, but the extent of it is becoming clearer and clearer. So is the pure evil involved in this ignorance and evil.

I have paperwork, emails, stories and even an internal documentary showing just how things are. Israel cannot even begin to understand why the outside world considers their treatment of the Palestinians abusive. After all – if they can hold anyone inside their borders – their own, and foreign nationals, then it is obvious to them that a similar treatment of Arabs is par for the course and normal behaviour. That to me is a large contribution to the Middle East problem.

This must be made public, and laws changed, so that men, women and children can be free. A semi European country which buys into our democracy should be made accountable for its behaviours. My husband had not one but 2 No Exit orders on him simultaneously, isn't one just one too many?

My life will never be the same, but if making this public helps one person in the future then I hope this is the time for it, as I have no more energy left to fight.

I don't know what to think. What is this system!? I get a judgment that I must have my money back, which was taken by the system in the first place, and then I find out it will cost me more again to enforce the judgment! No wonder people are in a panic when they are ordered to pay money! So I lose everything to pay money to release Ilan from Israel, it's taken and divvied up, and she gets to keep her part as she's a mum. It was my money. I'm a mum too.

I'm in Weston Super Mare. I've not been here since I was with Ilan. That first glorious week, was it real? We were so much in love, so fresh and new and it was like finding a long lost love and friend all rolled into one. We shared stories, laughed, cried and loved so much, discovering our thoughts and dreams like kindred spirits. No vocabulary could describe that feeling of coming 'home', back to your soul mate. This was the time you see in the movies. We talked endlessly, Ilan was euphoric to be in England and we melded or dare I say it welded our hearts together.

Everything from my past paled and faded in those days. So I sit, almost a decade later in a street café drinking cappuccino, alone in a grey day, remembering a place that was bursting to life in full technicolour all those years back, and now the sun is struggling to shine. I'm eight weeks from a court case I couldn't have imagined and the beginning of the end of what should have been. Ilan withered and died in the land he is in, the life sucked out of him and I sit here unable to find the nurturing I need for myself.

The connotations of the word husband, a worthless title. Now partner, lover, fiancé, those were real times, but the marriage actually destroyed what we had before we had a chance to begin. In December 2011 when planning to renew our marriage vows, this place and Somerset were the places we talked about returning to so we could pick up where we had started properly. Instead I sit here needing a proper ending not some fading out with no explanation or goodbye.

I'm searching inside for some feelings or emotions past or present, I really don't mind which, but there is nothing, it's just numb, nothing at all. As if none of this is really happening to me.

Hell, we all do break ups, or most of us but I cannot live in this space whilst he holds me as his legal wife, not accountable or taking responsibility for the theft of my money. 'A rope around his neck' he said, removing it by strangling my life for over a year. If I thought it was madness before then what can this be? My so called husband is now in the 4th year of our 5 year marriage with someone else, so they say, being funded by me? And there is no authority which will put this right for me? I cannot reconcile it with the memories of this place. Also, I know you cannot fool all the people all the time and I know that people around me didn't get it wrong too, not all at the same time, for years.

But whatever was the trigger or the defining moment, there is no escape for me, no real peace, my thoughts swimming around trying to put sense to a man with no sense, or idea of reality. Even out of sight out of mind doesn't explain it, nor revenge. I still need my answers.

I'd promised myself I wouldn't call, would do my own form of closure, by just leaving it. God knows I want to. . But the case is looming and I cannot afford to go really, I just can't. I want to have money for other things, normal things. It didn't work out, he still will not give any solidity to his words, and it's like a cotton wool ball, combusting into angry moments. I asked for photos and letters back, he wouldn't. I wanted to give some things he'd treasure, he'd replaced them already!

Then today I learn from a helpful friend who is in Israel that I won't get any recompense unless I keep throwing money at it. Defeats the object in one way, but I'm so angry. Who could do this to another person and then get angry at me! You can't argue with the dead, they've gone and it must be awful, unimaginable to learn things about them and not get your say. But this? It's not the marriage breakup, god knows I can do those, it's the breathtaking theft of my life, my money, my identity, my plans, my old age (pension) and no apology, no guilt, no shame? For if there was, then I'd get the three things I want; my divorce, my money repaid and my closure, all of which require the other half to comply, co-operate and act on.

This situation is driving me to despair, I can't see the point, it's all worthless to write, to tell, to ask, to plead, to insist, it all results in the same. The invisible woman, silence really is a deadly weapon. Cut my losses, it's an option but could I handle it. I know life is unfair, I do get it, and maybe Ilan was dealt a bad hand by this conspiracy, but he told me himself that his life had been threatened too. So that's the license to leave me like this?

Thank god for therapy, without it I'd be lost. But trying to find myself is going to be a long journey.

Chapter 25

2013 A life stolen – betrayal

My memories haunt me. I abandoned him too. He had put all his hopes, everything into getting out just after the wedding. We were both so wrapped up in our own grief and shock that we couldn't get it together and I didn't go back straight away. I should have gone back. His world had ended with that betrayal, he was separated from himself and I didn't go back.

I had seen over 18 months of him being castrated, I knew Ilan had been naïve. He had an innocence about him, he was never great with subtlety of other peoples' agendas; he just took it as he found it. He had a total belief that he would leave Israel. We both had thought justice would prevail and even more so that declared friends would be honourable. I can see, sitting here, I handled this all wrong. I left him there. He would say to me in the future 'how could you have left me here', but I was trying to help him be the man, the man who wanted to handle things and put everything right. Imagine yourself having to wave your new spouse goodbye, knowing that somehow, for some reason you couldn't even go with them, have a honeymoon, have your life and have to wave them away at the train station.

Lizzie's affidavit is the key. She saw it and I didn't know that observation fully until about a year ago. I can put myself even more now in his shoes, the love of his life, his reason detre just going away leaving him totally alone. His family all with their agendas:

fear, greed, jealousy, revenge, all having a piece of him and I was the one who had his love, his life, hopes and fears, all of it.

I left him there. Was I the mad one? It was his love for me and desperation that was to split his personality in half. If I'd known just how deep the vendetta was to go, I'd have used different tactics and given all the money I wasted in one go and forced the situation. Who in his situation would want to open the wounds over and over again, being made to endure endless helloes and goodbyes, smelling the fresh air of freedom on me, and staying in the rank stale mate. It was too cruel and his self-preservation instincts kicked in to my detriment and ultimately to the destruction of everything I had built and stood for as a person.

Each failure, each block, each twist and turn and mind game reinforced Ilan's self-image of a worthless half man. His emails showed that his efforts to stay normal in a crazy situation became weaker and weaker. He told me I was his life, but Israel, it was a place he had to survive in. He's said that I was too pure and clean to be connected to that. He told me that being in a dog eat dog world 23 hours a day now meant he couldn't switch on decency and love in that final hour before bed. He was disappearing into survival and couldn't imagine a normal healthy free life anymore.

So, after almost 10 years, my husband has abandoned me, just like that. From planning to renew our wedding vows to a brutal and cruel intermittent demand for a divorce, within 72 hours my world completely collapsed.

But 18 months later I'm still married to him. One and a half years since he wanted to die. Still married to an angry, bitter man, a man who was perhaps bigamously living with another woman, the one from the astrology chart I'd found, Elvira. He stole all my money, and the biggest perversion of all is he refuses to give me the very thing HE demanded, my divorce, using silence as a weapon just like his family, breaking me down to try and make me give up my own rights for once, the right to my money and my freedom. I'm being put through the same torment by him as the torment HE received and he seems oblivious to my pain.

Israeli Law, firstly preceding a divorce is an agreement to split assets, or in our situation to make arrangements to repay a court order which was made over 7 months ago. Since then, I have received not a penny, just a total disregard for this theft and my financial struggle. My money was put there to facilitate his return and our future and was used to facilitate his new life.

The therapy is working, he's nearly out of my emotional state, the grief being slowly replaced by some anger, a lot of frustration and needing even more faith in the universe to balance the books of energy and find my way forward. I married a weakened and selfish man who continues to finds ways to avoid me and by doing so abusing me right to this day. Hoping the Englishwoman will quit, walk away and have a 'husband' who is in a serious relationship with another woman for over 3 years. I feel like I'm in a relay! Pass the baton to the next fool waiting to be used. His first wife wouldn't divorce him so he does the same to me! I'm going to heal, from purpose and intent, not time.

Chapter 26

The beginning of the end

The beginning of the end. What will the ending be? Sunday 9th June. I rang him to check he'd be there, and he lost control, screaming and shouting. I remarked on how sad it was that he would be in Tel Aviv and wouldn't pick me up and how a decade ago things were so different.

He didn't hear me, just screaming about something else, just spewing out toxic poison. Holding the phone at a distance in disbelief, I wondered where he'd got the license to be so abusive. For me the trip was turning my stomach in knots. It was unknown territory, complicated and I was fearful of the emotional tirade I would get as his treatment of me was as if I'm a worthless human being. I just couldn't handle these outbursts.

My counselor called last night, her letter is fabulous. Her evaluation of him is so accurate but despite this I continued to question what I seem to do or say which triggers him to such hatred. He claimed he does want to meet but suddenly didn't know a single landmark in Tel Aviv. The Azriel Centre, he doesn't even know the name of it, never heard of it, doesn't know anywhere at the beach.

Come on girl, think clearly. I am on yet another flight to Israel, but this time I promised myself I would deal with it better.

I have to present a reluctant divorce due to family interference, and he is choosing only by ultimatums and his mother's demands as he has repeatedly told me. It really is a reluctant divorce, for in my heart and soul I cannot imagine the rest of my life without him. Not when we never had a chance with so much interference.

But flying British Airways means I'm not in Israel yet so I can hold on to British courtesy for five more hours. God help me, I really meant it, God be with me.

10th June. Yoram suggested I get the divorce, to let it all go and walk away as I'll never see my money again anyway. But why would MY divorce have to work like that? I've seen enough to believe it shouldn't. I tossed a coin, betting on Ilan's consistency of unreliability. He's consistent in avoiding, denying, lying and showing disrespect.

Recalling when we met; I'd been through years of development and I was at the peak of my self-awareness I thought through my work.

I had been open spiritually and my understanding of human behaviours had been at its sharpest. I had personal substance for many years, I'd been able to work on the personality factors that chained me and was trained to practice those skills on others. I was free, I had personal power, and presence, that's what people saw and commented on. It couldn't have been so true as this episode of my life had lit up my ignorance of just how deep one has to dig to really find out the truth inside.

I'm here in the country which has a collaboration of people, started by just one woman, who stooped so low with dirty tricks and a determination to break a man's spirit. She realised her ambition, he is now not just a prisoner of the country but a prisoner of his own mind. I arrived, a stranger in this country I've known so long, to fight for myself this time. There must be a price to pay for them. So I've tossed the coin and now I begin my journey to begin the end.

I cannot shake off the pain and the anxiety.

Will the real man please put up his hand? Ilan is not mentally ill, according to Israeli law, so I am refused the opportunity to disclose any weaknesses or vulnerabilities, this country does not listen. But now we are in the game and tomorrow maybe I'll bury the living dead so I can start to breathe again.

What is my dream? For a psychiatric report to be ordered to declare Ilan is in a desperate state of trauma. Then we can hang out the flags for it will be a result! What is my nightmare? A deliberate whitewash for I am now so well trained in systems here.

Is Ilan either a criminal or a broken man, purposeful in his intent or with a destroyed spirit and unintentional behaviour? I know best. He is fragmented. I have to listen to my instincts. There is no mystery. Israeli culture is on trial as far as I am concerned. I am on trial as far as they are concerned and I have only the truth as my defence.

10th June – pm. Words fail me. Ilan impatiently and rudely talked to me, agreeing to meet. Hot, sweaty, disconcerted and disorientated, I eventually arrived at the Azriel Centre, a gigantic shopping centre in central Tel Aviv. I had no clue how to find him as I walked inside but within half a minute I felt a tap on my shoulder and turning around I saw him. His eyes were shining and a big smile on his face. How long had he been there? He moved to embrace me but everything inside me contracted as my anger rose. I just shook his hand, feeling so unprepared and unkempt. I needed a cigarette to calm my nerves so we took a seat outside with traffic roaring behind on the main road. It was incongruent. Surely he must know he'd been shouting and impatient only minutes before on the phone. It just didn't seem possible that I'd spoken to such a split personality. He must know, he must.

No time for niceties or small talk, and needing answers I sprayed questions like bullets. I had travelled so far and couldn't be civil. I went straight in at the deep end.

But first, he asked me for a favour. "Please don't make me cry Mar"

"Me?! You should cry from your lies, your guilt and your shame, not from me. Let's start Ilan."

"I believed in you, and trusted you. If you wanted to make me happy, then you should have bought me a dog, not planned to renew our wedding vows. Our marriage was over within 72 days, I was dismissed so quickly, after 5 years of fighting for your freedom?"

"No, no, you're thinking isn't right"

I was boiling over. I had travelled thousands of miles for this drivel? My pain was real and present, his just blurred, his memories not recent nor his recollection of events in sequence.

The bottom line, I asked for the real reason.

"I was forced to choose, my parents or you. That's it. I was given an ultimatum."

His parents! I've lost to emotionally blackmailing hysterical parents, eight years into my marriage? I don't have enough punctuation marks or expletives to describe my feelings and reaction to this.

"What about me being here with you in Israel?"

"Here too, it's a straight choice. You don't remember that I escaped last time without telling them, I am not allowed to have you. I can't say exactly what the threat is but I have no choice."

"You were telling everyone who would listen Ilan that your children's' lives were in danger, after your suicide attempt." I was pressing more and more with questions, I needed to know.

"'They were having severe problems at home, I was worried about them."

My mind was racing. He'd claimed to a lawyer his children would be killed. Did he just have paranoia I wondered, but I couldn't stay calm.

"Work?" I asked.

"I live with Eitan and just get pocket money. He decides everything for me. People didn't want me to have a life. I tell them I love you, but they just don't answer and turn away." He said sadly.

His mother! Not only can he not leave with this blackmail and a no exit order, but then he said

"If they were not in the equation I would be with you in England. You have to believe me."

Sitting in a restaurant, after hours of travelling, listening to him just not connecting his own behaviour at all was too much for me.

However I started to understand. His reality is the ultimatum. *You cannot be married to her anywhere in the world. She will affect your thinking.*

He had promised to stay in Israel until either all who want him there are dead or they change their minds. It is the culmination of Matty's intention to destroy his life, ruin us, and leave him 'crazy' as she put it and the snowball effects have led me to this. My struggles, fights and battles were not just the system which was well used, but the mentality and culture of these people. He is a child in a man's body. I have gone through all this to be left to appease a dramatic hysterical mother! Oh please, it was utter nonsense but would be laughable if there were not lives at stake.

I found my way to my hotel and Ilan called repeatedly. I answered some calls, listening to him pleading and begging for us not to go to the rabbinate.

11th June. I didn't sleep all night as being constantly woken by vivid dreams. I'm so tired, as Yoram and I make our journey to Haifa to the Rabbinical Court. I need to be clear of my aims and objectives. In Ilan's heart and soul he cannot divorce and claimed he would tell the court exactly what he told me. I hope so. They will see instantly the absurdity and the tragedy of his broken mind. I needed this assessment to be ordered. No one in any reasonable state of mind could accept that Ilan is a healthy man.

I wondered *"What if these ultimatums are in his head? What if they are real? Will he really say the same again today?"* The answers would come today. He still claimed to me that I am not being held in this marriage. Of course he saw it this way because our relationship is in his memories as he sits frozen in the present, unable to understand choice.

We stood outside and then sat together inside. It didn't feel real. I fear there may be nothing I can do. We hugged outside the door of the building, he cried and I was numb. We enter. I hate this corridor. It is stark, full of the energy of hopes and dreams dying, full of empty and cold wretched endings. It was always a busy building. The divorce rate is high in Israel.

We are called in, a panel of rabbis seated high up, and two desks, one for each adversary. Yoram reminded me this is a preliminary hearing, nothing will be decided. But that was not so. I concentrated as it was obviously all in Hebrew. Yoram asked for patience so I can have things translated. They don't grant it. Immediately, I heard the decision. We must divorce immediately!

But we'd only just walked in, no one had spoken. It's all in Hebrew, and I couldn't believe what I was hearing. The process wasn't calm or measured, there was no chance to talk or present information, just a babble of Hebrew, people talking at once and I was standing with no voice.

They refused an assessment and started to discuss the money. Yoram told me they seem to want this over. I didn't know what to do. I was told to sit with Ilan and with tears rolling down his cheeks he translated the information. The times we had sat together on the same side, yet he was the only one who still helped me to understand. He had his arm around my shoulder as I leaned in to hear better.

"They want the ketuba, to know about the money from our marriage contract" he continued.

Just as Ilan had foretold a few days before, we are sitting together and as always, my considerate man doesn't leave me in ignorance of events. This was horrible. An older rabbi on the right was watching us and a separate part of me wondered how we can be divorcing when we'd said nothing, and why should I. Ilan was left to speak with them. Waiting outside, I worked hard on grounding myself, but I knew that it wasn't working. Ilan comes out, we go in.

They tell me, "Ilan is penniless, worthless and a low life and we must divorce. Perhaps a nominal symbolic payment of £10 per month might be acceptable. I should get a new husband. It is logical, all else is irrational. He is of no use to me. If I want to try and find assets, well do that, but a few shekels a month is best offer."

I observed in a bubble of horror. My life had been decided without my input. Just as a bride doesn't speak on her wedding day, I was dumb in my divorce case. How had they let Matty stretch things for 4 years I thought? They definitely wanted me out of Israel, of that there was no doubt. I asked over and over to Yoram of the decisions being made about my life.

Suddenly I decided, not this time, despite being told not to speak. I stood up, angry, empowered and determined. I asked the young rabbi if he'd throw his wife away if she had cancer? He replied no, so I explained that trauma couldn't be seen. I was a good woman, honest loyal and faithful as his wife, who had given everything. Ilan was worthless in their eyes but I knew it was because his spirit had been broken.

Yoram then spoke. "In the old days according to Jewish Law, the rabbis were sages and wise people and people came for help. We do not come here for your judgments; we come here for guidance and help. You should not be trying to break a thread, but to help someone in trouble, for their souls, according to our laws."

I looked at the elder rabbi and felt he had seen me. He was looking straight into my eyes. He knew this was true. I was standing defending a man with an unarranged marriage approaching, a disarranged brain and no justice for me.

"It was my duty, up to a divorce, to keep my promise, to help him when he didn't know who he was, as he had begged." I insisted.

I had pushed the record button on my phone in my handbag, hoping to keep the information for later. Something was wrong with the scene being played out.

We got it, an assessment, first by a social worker for both of us. It was a fantastic result. Yoram was delighted. Ilan was called in again and told the judgment. He nodded but gave no emotional reaction. It hadn't sunk in but I'd got exactly what I'd asked for in my heart. Ilan was happier when we left the building. We went for some food and spent a couple of hours together.

When it was time for me to go, I asked him for a lift to the train station. Suddenly he didn't know what a train station was. He offered me money for a taxi and the most heartbreaking sight was of him emptying his wallet, then scrabbling around in every pocket to find coins.

"I'm sorry, I'm sorry. I wish I had more, but I haven't got anything." He sobbed, as he poured coins into my hands. It was heart wrenching watching him searching for money. He had a total of just over £7, everything he had.

I mustered up my strength and composure and caught the train back to Tel Aviv, reviewing in my mind what had happened.

Why were they in such a hurry to split the marriage, I wondered. So did Yoram. We'd told them about this book and how I was writing the story so the world would know of the endless battles with the system and how we were broken. I realised then, an Israeli wife, she would have got it all, but I was not Israeli so I should go quietly with nothing. My money was lying in the hands of the jailors and I intended to get it back and as I wrote this I hoped the education would save many lives. There was another trip and so soon. Neither Ilan nor I expected things to move so quickly. "I'll see you in England, before you come here again" he'd said. "I'm a prisoner here, and I can't stand it anymore. I'm going to see someone to help me get out of here."

This was a first for Ilan in over a year. He'd not talked about leaving since before his suicide attempt apart from the few days after he'd last seen me in October.

"Just sit still Ilan." I'd replied. "It will all fall into place soon enough."

Seeing me had stirred him up again. Made him feel again, his hopes and dreams struggling to express themselves. It was on the same day as his call, the invitation arrived for a social services meeting, I'd only been home for a few days and it was set for 4th July. I only had two weeks to prepare myself and source money for the flight yet again. I'd visualised the outcome of the Rabbinate over and over, that they would take things further and dared to hope they'd seen my plea as urgent. It is very rare in Israel to have another case so quickly. In my mind's eye, I visualized Ilan, meek, compliant, perhaps hoping the trigger questions wouldn't be asked. My worst case vision was him aggressive, claiming again to be sound, preferring divorce to being found out.

I shook off the distraction of negative thoughts. I had all the evidence of danger to my life for being persistent, though the shadows hide those who may want to deter me so much. There could be a risk of suicide attempts again, he'd tried twice, the second time more serious and witnessed and I had my professionals and their letters. Then of course, the disc with countless conversations in which Ilan wanted to end people's lives as well as his own.

"So Ilan, you want to exist with no plans, dreams or hopes, no responsibilities or accountability, locked in against your free will and never think or feel?" I asked in another call.

"That's how I live every day Mar. It's my life now."

"You told me only days ago that you wanted to leave." I said. He was so mercurial.

"I do. I really do, but I don't know what to do anymore."

"I bring up your feelings when you see me, your mind clears for a while and you admitted that you are held by ultimatums." I replied. "Then a few days with people there and you sink down again."

"I don't want to feel Mar, that's the whole point. I cannot afford to feel." He sighed.

"We both decided we couldn't go through with divorce 2 weeks ago and that requires action. We can't just leave it, me here still trying to resolve things and you closing down into a different reality."

But all he said was he wanted to work things out, but who could know if it would last forever. He'd told me that when it came down to it he wouldn't be able to divorce me. I told him the same.

Chapter 27

3rd July

It's chilly this morning at Heathrow Airport, Terminal 1. Flights to Israel are usually distinct and separate at the airport, but fortunately security isn't as arduous as in the past. I can recall occasions when bags have been emptied, creams and powders destroyed and endless questions.

Its feels so ironic now, the endless interrogation and bag checking is all intensified on exit from Israel. Entering is so simple. No landing cards or visas needed, maybe a couple of questions at passport control, and then you are in. The ethos has changed, now it is the leaving that is the challenge.

I have goose bumps from the air-conditioning, there are grey skies outside and the plane isn't even going to be half full today. I'm told Wednesdays are usually quiet. I'm not bristling this morning; the familiar resentment hasn't shown itself yet.

I'm thinking about the upcoming meeting, trying to think in terms of it being a business pitch. The objections run through my mind, Ilan pretends for an hour that he is fine. Social services have a general apathy and won't drill down into the issue. I'm a foreigner, so feel second class already and of course there is the language barrier.

But my agenda is only to help, to present risks, dangers and my love for my husband and then holler as loudly as I can. But I fear the country will not help me as they haven't at any other stage. If there was no appreciation of Ilan's condition up until now then I have a mountain to climb.

They might decide as in October that after a few minutes Ilan will protect his vulnerability to great effect. The man I've known half my life will be ignored by a stranger who faces him for a few minutes I fear. The love and effort I've gone to won't be heard. I need them to understand why I'm there, I want to help, not hurt. I cannot for the life of me understand, how an assessment of a man who tried to die, should be such an impossibility. I was going to be facing the executioner, the authorities and I didn't hold out hope.

I arrived in Israel and for the first time in years I was a guest, to be collected and accommodated. It had been so long since I was welcome and everything felt different because of that. I'd met a wonderful person on one of my previous trips who had said if I ever needed help, it would be there. True to his word Yehuda picked me up and took me to his home. Entering the house, I was met by a huge dog, which I was told 'took to me straight away'. The entrance was beautiful, a very high ceiling in the lounge area, an open curved staircase straight ahead and to my right the kitchen with a breakfast bar sat Tia. I hadn't connected their relationship at all. She had worked in Yehuda's office, and I hadn't realised they were a couple.

What a woman, after my own heart she was. We were to talk endlessly during this visit as she let me pour my heart out. She was a fantastic listener, and was to become a part of a life changing watershed in my life. Perhaps it is all true, that I am an abused woman in this country and every act of kindness overwhelmed me, that people could be so helpful and kind and it was totally unexpected. No matter, what I just couldn't take in was I was worth their time and energy. I began to realise just how low I had got and how little I could accept and receive but although I was at a deep low the essence of me was seen and appreciated and from that place came their hospitality.

The first evening, until the early hours of the morning, they helped me to prepare until finally it was decided Tia would come to Haifa with me and translate as needed. I just couldn't learn all the words I needed in

Hebrew. But surely, Ilan's suicide attempt, the bridge from our love and hope to sudden despair would be noted. I was strongly advised to keep things simple and forget the whole story, just concentrate on the one aim, the rest was just too incredible and too much for a stranger to absorb.

I hardly slept that night but a niggling feeling that my justice and vindication might not come wouldn't leave me. It might not come from the same system which held him so readily. It was possible they wouldn't want accountability or to really check things. Worse still Ilan would not wake up in time to smell the coffee and lie to protect his vulnerability. DefinitelyI knew that it would be a life changing day, no matter the form it took.

4th July – Independence Day in the USA

Independence. For whom? Today I went to the rabbinate bursting with papers and proof to ask them to help me. Ilan needed an assessment for his depression and PTSD. My new friend Tia who had taken me to her heart was with me. There was no way I could have done this day without her.

We left early, around 7am to get to the court on time, expecting to have a 1-2 hour session. I could not have imagined the day would unfold as it did.

Ilan was in a rage on the telephone. I had called him when we arrived as he was not there. I had to hold the phone away from my ear and both Tia and the social worker could hear his raised voice. I knew he was scared which always brought up his anger. He shouted to me he would only give them a maximum of one hour as he had a busy day. Whilst we waited I tried to explain to the Social Worker exactly the seriousness of the situation with Tia translating all the time. I offered key questions to ask Ilan when he came. He arrived, very unhappy and wouldn't even greet me properly. He was immediately taken into the office to speak with the Social Worker.

Tia and I were seated on the landing at a grubby desk so we could smoke, and waited. It wasn't long before I was called in to join him. Ilan wouldn't look at me. She asked him about his plans. He wouldn't discuss anything but avoided eye contact with me.

He said. "I can't be with her anywhere in the world."

I knew what he meant. No one would allow him to be with me.

"This is my point. He's afraid. He says his mother won't let him be with me. He's a prisoner here; of course he will say this. He tried to die. Don't you understand?"

But that wasn't her interpretation. It was viewed as didn't want to, not can't.

The Social Worker then declared. "There is a judgment here from last month in which you both wanted a divorce. You both wanted an end to the marriage."

"It's not true! We are here because the judgment was to help him. To help us both."

Ilan said. "If that is what it says, then we should do it."

He didn't know the impact of his words. There was no more vitality in him. It was the same as so many times before in the face of authorities.

I reacted immediately, saying "We do it now, today, enough."

The words were barely out of my mouth when in an instant wheels were set in motion, papers typed and we were told we would have to wait outside for a court case. I went into an alternative reality. We waited. Then we were ushered into a room and they asked us if we both agreed to divorce. I was defeated. They were breaking their own laws. They were not going to help me. Ilan had been right all along. The system had broken him and was about to break me.

We both mumbled yes. I couldn't or didn't know how to stop this charade.

We were to be nearly 7 hours in this building and during all our waiting times I said over and over to Ilan

"Talk now, because when this is done, I can NEVER talk to you again, ever in this life."

He paced up and down the corridor, whilst I wept with anger and loss. Ranting and railing against him, full of hatred. He wouldn't talk.

"I have to. They won't let me live my life. It's over for me. I want you to be happy. We have no choice." he said reluctantly.

"Please Ilan, please, wake up. Don't let them do this. They are stealing my hope too. I beg you." I implored.

He couldn't converse with me.

We were back in another room, where a rabbi sat at a desk holding a form. He asked me the same question in as many permutations as he could find.

"What is your father's name? Does he have another name? Are you sure of his name?"

Over and over he requested the same information. I was so angry with events and was reacting very quickly. They said we needed a witness who knew our relationship as a couple and suggested Ilan brought a member of his family.

"Yes, let's get your brother, your father, bring them. They want this divorce. Let them be here to witness it." I said bitterly.

Ilan was in a complete state of shock at how things were unfolding but stayed tightly in control.

"My brother is in Tel Aviv, my dad is on a beach somewhere."

"Do you have friends locally?" the rabbi asked.

"No, I don't have any friends." He replied.

I knew he wasn't in control because he'd always behaved this way in so many previous cases with Matty showing his calm exterior, whilst his heart pounded. I'd seen it so often but this time I wasn't going to help him. Finally Tia was called in as my witness. I was spewing anger from every pore in my body. This wasn't just a row, this was really happening, a divorce. This wasn't my experience of Social Work or mediation. This was coercion.

Though I kept telling him in English and Hebrew to talk, he still wouldn't. I barely gave him the opportunity in truth. The rabbis, one of them with such kind eyes, told me to sit, as we entered yet another room full of very busy people preparing the end of my connection to Ilan. They asked me to stay in Israel a little longer but I refused to extend my ticket. They weren't going to pay, so why should I? Tia told me later, that she saw Ilan was totally traumatised. This was real and he had no one with him. His lifeline was disappearing. I didn't spare a thought for his condition, just as he never thought of me. We were both in our own worlds of grief. I had given him all day to talk. Just before we went into yet another room I told him.

"This is it, your last and final opportunity. Is there some piece of you inside, the part that loves me who will fight, will stand up and say no? This is YOUR decision; I am merely acting on it as decisions are to be acted on. I hate all of you. This wasn't the judgment last month but they can't wait for this. They want me out of here." Ilan didn't take his chance for just as he was about to speak in response to me we were called in.

Inside there were 4 people, the rabbi who had scribed the Get, another sitting by his computer, another who was 'cooking' the divorce agreement. He was heating it to dry the ink. He was trying to explain to me in

Hebrew the source of the ink, the quill and the process. I didn't care where the feathers came from, and as far as the ink, it felt more like this betrayal was to be written in blood.

A fourth rabbi, the kind one, told me to sit. It seemed everyone was pleased with this impending outcome, apart from the married couple. Just before we were to conclude this process, the social worker needed to see us one more time.

"He's got plans." She told me.

"Such as?" I barked.

"I don't know. He wouldn't say. But you can just tell by looking that he does. He seems well to me."

"Of course he's not well. It's obvious he's not well. None of this is normal." I countered.

Ilan seated in the corner said nothing.

"Tell me to my face, look into my eyes and say you don't love me and you want this divorce." I demanded. "If this is what we do, then I must have closure."

He wouldn't, he couldn't.

The Social Worker told him "Ilan, it's not fair, give Marianne her life."

But his eyes brimmed with tears and he choked on any words.

She told him again, "She loves you, this is not fair Ilan." Still nothing, so she said to me

"Marianne, take your life, don't ask him anymore."

She then went on to discuss 'compensation' for the marriage. She asked me for an amount I wanted repaid. My first amount was refused outright as unrealistic, absurd really, as it was only half the amount I'd invested. Eventually a sum of £70 per month was decided upon, to be paid monthly to me for the next five years. Ilan stumbled over the commitment and the Social Worker impatiently told Ilan to be clear as this was a legal requirement. I couldn't take it in. He couldn't even carry out a normal practical conversation, he was so unclear. It was funny how she didn't notice, despite her own frustration with the practicalities.

So the madness must be mine. All these people are saying I must divorce this abusive man, who has it seems, psychologically tortured me. But I don't see it. Am I so blind and deaf to this alleged abuse?

During all this time, Tia sat patiently in the same seat, waiting, as I came and went, taking it all in. During that day, initially she thought Ilan was a bad man but she watched, listened and came to the end conclusion that he was a broken spirit.

So back to the divorce room one. I sit, responding to their generosity of spirit. I look only forward, away from Ilan's eyes. But he is prodding me over and over again.

"Mar, Mar, we have to talk."

I keep my eyes focused ahead and the tears are rolling down, but I won't break down and actually cry.

He keeps asking, "We need to talk, please, let's talk." I'm frozen in self-preservation, my endless ranting of the day has gone; my questions and pleas unanswered as those around me feel sorry for me, 'Miskena' in Hebrew. Poor woman.

It seems I agreed a few weeks ago to this divorce and so did he; but that's not how I understood things then, nor did he, so how could this be happening? I'd never received the minutes of that case but it seems they were all set for this. Perhaps I could have saved this trip, had I truly known.

But no one can see the man he was. I believe he died the night he tried to. His heart beats, he is different and incapable, closed to me and closed to his own heart. I then learn about the Ketuba. This is the marriage document, a sum of money being pledged by the groom on the wedding day. My 'dowry' in case of divorce is one shekel! About 20p. Or in real terms the lowest silver coin, maybe that would be 5p in England. What his bride was worth. I pity myself. I asked him for the shekel. He laughed nervously, breaking his own tension.

"You still have your sense of humour!" he said but I wasn't laughing. Is that the secret? His words of helplessness and fear are for MY ears only, never uttered in front of a single witness this past year? If that is it, then what therapy I need. Is the denial mine?

I am so exasperated. I am given instructions now on how to receive the Get. They show me how to open the palms of my hands and how to place my thumbs, telling me when I receive this newly scribed document not to squeeze it. Ilan is told that once he hands me this paper we are divorced. But still we have to wait outside before we go back in for the final time.

I go back to Tia and I tell Ilan this is our final conversation. I tell him goodbye, but he responds with

"I don't say goodbye to anyone. " No closure from him, and no closure for either or us.

I ask him for the one shekel. He gives me ten. I refuse saying it's too generous, just give me the one. I feel so beaten, bitter, shocked. He actually gives me the one shekel. It's all so absurd.

Then into to our final room. How many times I already thought I was in the final room and now I am. My eyes are dry. Ilan is given something to read. He is stumbling over the words, reading each one slowly, barely able to speak. They are pointing a small stick at each word making him utter them. He is suffering but still doing his own request, his own outburst and regretting every second as much as me.

In English I am saying, "Just do it, do it, give it to me. Get it over with." As I stare out of the window. It's the last thing I really want, but I'm powerless.

He doesn't want to. It's taking all he has in inner resources to go through with it. He places the folded document into my hands and I am instructed to put my right hand on top and then put the paper under my right armpit, still holding it with my left hand, and walk a few steps to the window and return to my position.

It's done. We are now divorced. I'd told Ilan all day to talk before this moment or it would be too late. During the day I'd asked over and over for his permission to be in this book and give me the right to access all the legal documents to show this ten year struggle, which had ended in vain sometime after 3pm this day. He agreed, reneged, worried, procrastinated, unable to commit even to this, tells me to email him, but I have a printed document telling him over and over, just do it now. But he is afraid of Matty. He is afraid that if an extract of a judgment is inserted with all the documented facts, she might actually sue him and he was scared saying she would find more ways to destroy him. I reassure him that no one can sue over the truth, and the documents over the years proved it. He was still held in Israel, and she still refused to lift the Order, so how could it not be true.

He was scared of how she would use the corrupt system to finish him completely. I didn't think she had much work to do. Still it seemed it was all about Ilan. It was all about his fear of her. I leave it, go back to it and leave it again. I know in his heart that he is willing but see he is not capable or able. He runs off here and there for advice, warned not to sign, but suddenly he says yes. So I have access to all the legal papers which I paid for in money, blood sweat and tears, all for my *one shekel*!

He'd given it finally, signing the permission witnessed again by Tia.

As we left the room he begged to talk to me, begged me. Tia and the Social Worker called to me,

"No, don't look back Marianne, don't speak to him ever again." I walked away. But I do look back. Ilan looks bereft, alone in the empty corridor, a strangely empty corridor. Apart from one amicable couple there was no one else there. I note in my mind it is very unusual instead of the usually bustling of divorcing couples. But I can't, I won't talk. I have to stay cold and angry right now. He is in shock. I kept my word, that I wouldn't talk afterwards only before. It took all I had. I turned away, and I looked back once more. He stood in complete dejection then turned and walked down the corridor.

So I am told I am apparently the abused woman, crazy and obsessed to have gone so far for nothing. For a game player who is fine. I'm told I needed to get some counselling, as a lot of it could all be in my imagination. I protested strongly. They don't know him. They don't know me. My own therapist heard conversations and diagnosed from that alone he needed help. All they see is a dejected woman. If only I had been fluent in Hebrew then I surrendered the thought as it came. Ilan is fluent but it hadn't helped us.

So even though today it is over, I don't know what actually ended. I just don't know. It's been so long since things were 'normal' between us. I'd talked more with Tia in the last day or so than I had with Ilan.

I couldn't hold on to a marriage post mortem, picking out the bones of a few good years. There was a couple there, divorcing after 37 years of marriage, very amicable but Ilan and I both cried and in our hearts didn't want it. It was bizarre. I know Jewish Law doesn't break the marriages of those in doubt. Look at the contrast with Ilan and Matty. It had been the total opposite. I'd always known that divorce wasn't so easy in Israel, but surely if the couple don't want it then what their motives were I will never know. There was no help at all to keep our marriage intact.

But in the end I held myself together as events took such a quick turn. I knew if I hadn't made it happen today then this plaster would never be ripped from me and I needed the rip, not the slow painful plucking, taking out a follicle or keeping the wound in a putrid state.

But Ilan chose. He chose his mother, his brother and his children. To be honest, I don't believe it. There is no sense as it was a choice from a prison behind borders moments after a suicide attempt. Not from freedom and health. But from now on I need to learn to withdraw from the drug, the addiction I have to my husband, no now my ex-husband, the sweet and innocent love that was stolen from me by barriers and borders, external and internal.

But he blamed Matty and the system most of all. She wouldn't let it go and the system had helped her. The hatred won, the fear won, the greed won, power won, and yes, love actually lost the war. Matty could celebrate the destruction she had planned and carried out relentlessly with the undivided support of every legal authority in the land. It felt like legalized murder by the state.

We returned to Tel Aviv. Exhausted and drained, to good food and kind company. Yehuda and Tia were the most perfect hosts in the world. After a few drinks, whilst watching a movie, my mind slipped in and out. What does it mean now? Is he suffering or are his tears crocodile tears? Tomorrow, he'll be the usual, maybe, the only difference is that he cannot vent his frustrations towards me ever again.

I kept remembering how desperate he was to talk in those final minutes. I feel the pain. But what words could I have heard? Sorry? Let's be friends? I have NO idea, and it's better that I don't know them. So I have nothing reverberating in my mind. I only remember just before it happened, I'd asked as I touched his chest 'is there still YOU somewhere in there, any part of you that remembers why we suffered, why we battled, not to this end but for love and freedom.'

I'm drifting, the rooms in the scene of my mind are so vivid, all kindnesses given by strangers, Ilan in stark contrast. I think of the ordeal, another milestone in a babble of Hebrew. My life had been decided again without my full comprehension. Thinking how one word I didn't understand blanked the rest of the sentence.

I think. I don't want to but I do. His son goes into the army in two weeks, Ilan's focus of love, where he pours out all his good feelings. Ilan had taken or even made phone calls all that day, sounding calm, business as usual. I recall how much he'd celebrated his divorce from Matty, just a few short years ago, trying to arrange his marriage to me on the same day.

Not so today. There was no celebrating for anyone. I'd needed the anger, pouring my words out like a rainstorm. Tia told me Ilan barely had a second to answer to the barrage before I battered his brain again with reprisals.

I don't feel anything. But tonight I am educated about the Ketuba. I'm told if a small price is put down it indicates a low commitment. Ilan had tried over and over to explain or remind me what had happened and I don't recall it from the wedding day, but I refused to hear and closed him down today. One shekel, the smallest piece of silver in Israel! Yehuda was disgusted. They tell me 'mazaltov', congratulations, your new life is now. But it's not a celebration it's sad, tragic, and a waste. Pointless, at least today it is.

I remember now. Ilan finally had agreed he was not so arrogantly 'one million percent' ok. He told me he knows he is not. He accepted that he had treated me with breathtaking anger and abuse, it took him time to move from 'I'm sorry for what happened to you' to 'I'm sorry for what I have done to you' But I don't remember these things until later. Seven hours of hell takes time to filter through.

He was alone there, Tia was my rock, calm and patient, watching me parade all my emotions but impressed with my dignity. I feel the anger and the emptiness, the futility and the sensation of his head going back underwater like a sailor to the sirens and mermaids of folklore. He will be ok I think. I was just a dismembered voice to rail against. I was not real.

I don't expect to see any money but I'm informed it's not impossible, that someone will take care of it for me. Ilan has a job with poor income with barely any relationship to his captors and left the love of his life;

holidays, fresh air, his hobbies, music. He reined his emotions in today.

Tia tells me he is not bad, not a bad man, she has seen enough. 'Misken' – Poor man, not bad man. He needs pity, not vengeance. I know it's true, as not all of us who knew him were wrong. His safety is no longer in my love or my presence, it must be in the closure, not the closure of the marriage but in the massive exertion of closing down so he couldn't think or feel, just like he told me a day or two before.

5th July

It is day one of my 'freedom'. Hot, so hot. There are children playing and lazing about. I'm sweating again, whilst Israelis don't. It's not fair. Maybe when I'm home it will hit me. Who knows? Here, just a few miles from him, I feel safe, it's paradoxical.

I think I'm going to be empty forever. No more struggle, no mission, no war, just a normal life like everyone else. Do I know how to? I'm just not sure how to do it. Tia and I talked for hours and hours like old friends, now bonded for life. We are inside the house for the sun is too hot to sit in and my pale skin is fated to its washed out colour. I'm hot, disheveled and more comfortable than I've been for months. I don't want to go home.

I'm not sure of myself anymore, but as I sit in their beautiful home, so spacious, so gracious, I decide to read the story of our big day yesterday to Tia. I need to know if my written account of events is accurate.

As I read she gets goose bumps all over and tears fill her eyes. The account is indeed accurate, not exaggerated at all, it's exactly as she experienced it.

So now I am relieved. I am certain that truth is stranger than fiction. Tia reminds me. When she had come in as our witness she was asked for her ID. She'd opened her purse to retrieve it, and one shekel fell to the floor. *The* shekel, the ketuba! She'd bent to the floor, picked it up and exclaimed

"Ilan, here!One shekel, your ketuba payment." It was like a parody, a comic tragedy. She reminded me that culturally this was an insult of the highest order to a wife. Today she is still shocked with the audacity of it all. Better that he had written zero as that perhaps it could be interpreted as priceless. But culturally this had stripped my value and worth to less than nothing.

We sit drinking vodka and grapefruit and she tells me that had it not been actually true, the shekel falling from her purse, it would have been too corny!

But I am reassured, as each major event with friends had been written to exact detail and her verification confirmed that all I had written of other events was true. Tia urges me to continue to write, to tell the story and share others' traumas, to open the minds and eyes inside Israel and to the world.

She reminds me that the Social Worker didn't want to accept the suicide rate was true. She'd refused to believe there was an increased risk for divorced people combined with no exit orders driving people first to insanity then to total compliance or death. Of course she wouldn't listen. They already knew. It's like a flea circus, when the lid is lifted the conditioning is complete. Animals that pace in small cages then moved to a larger space still spend initial time only walking within the original parameters. Israel is not a country, it's a cage.

That is why freedom and choice couldn't be registered in Ilan's psyche. The damage was already done.

I've lost him a long time ago but officially now on paper my failure is official. When Ilan resigned himself 18 months ago, I was fighting in an empty arena for what was truly an invisible hostage. I'm assigned to his memory banks, of that I'm sure, but my work is to begin what he seems to have accomplished for so long, to somehow recover. My grief starts now.

I must accept the dice have been rolled, all the cards played and I had to act on the court's decision. He uttered the words and I forced his hand. They forced us both. I ache inside imagining that for Ilan it was a bad day, just that. For me it was a life changing moment, the severing of our connection in this lifetime. It is compulsory for my wellbeing, but I am truly awake to the consequence of legal severance. I ache with the fear and pain of it meaning nothing to him, or it could have been the final nail in his coffin. I don't know. Maybe for him the true loss of me won't hit home for months, years, or maybe never.

He has been in my life for half of it, on the periphery of my vision for many years, then in the centre, and all other issues sidelined for almost a decade. An assessment of his trauma would have been true freedom for us both but Ilan will maybe cope better as a somatised victim because for him to truly absorb his anger and abusive behaviour would make his life impossible. His suffering ends as mine truly begins in a new form.

But what is important is there are more 'Ilans', more 'Mariannes' waiting to happen, or in different stages, all heading in the same direction until the truth is told. Somehow, someday, I may find true peace. Ilan is broken into different pieces now; the essence of him was mine and a part of me. No divorce can break that. Bit by bit my honey was stolen, my sweetheart was soured.

All that is left is the bittersweet taste of it all. I want the truth of this tragedy, not unique, but certainly extreme to bring enough voices with more stories to change the future. Israel, with the banner of 'the right of return' has a flipside, 'no right to leave'.

So what started in Israel ends in Israel. One more citizen safe inside the borders, many more outside afraid to return and others choosing death as their freedom.

If this story of sacrifice and unconditional love can encourage just one person in the world to turn a corner and fight for love, hope and freedom of choice, stand up and become whole, then it will have been worth it. I pray that MY voice will be heard and one decade of my life was not in vain.

Chapter 28

I didn't know how to finish this unfinished story. Ilan carried on trying to communicate as if the divorce had never happened, oblivious to judgments and court orders, still unable to make any rational statements.

"No piece of paper can finish our marriage. You are still in my heart and soul. I gave you my heart forever and it hasn't changed." He declared.

No mention or declaration of intentions or love nor plans. Just disconnected statements showing he still was no nearer to reality than he had been when he'd tried to end his life. I wasn't sure how to move on, as his ignoring the divorce and financial orders meant I was no nearer to an ending than before, yet my love had stayed pure and open throughout. I had no choice but to try and put things to one side and finish my book. 'There is one chapter left' my friends said to me. 'One you cannot imagine, or create, but one which will emerge as the whole saga has been stranger than fiction from the beginning.'

The Israeli system had done its job. Ilan was disjointed, disconnected and totally emotionally closed. He was unable to empathise or understand anything normal people could. His answers and reactions proved it. He couldn't access his emotions, never mind express them. An open door, a border release and a plane ticket would not move Ilan from his mental prison and long term conditioning. He had no plans, no future, no dreams, and moved from a comatose state to fragmented memories. To hear him was too much to bear and my heart still cried with the pain of loss.

Determined to find some peace, tell my story and pray for miracles, I pressed on with an urgency engrossing my every waking minute. It was finally done. I had completed my work, and with an inner knowledge my life was about to change, I rested and waited.

I contemplated a holiday, somewhere to go and recharge my batteries. After almost ten years of struggle I needed to find some balance. Ilan was contacting me with statements of coming to England. It seemed now we were divorced and he'd proved to be obedient and well trained, his brother was prepared to sign for him to visit Germany to a business exhibition, chaperoned to ensure his three day pass would not give him full rights to make choices, but at least the leash was being loosened. It was tragic to hear. But there was no more capacity in me to listen to his ramblings. It was the first time he'd mentioned leaving Israel since his suicide attempt so no matter how unrealistic, this was a major shift in his thinking.

I knew I wasn't well. Overcome with a fatigue which overwhelmed me, I got a course of antibiotics and a blood test ordered. I never got the chance, as an allergic reaction took control of my body the weekend I was going to see my terminally ill mother. Instead of the intended visit, whilst contemplating where to relax for a week or two, I found myself in intensive care in hospital fighting for my life. My body was breaking down; a culmination of years of relentless stresses and pressure. The situation had finally taken its toll.

There was a real chance I would die. Die as a result of enduring the heartbreak and injustice, ignoring my health to arrive at a critical state. I fought hard, delirious, in a hallucinatory state whilst still aware of everything happening around me. I knew I was in hospital but the hallucinations told me different. I was paranoid, believing everyone was suspicious, claiming to have killed people, claiming doctors and nurses were not what they seemed. All the years of documenting this fantastical story, and then caught in a delusion, knowing it; fighting it whilst having to surrender to it. It was the most challenging time of my life.

In the middle of my stay, my dear mother, the best friend I ever had, finally passed away, the day after I was moved from the ICU. It was just too much to bear as my body relapsed, with a perforated colon. For the first time the battle was mine, the grief was mine and Israel was not on my agenda.

Ilan called many times, finally reaching me, as I gasped for air on oxygen. They let patients have mobile phones in hospital these days. I explained:

"I'm fighting for my life Ilan, I'm very ill; I have no time for you."

"What are you talking about? I'm thinking of going to Germany soon. Maybe I'll go to court and try and leave Israel."

All I could hear were disconnected statements with no understanding of my plight. I told him my mother had died; he didn't even assimilate the information. He had loved her with all his heart, yet didn't react at all. He was lost in his own world of impatience and anger not understanding a word I was saying. Grief overwhelmed me with the enormity of my mother's passing. My failing body wasn't responding to my will, and my loss was complete.

"Where are you Ilan? Come to me, help me." I begged.

"I don't understand you Mar. Why are you talking like this?" he replied.

Then, and during my stay, I truly understood. The destruction of Ilan's humanity was complete. The kindness of strangers was sweeter than his words. No worry, no understanding, no comprehension or compassion came from him. His life force was blocked. As I fought for air, I felt more alive than him. I had never blocked love, the noisy, determined and loud state of love. I never allowed it to be silenced and never let my mind take control completely. The imponderables I'd been pondering were clear. He was an empty shell, still married in his own mind, yet unaccountable and unable to plan or understand the basics. The tragedy was his too, if he only knew it.

"If I do die Ilan, it will be with no regret." I said. "I've lived my life to the full, and love is all there is. I knew it as a child, and lived by the value all my life. It's got me into trouble I know, but I acted from love."

"What are you talking about?" he asked impatiently.

"Do you have any feelings at all? What do you feel about my predicament?" I asked.

"I don't understand those questions, they are too difficult." He retorted angrily.

I am a widow. My lover has a heartbeat still, but no life or love in him. He is a dead man walking. He has no passion, no dreams and no humanity left. Without treatment, he will never recover. The task was successful. The aim to destroy his spirit was achieved, by those who perpetrated the crime against his soul, and the system who helped. The system in Israel is a money making machine, which told me, he can live as a pauper in Israel, and the state will feed his children. But he will never breathe the air outside Israel unless he pays in full, and then some.

Yes, 36 years child support ahead was the request, until his child was older than he was at the time of the judgment.

Israel has my money, took my husband, and the fight to save him nearly killed me too. My judgements are worthless and unenforceable, as I am a foreigner without the resources for a never ending court battle.

So it's time to recover, bury my mum – my best friend in the world - thank her for instilling the fortitude and courage which enables me to learn to forgive. I am the product of my parents who loved each other unconditionally, and taught me that love is really all there is.

Justice will prevail, of this I am sure, and no one should endure one minute of this suffering in Israel any more. Not one man, woman, or child should be imprisoned in the land of Zion for money and paranoid guarantees that no human being can fulfil.

Shame on them, these people have forgotten how to show human kindness, to their own people and their neighbours in other regions. It is not the Jewish way. Jewish people are supposed to help each other and look after each other according to the religion. Many voices are beginning to speak out against the paranoia and impingement of freedom of Palestinians, standing at check points and marked out, disrupted from a peaceful life. But we cannot forget those inside Israel, who have no voice and no one to speak for their suffering. The regime rolls on oblivious to the damage, and all those caught up in the region are paying.

I have paid as a European, the highest price. Love is absent in Israel, and I pray my words will wake up the slumber and greed and revenge will be replaced with compassion and humanity.

As I close this chapter on my life, I heard a phone call between Ilan and Matty. She finally needs something from him, a signature to allow her to take her daughter abroad. After a decade, her shouting is just as loud, and Ilan just as intransigent. He wouldn't sign on principle. It would require a character of such magnitude to rise above his predicament and unconditionally give freedom to another. Their war continues, and I heave a sad sigh of loss yet relief that I don't have to take part in the drama from this day on.

The next generation in his family are already paying the price, with freedom of movement the on-going tool for hatred and revenge. She still holds the key, and now it is a useless weapon in her hand. The game had no winners.

There is a moral bankruptcy in those people and particularly the regime in Israel, breeding more hatred and warmongering between citizens.

It takes one person to start a war, two to fight it, and just one to end it. Yes, Israel's system is barbaric, the citizens doing disrespectful and hurtful things to each other with full compliance of the courts. I will be the one who ends the tug of war, by letting go and forgiving. Not forgetting, for its not possible. If the behaviour in Israel is classed as normal, then I'll choose crazy instead. I gave everything I had for unconditional love, the principle of human rights, and now I have to begin my own journey to wholeness by telling my story.

I thank my mum for believing in me, inspiring me, and supporting me. She picked me up every time I fell, with unwavering love for me, and also for Ilan, who she considered her son. She is with me in my heart, reminding me that I can make a difference with the right amount of courage.

Just as she foretold when I was a child, there was a book in me after all!

There is a story in the Bible of the Good Samaritan; the only one who picked up a helpless man lying on a road, as many more passed him by. The seven years I spent trying to help Ilan were not wasted. I learned it takes no responsibility or accountability for individuals to declare him corrupt or a bad man. It takes much more to enquire and check on someone's behaviours being synonymous with trauma and depression. All I ever asked was for a professional to check it out and confirm what was, and is obvious. But I was never going to get it. His case would have opened the floodgates for people who need psychological help in their entrapment. It was far easier to bury us both in red tape, only allowing Israeli money and earnings to pay the ransom. Reciprocal laws between our countries were ignored completely.

I know without a single doubt I took on the accountability of any decent person, to help him. Trying and often failing to hold on to the values I was brought up with, I pressed on and shouted from the rooftops for help, for both of us. It almost cost me my life, but I have no regrets. Having a spiritual outlook on life, it has taken all this time to realise that although married and caught in a nightmare, I had my journey and lessons to learn independently. Ilan's despair and avoidance focused me more and more on fixing his problem, or fixing him without realising there was a 'me' in the story. No one should have the right to keep someone prisoner, hold them against their will, and destroy their spirit just for a few shekels. I just assumed everyone would rally and rail against the barbarism in a modern country but as it transpired, it wasn't so.

Money is the root of all evil, the saying goes. It is incomplete, as many know it is the 'love' of money which is at the root of the evil. In Israel, the desperation for an ironclad future filled with money and security has wiped out compassion. Unless it happens to them personally, it can't even be understood and empathy plays no role. As Ilan continues to use the only weapon of choice for the next generation in his family, I am filled with sadness that lessons in Israel have not been learned with their own people and their neighbours. He still talks to me of leaving Israel in occasional moments of clarity, but lacks the energy. His inner resources remain depleted, as mine are starting to recover.

I am still filled with hope for my own future having learned unconditional love really has no strings attached, and doesn't require my partner to be in my presence. This love filled me with courage at my lowest ebb, and inspired me when needed. I received a wonderful gift, and in writing this story I have learned what my journey is. Ilan's journey back to himself is just beginning, and at this moment as I write, he still yearns at times for his life, but is held back by the emptiness and emotional walls he has built, a walking contradiction every day with survival being the objective.

I have gone further than many would have, and have survived, with my optimism, gratitude, and openness still intact. No matter what damage is done to us, with hope and love we can turn the page, get a blank sheet and start again.

Life is life, and I don't intend to endure it or survive it, I intend to live it, and by finding the laughter and joy again, my dreams and plans for the future start to take shape. I welcome those dreams like a long lost old friend.

End

A letter to my reader:

Dear Friend,

I want to thank you so much for reading my book and coming on my journey with me. The story has ended for you now, but for me it is not yet over. I understand that the largest majority of readers choose not to review books, but if you could make an exception on this occasion it would mean a great deal to me. Reviews are the lifeblood of the publishing world, on and offline. And as a new author it is an important aspect of building my readership. Please spend a few moments sharing your views and feedback with a review.

You can also visit my website www.marianneazizi.co.uk and keep up to date. And you can find me on Facebook and Twitter.

Thank you so much for reading. I hope my story has touched you in some way, enough to tell your friends about it!

Marianne Azizi

Printed in Great Britain
by Amazon.co.uk, Ltd.,
Marston Gate.